Hostile Forces

Hostile Forces

How the Chinese Communist Party Resists International Pressure on Human Rights

JAMIE J. GRUFFYDD-JONES

Oxford University Press is a department of the University of Oxford. It furthers
the University's objective of excellence in research, scholarship, and education
by publishing worldwide. Oxford is a registered trade mark of Oxford University
Press in the UK and certain other countries.

Published in the United States of America by Oxford University Press
198 Madison Avenue, New York, NY 10016, United States of America.

© Oxford University Press 2022

All rights reserved. No part of this publication may be reproduced, stored in
a retrieval system, or transmitted, in any form or by any means, without the
prior permission in writing of Oxford University Press, or as expressly permitted
by law, by license, or under terms agreed with the appropriate reproduction
rights organization. Inquiries concerning reproduction outside the scope of the
above should be sent to the Rights Department, Oxford University Press, at the
address above.

You must not circulate this work in any other form
and you must impose this same condition on any acquirer.

Library of Congress Cataloging-in-Publication Data
Names: Gruffydd-Jones, Jamie J., author.
Title: Hostile forces : how the Chinese communist party resists
international pressure on human rights / Jamie J. Gruffydd-Jones.
Description: New York, NY : Oxford University Press, [2022] |
Includes bibliographical references and index.
Identifiers: LCCN 2022010846 (print) | LCCN 2022010847 (ebook) |
ISBN 9780197643198 (hardback) | ISBN 9780197643204 (paperback) |
ISBN 9780197643228 (epub) | ISBN 9780197643211 | ISBN 9780197643235
Subjects: LCSH: Human rights—China—History. | Communism—China—History. |
Authoritarianism—China—History. | Civil rights—China—History.
Classification: LCC JC599.C6 G78 2022 (print) | LCC JC599.C6 (ebook) |
DDC 323.0951—dc23/eng/20220412
LC record available at https://lccn.loc.gov/2022010846
LC ebook record available at https://lccn.loc.gov/2022010847

DOI: 10.1093/oso/9780197643198.001.0001

Contents

Illustrations	vii
Acknowledgments	ix

PART I: THE ARGUMENT

1. Introduction	3
2. A Theory of Responses to Human Rights Pressure	17

PART II: THE REGIME

3. Pressure as Propaganda: From Mao to Hu	41
4. Hostile Human Rights: Tibet, Hong Kong, and Beyond	54
5. When Does Pressure Become Propaganda?	71

PART III: THE CITIZENS

6. Experimental Activism: How International Pressure on Women's Rights Affects Public Attitudes	97
7. People on the Street	118
8. Pressure in Real Time: Meeting the Dalai Lama	133

PART IV: THE IMPLICATIONS

9. Implications for China and Beyond	149
Appendices	173
Notes	183
Bibliography	229
Index	243

Illustrations

Figures

1.1. International attention given to country's human rights, 1990–2000, and proportion who believe that human rights are not well respected in their country, 2000–2004   8

1.2. A simplified model of how people respond to foreign human rights pressure   24

4.1. Number of Dalai Lama meetings with foreign heads of state, and number of meetings reported in *People's Daily*, 1989–2016   60

4.2. Proportion of human rights pressure reported in the *People's Daily*, and percentage of Chinese population with access to the internet between 2000 and 2011   69

5.1. Instances of foreign human rights pressure on China, and instances of pressure reported in the *People's Daily*, 1979–2011   74

5.2. Number of articles in *People's Daily* each year about US State Department human rights reports on China, and years with no bilateral presidential or foreign minister visits   86

5.3. Articles about Human Rights Watch reports on China in the *People's Daily* and *New York Times*   93

6.1. Change in grievances over women's rights after reading about foreign pressure   108

6.2. Translated control, and translated basic "shaming" treatment   110

6.3. Respondents could choose to "like" this *Weibo* post   110

6.4. Change in grievances over women's rights after reading about foreign pressure that addresses Chinese leaders only   113

8.1. Google searches for "Dalai Lama" and "Hu Jintao" in China   137

8.2. Quasi-natural experiment   138

8.3. Results for regressions on either side of twenty-one days in July, on whether China is democratic or not   143

9.1. Percentage of the Ugandan population who have positive levels of trust in the president, and percentage who believe people are treated equally   158

9.2. Trust in president and satisfaction with democracy in Zimbabwe   161

9.3. How Hong Kong citizens identify, 1997–2019   165

Tables

2.1.	Implications and Tests of Hostility Hypothesis	35
2.2.	Main Predictions of the Three Theoretical Frameworks	37
5.1.	Impact of Different Types of Foreign Human Rights Pressure on Probability That the Pressure Will Be Subsequently Reported in the *People's Daily*, 1979–2011	77
5.2.	Impact of Different Sources of Foreign Human Rights Pressure on Probability That the Pressure Will Be Subsequently Reported in the *People's Daily*, 1979–2011	81
7.1.	Percentage of Interviewees (in China) Who Said That Foreign Pressure on a Given Issue Is "Justified" When Asked	122
8.1.	People's Ratings of the Level of Democracy in China on a 1-to-10 Scale before and after the Dalai Lama–Obama Meeting	140
9.1.	Resonance of the Narrative That the International Human Rights Community Is "Hostile" toward the Country and the Ruling Party's Relative Ability to Control This Narrative in Four Case Studies	156

Acknowledgments

This book has been a fulfilling and miserable experience. I would like to sincerely thank everyone who has made it easier for me, in any small or big way—not least to my advisors at Princeton, Gary Bass, Thomas Christensen, Rory Truex, and Amaney Jamal, for their advice and inspiration, and to my professors from Oxford, Hélène Neveu Kringelbach, David Anderson, Ann Dowker, and Dick Passingham, for their support over the years. As I was drowning in a swamp of ideas I had the help of dozens of interviewees in China, many not quoted in this book, from women's rights activists to Hong Kong lawmakers, who gave me a firm footing and a clear direction. My research assistants, in China and the United States, whom I will also not name here, were truly fantastic. I'm also grateful for all the support from Princeton China Center in Beijing and want to extend particular thanks to David Kiwuwa and Greg Moore at the University of Nottingham Ningbo China, who were helpful and welcoming beyond any of my expectations. All of this research and travel received generous funding from Princeton University's East Asian Studies, the Princeton Institute for Regional and International Studies, the Lynde and Harry Bradley Foundation, and the Center for International Security Studies.

Thank you to many, many others from Princeton University, the University of Kent, George Washington University, the University of Nottingham Ningbo China, Hong Kong University, Peking University, the London School of Economics, and beyond, who provided words of encouragement and discouragement over the years. Thank you to my family and friends for not asking too much about how this book was coming along, and to Zara and Leyla, without whom this would all have been possible, but would have been much more miserable.

PART I
THE ARGUMENT

1
Introduction

> Interfere more and more. Interfere as much as you can. We beg you to come and interfere.
>
> —Aleksandr Solzhenitsyn, Speech to the American Federation of Labor and Congress of Industrial Organizations, Washington, DC, June 30, 1975[1]

The European Union denounced it as "brutal repression." The US House of Representatives called the behavior "disproportionate and extreme." German Chancellor Angela Merkel and French President Nicolas Sarkozy suggested that they might not attend the upcoming Olympic Games opening ceremony in protest, and mass demonstrations suffocated the Olympics torch as it voyaged across the globe.

Chinese security forces' March 2008 crackdown on riots in Tibet sparked an outpouring of outrage and condemnation of the Chinese Communist Party (CCP) in the West at a level not seen for almost two decades. For some observers, the international campaign was a vital way of shining a light on authorities' repressive policies in the region.[2] In the previous century, many Soviet dissidents—like Solzhenitsyn—had appealed passionately for Western leaders to speak out in this way against their own regime. Condemnation from abroad sustained them in their fight, not least because it passed on information about their government's abuses of human rights to the Soviet people.[3]

And the Tibet campaign did indeed inspire Chinese citizens to launch their own mass online outcry and join in demonstrations around the world. But the outcry was not over the repression in Tibet. Instead, it was directed at the West, and directed against what for many was a provocative crusade of harassment and hostility against their country. Online campaigns sprung up to target foreign media organizations for their purported bias in covering the riots, mass boycotts squeezed French businesses over President Sarkozy's threats to shun the Olympics, and marches outside embassies assailed Western leaders for their perceived support for the Dalai Lama, the exiled Tibetan spiritual leader. Many protestors focused their ire not on authorities' use of violence against their fellow citizens but on the Tibetan activists and rioters themselves, and particularly on the Dalai Lama for his alleged role in organizing them.[4]

Hostile Forces. Jamie J. Gruffydd-Jones, Oxford University Press. © Oxford University Press 2022.
DOI: 10.1093/oso/9780197643198.003.0001

Of course, when we look at China's recent relationship with the West, the tensions of 2008 are hardly unique. From authorities' attempts to control how many children their citizens have to their belated response to the emergence of the COVID-19 virus, there are few areas that have not been touched by very public international disapproval. UN resolutions, US presidential debates, even Nobel Peace Prizes have all locked their gaze on the Communist Party's treatment of its people's human rights at some point. Yet despite all this attention and condemnation, we have, surprisingly, almost no idea what happens to it within China itself. How do these kinds of international human rights campaigns matter inside authoritarian countries like China or the Soviet Union? Do they even reach people? And if so, do they really help to strengthen domestic calls for liberty and democracy? Or do they backfire, turning people against human rights movements?

In this book I argue that to understand why human rights in places like China have improved, stagnated, or worsened in the face of international pressure, we need to understand how these countries' rulers—and their citizens—deal with that pressure at home. I show that while Chinese leaders have decried attempts to put pressure on them over human rights on the international stage, they have also sought to use that pressure as a tool to bolster their own domestic support. The Communist Party has, at times, strategically employed external pressure to help soften the public's concerns about human rights violations in their country and reduce their support for efforts to address those violations.

The goal is that by tracing what happens to human rights pressure within authoritarian countries, this book can tell us something about how that pressure succeeds, but also how it fails. And China is not normally counted as one of international human rights campaigners' (well-documented) success stories.[5] Many observers have applauded how the CCP has signed on to human rights treaties and released prominent political prisoners when the eyes of the world have been on it,[6] but evidence of underlying change has been far less promising.[7] As we begin the 2020s, the CCP is as intolerant of challenges to its rule as it has ever been. In global rankings of civil and political freedoms, the country is rooted near the bottom: the fourteenth least democratic,[8] the third worst political rights,[9] and the fourth least free media.[10]

And despite increasingly powerful international human rights norms, laws, and transnational networks, China is just one of a growing number of high-profile failures. Leaders from Ankara to Manila have fought back against human rights activism, reversed past liberalizing changes, and steadfastly refused to submit to international demands.[11] What explains these failures? The scholarship so far does not tell us how these countries have successfully fought off foreign activism but instead has treated them as places where the power of human rights has not yet achieved fruition due to some roadblock or other.

For China, the popular story has been precisely that—the conditions behind the human rights community's triumphs in other countries are simply not present. Some argue that the CCP's growing international power means that its leaders have no need to give in to economic or diplomatic threats[12] and as such are just less vulnerable to coercion or shaming.[13] For others, the failure comes down to the fact that repeated criticism from foreign actors has not been accompanied by a similarly strong push from the domestic population.[14] One of the foremost scholars of China's human rights, Andrew Nathan, maintained back in 1994 that the only time foreign pressure had been effective in the country was when "it pushed in the same direction as internal forces"[15]—in other words, when foreign efforts to push the Chinese government to respect human rights were also supported by powerful movements within China. And when surveyed, Chinese citizens do express remarkably few concerns about the state of human rights in their country. In the face of rising crackdowns on legal, civil, political, and religious liberties, in recent polling almost 80% of the public said that their nation was democratically run, and over 87% said that they believed human rights were well respected, a higher figure than liberal democracies like Australia and Taiwan.[16] The argument is that since Chinese citizens and activists have not expressed widespread grievances over human rights and democracy in recent years, international efforts have had little domestic unhappiness to tap into.

What this argument misses, however, is that the international efforts themselves may have had an impact on that unhappiness. Foreign pressure may raise citizens' awareness of human rights violations, feed into their beliefs about whether those rights need to be improved, and build their support for domestic activism—or it may spark nationalist sentiments, lead to a backlash against the international community, and drive support for their government's actions. Either way, foreign pressure can influence the direction of internal forces.

The Importance of Citizens

I assume that ordinary people and their concerns about the state of human rights in their country can make a difference. Even in China, a country that scores the lowest mark of zero out of fourteen on the Cingranelli and Richards (CIRI) international rankings of political freedoms,[17] the weight of public opinion has sparked changes in government policies over human rights. In late 2015, for example, following a concerted campaign over many years by women's organizations and feminist activists, the legislature passed a national law banning domestic violence. The campaign had gradually picked up publicity over the previous decade in part due to the high-profile cases of women like Kim Lee, an

American woman living in China who publicized the abuse she suffered at the hands of her husband on *Weibo*, China's Twitter.[18]

The Chinese government has also taken steps in recent years to control its use of the death penalty, instituting reforms that led to a 75% decline in convictions from 2002 to 2013.[19] Domestic opposition, in the form of public uproar over high-profile wrongful executions, has been the driving force behind these changes. See the famous case of Nie Shubin, who was exonerated of the rape and murder of a woman in Hebei province when another man came forward to confess his guilt—ten years after Nie was executed. The mass outcry, negative media coverage, and appeals from the legal community sparked a chain of events that led to reforms in the death penalty law.[20]

Interestingly, the public has not just demanded that courts show clemency,[21] but in some cases called for them to impose the death penalty.[22] After social media campaigners protested the perceived lenient life sentence given to Li Changkui, a Yunnanese farmer convicted of murder in 2011, the court ordered a retrial, and Li was sentenced to death.[23] This led some, like prominent legal scholar Liu Renwen, to worry that the public may have *too much* sway over judicial decision-making: "On one hand, when the public holds the courts accountable, it prevents problems like corruption, and that's a positive function. But on the other hand, [in this case] it seems like popular will has too much power."[24]

Perhaps we should be wary of putting too much weight on what members of the public think. Often what really matters for shifting government policy are the actions of a small number of dedicated human rights activists.[25] But we should not forget that public opinion can have seismic effects on the success of those activists. Public awareness and support for the human rights of vulnerable groups can profoundly affect activists' ability to advocate for policy changes.[26] This is particularly relevant in authoritarian places like China, where small interest groups by themselves are likely to have very little sway on government policy. Activists in China who call for the reduction of the death penalty or for laws against domestic violence may have some limited success in changing government policies, even without any public interest in their actions. However, those issues on which the CCP has quickly implemented reforms in recent years, from abolishing detention facilities for migrants to cracking down on corruption, are often precisely those that have also seen a large public commotion.[27] At a minimum, governments should be far more likely to release a prisoner or change a law on family planning when the action is backed by a public outcry, and far less likely to do so when the reform is opposed by the public. If we are to fully understand how international pressure affects human rights in China and elsewhere, we should know how it affects the people of that country.

Impacts of International Pressure on Citizens

The obvious answer is that it does not affect them. As a PhD student, I was sometimes questioned on why I was writing my dissertation on this subject. The CCP, with its vast censorship system, does not let its people hear about foreign countries' criticism of their human rights violations—so why try and study something that does not happen.

The logic behind why the CCP would do this is quite straightforward: when people find out something that is critical of their rulers, they will become more critical of their rulers. For many human rights scholars, the international community can play a key role in this process.[28] From the international community citizens hear about foreign condemnation of their government's repressive acts, learn about international human rights norms, and become more aware that their leaders are not respecting those norms.[29] As a result, they show their support to activist groups protesting those repressive acts or voice their own displeasure online or on the street.[30] For authoritarian regimes like the CCP, this kind of dissent can be highly dangerous. The more people protesting the government and its actions, the more that others will be emboldened to join in and publicly announce their own grievances. At its most serious, this may lead to what Timur Kuran calls a "revolutionary cascade" of anti-government protests.[31]

So regimes should cut the problem off at the source. They should use their powerful repressive and censorship apparatuses to strangle any dissenting voices, whether they are domestic or foreign. Any condemnation should be suppressed. In this way regimes can maintain the illusion that they enjoy widespread support at home and abroad and minimize any public discontent over their behavior.

The need for authoritarians to limit criticism in this way has become almost tautological. Part of the way that political scientists define what makes an authoritarian an authoritarian is the way they "stifle independent criticism and analysis"[32] and "limit criticism of official policies and actions."[33] The watchdog organization *Freedom House,* responsible for monitoring political and press freedoms around the world, codes governments as authoritarian based in part on their willingness to "censor or punish criticism of the state."[34] Stopping criticism is what these regimes do.

And this seems to be why the Communist Party has chosen to hide some of the most high-profile criticism of its actions. When Xi Jinping visited Britain in October 2015, he was met with remonstrations over his treatment of human rights from members of the public, nongovernmental organizations (NGOs), opposition leaders, and the British media.[35] While the visit itself was heavily advertised at home, none of these protests (front page on British newspapers)[36] were even mentioned in Chinese media. It is why, when Reporters Without Borders ranked China as 175th most free country (out of 180) in its Press

8 HOSTILE FORCES

Freedom Index, authorities decided to censor the news.[37] It is also why, around the Asia-Pacific Economic Cooperation (APEC) annual meeting in 2014, they issued instructions like this:

> All websites in all locales are forbidden from reporting on U.S. President Obama's call at APEC for China to open the Internet.[38]

It has a nice touch of irony, but it is exactly what we would expect an authoritarian regime to do. And this level of censorship might explain why, after all the international efforts through the 1990s to publicly shame China for its human rights, at the turn of the century Chinese citizens still expressed fewer grievances about their human rights than those in most other countries (as shown in Figure 1.1).[39]

I chose to write the dissertation not just because of those citizens who are willing to breach the internet firewall and visit forbidden foreign websites, but also because, in contrast to the prevailing wisdom, Chinese authorities have made foreign condemnation of their human rights violations quite freely available to the

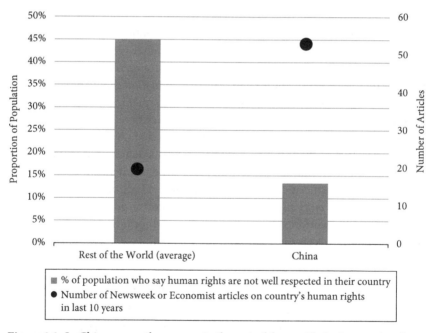

Figure 1.1 In China versus the average in the rest of the world, the international attention given to the country's human rights in the period 1990–2000 (measured by the number of *Newsweek* or *Economist* articles), along with the proportion of people who believe that human rights are not well respected in their country in the period 2000–2004 (according to the World Values Survey).

public. As discussed in the coming chapters, even Communist Party mouthpieces like the *People's Daily* have chosen to regularly feature news about international efforts to pressure China on its human rights.[40] These reports have often touched on extremely sensitive topics. On October 11, 2016, for example, Ilham Tohti, a well-known academic from the Uighur minority in China's northwestern Xinjiang region, was given the Martin Ennals Prize, an international award that honors human rights defenders.[41] The prize was notable, since at the time Tohti was languishing in a Chinese jail, having been imprisoned by authorities two years earlier for separatism. Despite being celebrated at the time, is it unlikely that the prize had any effect on Tohti's conditions,[42] just as receiving the Nobel Peace Prize had few obvious impacts on Liu Xiaobo's treatment in his own cell in 2010.[43] Indeed, on Tohti's arrest in 2014, Beijing paid scant attention to the entreaties of foreign states and organizations calling for clemency,[44] instead sentencing him to life imprisonment. The Martin Ennals Prize received little coverage in Western press outlets, but in China, the Communist Party allowed its domestic media to play up the news. State news agency *Xinhua* called the prize a "blasphemy and mockery of human rights,"[45] while nationalist tabloid the *Global Times* fulminated that the West was using the issue to "tear up" China.[46]

In early 2019, one popular interpretation of Chinese authorities' clumsy initial attempts to conceal the coronavirus disease outbreak was that it was the regime's "Chernobyl moment."[47] The spring 1986 nuclear meltdown at Chernobyl, and the Soviet government's subsequent attempts to downplay it, was in then-leader Mikhail Gorbachev's own words "perhaps the main cause of the Soviet Union's collapse."[48] The censorship of the disaster and of the subsequent foreign outcry was the archetypical authoritarian's reaction—smother any negative coverage of their actions.[49] Yet in 2019, as discussed in chapter 5, once the initial blanket censorship had subsided, authorities were only too happy to pass on news about Western criticism of their reaction to their public. Ironically, even foreign commentaries comparing the disaster to Chernobyl were freely discussed in state media, the *People's Daily* itself posing the question to its readers: "Will the current crisis crush Beijing?"[50]

If criticism is as damaging as we have been led to believe, why does the Communist Party allow its official media outlets to discuss these sensitive stories so freely—and why some stories but not others? What does this tell us about the role of international human rights pressure? In this book I challenge the assumption that criticism always damages authoritarian leaders. To understand its impacts, we need to go back to the foundations of how citizens respond to pressure on their country and how authoritarian leaders use their control of information to manipulate those responses.

Some human rights pressure may indeed have the effect we expect, sparking public grievances about human rights violations in their country. But this will not always happen. Hearing foreign actors pressurizing their country over a human rights issue in a way that appears to be a deliberate attack on their nation may qualitatively change the way that people think about the issue. Instead of considering it in terms of reducing injustice at home, they consider it in terms of defending their country against hostile outsiders. By fighting back against this pressure, they strengthen their belief that the treatment of human rights is acceptable in their country and become less willing to support efforts to change or improve that treatment.

This defensive reaction will be more likely the more "hostile" the pressure appears to be: the more closely linked it is to international competition, and the more divorced it is from real-life injustice or abuse. This includes pressure that comes from a geopolitical opponent at times of high tension, pressure that addresses issues intimately tied to the integrity of the nation, and pressure that vaguely rehashes general attacks rather than providing new information about specific rights violations.

We should not forget that the targets of human rights pressure are not passive recipients. They are governments, organizations, and individuals who can manipulate that pressure for their own advantage. Since authoritarian regimes have strong control over the flow of information, much of the information about human rights that reaches members of the public comes ready-filtered through their censorship and media apparatus. This means that news about police shootings of protestors that comes from authoritative neutral sources is unlikely to get through. Instead, regimes will only allow their state media to report to their public the human rights pressure that appears to be the most "hostile"—and they will make it look as hostile as they can.

Regimes will use this hostile pressure to push their citizens into seeing human rights violations in terms of fighting back against international threats, rather than as a matter of government oppression. But this will only work if the populace believes that their rulers represent their nation, and so any criticism of government policies is automatically construed as criticism of the nation as a whole. It is precisely because the CCP has been able to cultivate among its public this tight link between the party and the nation as a whole that it can so successfully weaponize international pressure for its own propaganda purposes.

Public International Human Rights Pressure

In the above conversation I sifted through a few different terms—"pressure," "criticism," "condemnation," "shaming," "diplomacy"—without really defining what we are talking about. These concepts each capture some of the focus of the book, something I less mellifluously call "public international human rights pressure." This is anything (made) public from an international source that seeks to make an actor—normally a government—protect human rights in a way that it would not otherwise have done.

The public instruments of pressure vary widely. At one end we have the blunt, direct tools. These are measures that tie behavioral change to economic relations,[51] or indeed measures that implement or threaten any kind of direct material punishment, from military action to the delivery of medical supplies. This kind of pressure is generally imposed by the most powerful actors in international relations, the states, but could also come from the threat of exclusion from international bodies like the World Trade Organization or even from the public or corporations in the form of consumer boycotts.

Then we have the softer tools—naming and shaming countries over their treatment of human rights. These are the instruments of human rights pressure that we most commonly see: UN condemnations of crackdowns on protests, Amnesty International's calls for the release of political prisoners, mass public protests for gay rights. They do not impose direct punishments but rely on "unleashing opprobrium,"[52] using international or domestic norms to persuade states to change their behavior. This is generally a more democratic kind of pressure, coming not just from states but also from the media, NGOs, and the public, and may range from harsh tongue lashings to mild disapproval, or even just starkly stating the injustice of the abuses. Some persuasive tools may not even be particularly critical, instead relying on emotional appeals for states to have restraint or to take steps to improve the treatment of their citizens.

Finally, we have the least explicit form of pressure, what Moravscik calls "cooptation."[53] This is when the international human rights community works (visibly) with domestic actors fighting for human rights within the target country. This might include announcing funding for human rights activist groups, publicly meeting with opposition groups, or giving dissidents high-profile international awards.[54] Regimes may feel shamed by the prestige given to the activists or worried by the challenge to their rule from more empowered opposition groups.

Of course, some pressure is imposed secretly or in private, but unless it is leaked or otherwise reaches the public sphere, it is not the subject of this book.[55] If pressure is public, then it is information that is potentially available for the public to find out about, and therefore information that needs to be dealt with by regimes like the CCP.

Authoritarian States and China

As one of the most high-profile targets and failures of human rights diplomacy,[56] China is a good case study. It is a common example of a repressive regime subjected to over three decades of all the tools in the human rights textbook, but also a case of uncommon importance as the world's largest authoritarian state.

One notable feature of authoritarian states is the regime's control over information, including any information coming from abroad. Rulers can take steps to manipulate any information about foreign human rights pressure, which means that the pressure citizens hear about is likely to be dependent on what their authorities choose to let through. This means that how regimes like the CCP deal with human rights diplomacy deserves special attention. And more often than not, it is these kinds of regimes that are in the crosshairs of the international human rights community. In 2016, for example, eight of the nine countries targeted for draft resolutions by the UN Human Rights Council were countries whose media was rated by the Freedom House watchdog as "not free."[57] Five of these were in the world's top ten offenders. Shaming human rights abuses may in fact be most effective in these kinds of states precisely because the information will have more of an impact in such a restricted media environment.[58] Yet we have very little understanding of whether, and in what form, international pressure reaches citizens living under authoritarian rule.

So while this is a story about what happens to international human rights pressure in China, the findings should also tell us something about authoritarian countries more generally. And in the book's concluding chapter I use the theory to make some tentative predictions about what should happen beyond China and why some countries' governments should be better able to exploit international pressure for their own benefits than others.

Looking at only one country of course has its limitations, since we cannot explore in detail how cross-national aspects like regime type, histories of colonialism and anti-Americanism, press freedom, and even past levels of government repression affect the reaction to international pressure. But an in-depth single-country analysis also has its advantages. Using a mix of historical and statistical analysis of state media reports, nationwide surveys, survey experiments, and mass interviews with members of the public, I can instead explore more deeply the impacts over time, between sources, issues, and individuals.

A wide range of approaches also makes it possible to address one of the most serious concerns about this kind of project, that of research ethics. The research environment at the best of times in China prohibits research into the sensitive arena of human rights, and this is especially the case under Xi Jinping, who has cracked down further on civil society since coming to power. In my research for this book I carried out surveys and interviews in China, so I had an ethical obligation to ensure that I did not ask respondents any questions where their answers would potentially put them at risk. Throughout my fieldwork, there was an ever-growing possibility that survey respondents or interviewees might be subject to attention from the authorities if they were to talk to a foreign researcher about human rights issues. There has been no clear guidance for foreign researchers or for the public over which topics or actions might attract unwanted attention. Given this uncertainty, I needed to be overly cautious about the types of questions I asked people in surveys and interviews.

In any case, asking people directly about most of their civil or political rights in recent years has become next to impossible, even in government-approved surveys. While I have taken advantage of some surveys that ask about political attitudes from the times before suspicion of academic research reached the fever pitch of Xi Jinping's leadership, in my two experimental surveys and most of the interviews I use the topic of women's rights. While women's rights in China have become a big part of Western condemnations of human rights in China since the arrest of feminist activists in 2015, I chose this issue primarily for ethical purposes. The CCP has, since its inception, portrayed itself as a liberator of women,[59] and as a result party propaganda can ill afford to condemn support for women's rights. At the time of my surveys and interviews, at least, it was relatively freely discussed in academic research and on traditional and social media.

This Book

In the next chapter I begin with the dilemmas facing authoritarian regimes like the CCP in how to deal with international pressure over their human rights. Social psychological theories of motivated reasoning and social identity illuminate how different kinds of international pressure may influence citizens' attitudes toward human rights and give us some concrete predictions about how regimes will approach that pressure.

The first half of the book examines how the CCP manages international human rights pressure. Chapters 3 and 4 analyze in detail the history of foreign attempts to target China over its human rights. I explore key case studies, from the massacre in Tiananmen Square in 1989 to the military crackdown in Tibet in 2008, that shine a light on how state media has chosen to pass on or censor highly sensitive information about human rights pressure to the public. The cases highlight the opportunities and risks of foreign criticism. Despite authorities' efforts to cover up their human rights abuses, extensive foreign media and NGO coverage does sometimes force state media to address those abuses. Once the abuses are in the open, however, authorities then do their best to play up and weaponize any subsequent foreign pressure.

In these chapters I rely primarily on the CCP propaganda mouthpieces the *People's Daily* (人民日报) and *Xinhua* (新华) but in more recent years also refer to state-owned commercial newspapers, most notably the *Global Times* (环球时报). The paper is a state-owned subsidiary of the *People's Daily*, and its commentaries are often written by military and government officials.[60] While the newspaper's paper and online circulation is less than twenty million,[61] the website is the third most popular in the country, and the paper is hugely influential on international affairs, with much of its copy picked up and repeated in provincial newspapers.

The *Global Times* is worthy of caution here, as it is not only driven by commercial imperatives but also unusually nationalistic in its commentary, and the newspaper's editorials sometimes push at the margins of what is acceptable in state-owned media.[62] Some editorials have been later deleted from online editions if they cross that margin[63] and the nationalistic tone has been criticized by former government officials.[64] We should, therefore, be extremely careful of saying that the *Global Times* speaks for the leadership.[65] However, while the paper's views and language are often more hard-line than official government standpoints,[66] it is unlikely that content containing news of sensitive government human rights abuses could be featured in the paper without some form of central approval. Indeed, stories about human rights are some of the news most likely to be censored by authorities.[67] Xiao Gang, founder of the *China Digital Times* website, gives the example of propaganda instructions over the Nobel Peace Prize given to Liu Xiaobo:

> When dissident writer Liu Xiaobo was awarded the 2010 Nobel Peace Prize, the CPD [Central Propaganda Department] ordered all websites not to create or post stories about the prize and to delete any that already existed. The SCIO [State Council Information Office] also issued a directive forbidding all interactive online forums, including blogs and microblogs, from transmitting prohibited words relating to the prize.[68]

Chapter 5 takes the lessons from the previous two chapters and studies them statistically. Under what conditions does the CCP choose to report international pressure? I combine two original databases, of all instances of international pressure on China's human rights and all reports of international pressure on human rights in China's state-run *People's Daily* newspaper, between 1979 and 2011. I find that the newspaper has been far more likely to write about pressure that comes from the United States, particularly at times of bilateral tension, on issues of territorial integrity, and when that pressure provides little new information about specific human rights issues. It even does so for obscure pieces of foreign criticism that would have been unlikely to have reached the public through other means. Together these three chapters provide strong evidence for the argument that China's leaders see real propaganda benefits from certain types of foreign criticism and choose to pass this information on to their public.

But why does it do so? What are these benefits? Looking at the regime's actions alone only tells half of the story. The second half of the book looks at how the citizens react. In chapter 6 I examine the case study of women's rights. While foreign pressure on women's rights in China has had a relatively successful history, I use two online experiments to show that pressure from the United States reduces Chinese citizens' concerns about the state of women's rights in China and their willingness to take action to support domestic women's rights activism. But when pressure comes from the African Union or is explicitly directed against Communist Party leaders rather than against the nation as a whole, this "backfire" disappears or may even be reversed.

I explore the thought processes behind these reactions in chapter 7, using over two hundred interviews with citizens approached randomly on the street in an eastern Chinese city. These interviews asked not only about women's rights but also about international pressure on air pollution and the use of ivory in traditional Chinese medicine. Together, the interviews shed light on the logics that people employ when they encounter foreign pressure on a wide range of issues and how they use it to form attitudes about their country.

One concern with these interviews and experiments is that they do not reflect how people hear about foreign pressure in real life. In chapter 8 I address this concern with a quasi-natural experiment. I make use of a nationwide attitudes survey that was conveniently carried out in China around the time of President Obama's meeting with the Dalai Lama in 2011. The timing of the survey allows us to explore how this highly publicized piece of international pressure affected people's beliefs about their rights—in this case making them significantly more likely to believe that their country was democratically ruled.

Finally, chapter 9 explores how these findings extend beyond mainland China, from Zimbabwe to the United Kingdom, and what this means for how we think about successful and failed international pressure. Pressure may backfire anywhere, but regimes that have the history and propaganda apparatus to be able to convincingly portray themselves as the sole, legitimate representatives of the nation and portray any external pressure as "hostile" are the most likely to be able to successfully elicit that backfire.

Most books on this subject are, quite justifiably, highly optimistic about the multiple successes of international pressure on human rights. They view its failures, places like China, as places where pressure has not been powerful enough, not reached far enough, or not resonated enough. But failures of human rights diplomacy are not just an absence of success. Cases like China may betray a fundamental contradiction of the global human rights movement in some environments—the need to both coerce the leaders and persuade the public. Pressure does not push in the same direction for everyone. For some, it may stifle their willingness to support improvements in human rights and increase their support for authoritarian, populist, and nationalist leaders.

Despite this, Chinese NGOs and activist groups have called out to the United States to publicly criticize their government,[69] and on a few occasions, the CCP has allegedly given in to foreign pressure, from foreign policy on Darfur[70] to releasing political prisoners.[71] In the coming pages I do not argue that this kind of pressure is not effective or has never had powerful and crucial impacts on human rights. Instead, the fundamental point is that states and organizations need to pay close attention to how their efforts may have different consequences for different members of China's domestic audience, and that what may work on the elites may have counterproductive effects on the citizenry. This has important implications for the sources, timings, and content of messages that are most likely to be successful in improving human rights in the long term.

2
A Theory of Responses to Human Rights Pressure

What is the impact of international human rights pressure in authoritarian states? How do members of the public respond, and how do their governments deal with the possibility that their citizens will hear this information?

As discussed in the previous chapter, studies of human rights and autocratic politics tell us that foreign criticism of rights violations should pose a challenge to autocratic leaders. At its most basic level, this rests on the common-sense assumption that their citizens are rational individuals, who want to develop accurate opinions about their surroundings. They evaluate all the information they have been given to do so. When they hear condemnation from abroad telling them that their human rights are not well respected and they believe it comes from a trustworthy or authoritative source, then they update their views about human rights in their country. They become more likely to believe that those rights are not well respected. If they care about their human rights and those of their fellow citizens—another assumption—then they will be more likely than before to try and put pressure on their government to improve those rights, by adding their own voice to criticism or by providing support to domestic activist groups calling for changes in policy.

Authoritarian regimes like the Chinese Communist Party (CCP) do not want any challenges to their policies and are equipped with powerful media and censorship apparatuses. They should, therefore, use those apparatuses to prevent their citizens from encountering any news about foreign human rights pressure.

How Do People Respond to Criticism?

This is a pleasingly straightforward explanation, but it does not tell the whole story. To understand this, we need to start from the psychological foundations of how people respond to critical information about their country, and then see what these foundations can tell us about how the Communist Party might deal with different kinds of human rights pressure in China.

The problem is that people are not merely rational individuals, adding together all available information to give themselves the most accurate depiction of

Hostile Forces. Jamie J. Gruffydd-Jones, Oxford University Press. © Oxford University Press 2022.
DOI: 10.1093/oso/9780197643198.003.0002

their environment. Many of us have justifiably berated a referee for wrongly penalizing our team but nodded sagely when the very same decision was quite reasonably given against our opponent. Many of us have avoided opening an email that may bring bad news about a job application or refused to accept that it was our poor timekeeping that caused us to miss a train. We all have different motivations in dealing with new information—we do want to try and develop the most comprehensive picture of what is going on in the world, but we also want to make sure we ward off anything that makes us feel bad about ourselves and seek out anything that might bolster our self-esteem. This is a phenomenon known as motivated reasoning.[1]

Numerous studies have found, for example, that rather than adjusting our beliefs based on new information, we try to fit the information into those existing beliefs.[2] We have an emotional attachment to our beliefs—maybe we have vigorously maintained the virtues of a particular politician to our family, furiously dismissed their detractors on social media, and traveled miles to proudly vote for them. Suddenly relinquishing those deeply held beliefs would hurt, so when we hear that the newly elected leader's policies are hurting the economy we deny the reports, blame others for the failures, or argue that the economy is not that important in any case.[3]

However, we are not just motivated to protect our existing beliefs. One of the more influential psychological theories of the last century is Henri Tajfel's social identity theory. This theory argues that our memberships in social groups like political parties, football teams, or nations are an important way by which we define who we are.[4] In China, as in many countries, the nation is one of the most firmly held social identities.[5] Indeed, Chinese people of all ages, genders, and ethnic groups show some of the strongest national attachments in the world.[6] In the World Values Survey conducted in 2018, 89% of Chinese citizens said that they felt close to their country and 93% said they were proud of their country.[7] This attachment has been heavily promoted in recent decades by the CCP[8] and nationalist protests have been an important way by which citizens have expressed their political opinions in public over the last century.[9]

A big part of our self-esteem, our sense of self-worth, comes from those groups—how well our football team is doing, how highly respected our political party is, or how secure and prosperous our nation is. If we think our group is performing badly, we feel hurt. If we think our group is being unfairly maligned, we feel personally attacked.[10] This is a feeling that we all recognize—a newspaper columnist excoriates our chosen political party for its poor policies, or a rival manager tries to have our team banned from a competition for flouting financial penalties. The pain is personal.

In simplest terms, this means that we are heavily motivated to protect and defend our group—against perceived attacks, against disrespect, against anything that might make us feel badly about the group (especially in comparison to other groups).[11] Like, for example, international pressure on our country's human rights. International pressure tells us that others are targeting our country for its behavior, that they disapprove of it and judge it to be below the accepted standards of other countries, and that they are trying to put pressure on it to change its behavior. According to the premises of social identity theory,[12] this pressure on our country may make us feel that we are personally under attack and that our own self-esteem is being threatened.

One way to protect ourselves is to lash out, to blame other countries for the problems, or to vilify them to make our own country look better in comparison.[13] Another way is to assert our love for our country even more strongly.[14] This is popularly known as the "rally 'round the flag" (or "rally") effect, often used as an umbrella term to describe the common phenomenon of publics rallying around their political leaders in times of national crisis or war.[15] In this case, it means that when people feel that their country is being threatened or attacked, they unite against a common enemy. If the international community is attacking our country over its human rights and this threatens our self-esteem, then we may reflexively seek solace in our common national identity and uncritically lend our support to our country's leaders.[16]

But we also protect our group through motivated reasoning of the criticism itself.[17] There is plenty of evidence to suggest that we reject out of hand information that attacks our ingroup or threatens its positive image, even if this information would help us form accurate opinions.[18] And if this critical information comes from "outsiders," like other countries or international organizations, then we are even more likely to reject it.[19] One study shows, for example, that Australians were far less willing to agree with someone telling them that their country was racist when they believed the commentator was from overseas than if they thought the commentator was a local.[20] This does not seem to be because they simply mistrusted any information that came from foreigners—indeed, they were quite happy to lap up praise of their country, regardless of who it came from.[21] Criticism, from outsiders at least, is unique because it hurts.

Fighting Back

Does this mean that people will simply ignore any foreign condemnation of their country? After returning to the United Kingdom after graduate school across the Atlantic, I found I was much more enthusiastic about British food than when I had left. What had happened? It had nothing to do with the quality of the American food I had faced; it was because almost as soon as I moved abroad, I was informed by my friends—French, Indians, Americans, even Australians—of the blandness of British cuisine. While I was quite sympathetic to this, as a wavering patriot I did not particularly like hearing others tell me so, and it made me defensive. So I pushed back, insisting on my appreciation of the food. I thought about counterarguments and even did some research on the new wave of British gastronomy. Very soon I was convincing myself.

The moral is that people do not just reject out of hand information that criticizes their nation. They often look to fight back, to take steps to actively defend it, especially when they feel like it is being deliberately targeted. An analogy often used to describe political partisanship is that each side sees their party like a sports team in a competition—they want to demonstrate that their team is superior to others.[22] Whether this is Republicans versus Democrats or the Soviet Union versus the United States, they want to feel (and show) that they are winning the contest, because if they lose, they will personally suffer. Criticism—especially if it seems to be deliberately trying to put down the team—is a direct threat to the team's performance in this contest, and as members and supporters they will look to fight back, to show that their team is better.

Part of this reaction comes down to simple belligerence: people are angry that their group is being attacked and just want to do something about it, to respond in some way. Studies have shown that one of the main reasons that people support their leaders more in times of war or terrorist attacks is anger—they rally around their commander in chief or they start preferring hawkish politicians or aggressive policies, things that will allow them to best fight back against that attack.[23] In the same way, it is a natural reaction to "cheerlead" for the nation, to play up the country's positive qualities as a way of expressing allegiance and drumming up others' support.[24] When it is being denigrated, vilified, or made to look bad in the eyes of the world, this is when cheerleading is most needed,[25] and this is when the citizens must fight back.

They also fight back by thinking through counterarguments to the criticism. There is plentiful evidence that our membership of some social groups is so valuable to us that we use all our mental resources to protect that group and our position in it.[26] Studies have found that when we encounter information that criticizes that valuable group, we process the information for longer than we would otherwise, spending time to go over it and develop counterarguments.[27] And by thinking through these counterarguments, we may end up developing stronger opinions in the opposite direction.[28] In the United States, for example, Republicans surveyed after news of the drop in the unemployment rate in October 2012 under President Obama believed that the level of unemployment was higher than those surveyed before the news.[29] The information clashed with their identities as Republicans, identities that are partly bolstered by the belief that Democratic presidents are bad for the country, but also the need to demonstrate that belief whenever they can around the time of a bitterly fought election campaign.

So on encountering human rights pressure, people may manage their emotional distress by fighting back, asserting the positive qualities of their country, and insisting that it does indeed respect human rights. If they have the will and energy, they may develop counterarguments, find logical flaws, or search their memory for evidence that their nation does not violate human rights, all making them more likely to believe that human rights are indeed well respected. They may also cheerlead for their country—verbally fighting back against its critics— even if they do not truly believe in their own words.[30]

But even insincere cheerleading may have real consequences.[31] One study found that while Americans do cheerlead for their Democrat or Republican teams when they evaluate whether their economy is good or bad, this cheerleading genuinely influences their behavior—it makes them significantly more or less likely to choose to go out and spend their money.[32] Another study found that when "strongly identified gamers" read articles that linked playing video games to aggression, they not only felt that their identity as a gamer was under threat but also became more likely to post comments online to try and discredit the articles.[33] The information challenged the gamers' identity; brought confusion, anxiety, and frustration; and motivated them to take action to fight back.[34]

Let's take a stylized example. Imagine that the US president issues a statement criticizing political freedoms in, say, Venezuela. The statement provokes feelings of anger and anxiety for Luis, a Venezuelan citizen, as it challenges his proud collective identity as a member of a country that values political freedoms, and the president's words feel like a deliberate effort to denigrate or even subjugate his country. As a result, Luis seeks to fight back against this attempt and reassert his country's positive qualities. He angrily denies that there is any problem with political freedoms in Venezuela and says that there is no need to improve them. He searches through his memory for ways in which his country has supported political rights over the years, by freely allowing popular votes or by allowing media that is critical of the regime. He then comes to believe even more strongly than he did before that there is indeed political freedom in Venezuela and publicly voices this belief on social media, announcing his support for the government and his opposition to activist groups.

Authoritarian Dilemma

There is the potential, then, for international pressure to backfire. If citizens react like Luis, then pressure may reduce their grievances about their country's human rights, make them less likely to support domestic human rights activists, and make them more willing to throw their backing behind an authoritarian government.

If so, these governments may benefit from revealing news about international pressure over their rights records to their citizens. The revelations may encourage more public support for their rule but also may help manage the fallout when their human rights violations are exposed. Autocrats cannot always hide human rights violations. In some cases, this will be because the violations are vital to a government policy that the public needs to be aware of, such as a ban on a particular social media application or a policy to reduce electoral competition. In other cases, it will be because the incident or policy change is so significant that the information has already spread across the population through word of mouth, social media, domestic media, or even international media and nongovernmental organizations (NGOs).

While these kinds of human rights violations may sometimes be effective methods of deterring activism or opposition,[35] they also risk sparking public dissatisfaction.[36] Foreign human rights pressure may help to resolve this. Imagine a budding dictator. He has just abolished a rival opposition political party and arrested its leaders. His regime needs to inform the public that the group no longer exists, and in any case the news has been widely covered in foreign newspapers so is difficult to hide. There is extensive foreign pressure on the regime to reverse its decision, and widespread criticism of how the crackdown harms democratic norms. By using its state media to report foreign pressure to its public, the regime induces members of the public to be more vocally supportive of the crackdown and less willing to support any activists protesting. In the social media age, this nationalist cheerleading may be especially useful. Framing news stories about human rights violations as attacks from hostile rivals may allow the regime to co-opt vocal cyber-nationalists—in China sometimes called "little pinks"[37]—inviting them to flood comments about the article on social media with defensive nationalist rhetoric.

But there are risks. Citizens may well be motivated to defend their nation, but this does not mean they do not still also have the desire to seek out accurate information about the world. Many will still respond to foreign pressure as rational individuals—they will evaluate the negative stories about human rights in their country and update their views on how well those rights are respected. Moreover, advertising international opprobrium over human rights abuses does not just tell people about foreign effort to criticize their country, but also risks telling people news about the human rights abuses themselves, abuses that they might not have otherwise heard about.[38] Take the case of Morocco in 1990. In response to an Amnesty International report that heavily criticized their respect for human rights, the Moroccan government launched a domestic advertising campaign to denounce the story. But the campaign backfired, because instead of winning supporters, it just served to spread the news around the country about the human rights violations contained within the Amnesty report.[39]

And we should not forget that the ordinary citizens are not the only domestic audience that a government needs to worry about. People on the front line—activists, dissidents, and protest leaders—enthusiastically seek out international solidarity for their cause.[40] There is evidence that this solidarity, from official statements in support of protests to threats of sanctions on leaders if they do not respect civil liberties, can galvanize activists.[41] The international attention reminds them that their cause is a legitimate one[42] and bolsters their feelings of power against a vulnerable government,[43] which may boost their confidence to come out and protest. In late 2007, for example, the US Congress awarded the Dalai Lama the Congressional Gold Medal. Despite media blackouts, Tibetan monks who had found out about the award through foreign radio broadcasts and Tibetan websites came out and celebrated—and were promptly arrested. A few months later, local authorities cracked down on protestors calling for the release of those monks, sparking mass unrest across the region.[44]

So for regimes like the CCP, international human rights pressure poses a dilemma. If some pressure does indeed backfire, making citizens less likely to express dissatisfaction with their human rights and less likely to support activists and dissidents, then rather than censoring all foreign pressure, it is in regimes' interests to make sure that their citizens hear and read about this information. On the other hand, these regimes also need to prevent their citizens, activists, and dissidents from finding out about any pressure that they might respond to as rational actors, increasing the risk of dissatisfaction and unrest. In other words, highlighting foreign pressure can have a propaganda value but carries risks.

For governments that rule over open societies, the free press and internet mean that citizens are going to hear about all sorts of information, information that damages the government as well as information that backfires. But authoritarian regimes can do something about this. They can use their control of the media and the internet to manipulate foreign pressure, to make sure that their citizens only find out about the pressure that will backfire—and not about the pressure that will damage—and to frame it in a way that encourages people not to seek accuracy but seek to fight back. The question then is: what to censor and what to pass on to the citizens?

Human Rights as Hostility

People have a range of motivations when considering foreign pressure (as shown in Figure 2.1)[45]—from the desire for an accurate picture of the world, to protecting their previous beliefs, to defending their important social groups (including the rights of their fellow citizens), to personal interests in the issue itself.[46] When these motivations conflict with each other, as often happens when

24 HOSTILE FORCES

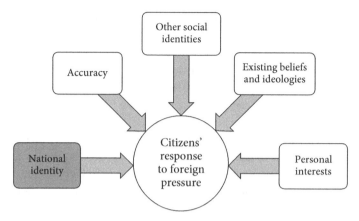

Figure 2.1 A simplified model of how people respond to foreign human rights pressure.

people hear criticism of their group, their response will depend on which is most salient and important to them.

For example, when highly popular local activists are arrested, people's empathy and solidarity with the plight of their fellow citizens may overwhelm any concerns about national pride or even personal interest. Or on ultra-politicized issues like climate change, around elections, in highly partisan countries like the United States, people's political identities may well subsume any other considerations. Studies showing how Americans fight back against information that threatens their previous beliefs and identities, for example, have found that this backfire only seems to happen on a very small number of emotional, controversial issues that have come to symbolize bipartisan competition in the United States,[47] like the war in Iraq,[48] the Affordable Care Act,[49] or the unemployment rate at the time of a presidential election.[50] On issues less obviously linked to bipartisan competition, people generally relegate any partisan concerns and look for accuracy.[51]

In China, like many one-party authoritarian states, people do not hold partisan political identities in the same way as in the United States. A huge online survey carried out between 2012 and 2014 found that Chinese citizens' ideologies do broadly fall somewhere along a spectrum from "authoritarian-traditional-nonmarket" to "liberal-nontraditional-market," but there is no clear partisan divide on this spectrum, no clear divide between right and left or between regime supporter and regime opponent.[52] Perhaps because political opposition is almost nonexistent in China, distinct partisan political identities have not been able to take root. Instead, as discussed above, the most powerful social identity is the nation. So rather than partisan competition, in China people's response to foreign pressure is more likely to be determined by the salience of national competition. Their response will depend on whether the pressure taps more strongly into their motivation to defend their nation in this competition or their motivation to form accurate opinions about the state of human rights.

To strip this argument down, if people's motivation to defend the nation is not activated (and nor are their other competing motivations like strong existing beliefs or personal stakes in the issue), then they should judge the content of the foreign criticism on its own terms—as something that tells them about ongoing injustices and abuses. If they then judge this criticism to be important and accurate enough, they will become more negative about their country's human rights, increasing the likelihood they will support activism to fight those injustices and abuses. Autocrats should use their censorship apparatus to prevent the public from hearing about this kind of pressure.

If the motivation to defend the nation is activated, however, people will bypass the content and consider the pressure not as a piece of information about human rights issues, the individual injustices or abuses, but as an attack on their nation's standing. They fight back against the threat, asserting their country's respect for human rights or forming counterarguments against the criticism. They will be less likely to support actions that protest those conditions and will be more likely to take "positive" actions like posting pro-regime comments on social media. Autocrats should use their control of state media to strategically pass on to their citizens pressure that achieves this.

To put this another way, certain kinds of international pressure can qualitatively change how people react to a human rights issue. Let's imagine that your own government has cracked down on peaceful protests across your country. News about what exactly has happened is hazy, at best. Now consider two hypothetical pieces of international pressure on your government over these actions. On one side is a statement from your neighboring country's populist leader, a country with which you have numerous territorial disputes (an emotional issue for you) and that has sponsored separatist movements in your homeland in the past, denouncing your countrymen as human rights abusers and calling for mass international sanctions. On the other side is a statement from a coalition of local and international human rights NGOs highlighting the pain of the arrests, the beatings, and the tear gas and calling out the government for its failure to protect its own people.

Clearly this is an exaggerated case, and there are numerous other differences between the two pieces that might affect how you interpret the pressure. For the purposes of this argument, however, the point is a clear one—in comparison to the second, the first piece focuses the mind on the threat to the nation and its standing. The injustices and pain from the human rights abuses are relegated behind the motivation to defend the nation against this attack from abroad. This framing of the very same crackdown changes the way that citizens respond.

My argument is that for an under-pressure government to successfully weaponize foreign pressure over a human rights issue and encourage its people not to fight the issue but to fight back, it needs to make them see the issue as one of international competition, and not individual injustice, to make them focus on the threat to the nation's standing rather than the content of the human rights violation. To do so successfully, it needs to be able to present the pressure as a hostile attack on the nation and its standing. On some occasions it is easy to frame pressure as hostile in this way, and the regime will happily highlight this pressure for its public. On others the source, the target, the issue, and the timing all make this strategy far more difficult, and when this happens, the regime will do what it can to stop its people from finding out.

The question then is: what lessons can this general insight tell us about the real-life impacts of international pressure in China? What does this mean practically for the kinds of pressure that the CCP can successfully weaponize to bolster its position? And what does this tell us about the actions that the international community should avoid, to prevent them from being used as domestic propaganda? This book is about China, an authoritarian state with a peculiar history of colonialism, nationalism, and geopolitics, so in the following I draw out some of the practical implications of my argument for China. What about other countries? The dilemma of foreign pressure applies to any regime around the world, and I will come back to what it might mean for countries with different histories, political systems, and international relations in the final chapter.

Implications for China

Source

The first indication of hostility is where the pressure comes from. It should be easier for regimes to make their citizens see foreign pressure as a hostile attack on their nation's standing when it comes from a major geopolitical rival. In fact, one of the key reasons people are much less amenable to criticism of their country from outsiders than to criticism from their fellow citizens is because they believe that outsiders have destructive or hostile motives toward their country but assume that their compatriots have the best interests of the nation at heart.[53] The perceived motives of the criticizer are crucial. If people believe that another country is deliberately using human rights pressure to denigrate their nation, then the threat to their nation and its standing becomes clear and salient.

A natural extension of this is that some outsiders will appear to be more hostile than others—most notably those who have a history of antagonism or who appear to have something to gain geopolitically in denigrating the nation. Citizens of the Soviet Union would have been far more likely to view pressure coming from the United States, its major geopolitical opponent, as a deliberate hostile act against the country than pressure that came from an ally like Cuba. The perceived hostility of a foreign country will also vary over time, as the bilateral rivalry increases and decreases in intensity. At the height of the Cold War, when the Soviet Union and the United States were trading barbs in the Cuban Missile Crisis, for example, the sense of international competition would have been even more salient for Soviet citizens, and pressure from the United States on their country's human rights would have been seen as even more hostile. Regimes that wish to use the pressure to evoke a feeling of defensiveness among their citizens will have a relatively easy job at these times.

Pressure that comes from a long-standing ally or a scrupulously neutral party, on the other hand, is much less likely to evoke this sense of hostility. Even with a geopolitical opponent, there are times when relations are more benign or positive, where both sides are seeking to sign a bilateral trade deal, for example, and the news is full of stories of cooperation and friendship. It is particularly difficult to accuse a criticizer of hostility if they seem to have a genuine interest in improving that human rights issue. Close allies, by their nature, have no obvious material gain from bringing down their partners, so any criticism is far more likely to be motivated by an honest concern with human rights. Others may have an even more palpable interest in improving the issue itself: organizations whose sole job is to work to eliminate a particular human rights violation, or countries whose citizens are being physically affected.[54] The point is that it is much more difficult to frame as "hostile" those whom you have been calling your friends and partners, or those who have seemingly genuine reasons to want to improve the human rights issue.[55]

The United States is China's most prominent geopolitical rival, a rivalry evoked repeatedly by state media and reflected in public opinion.[56] In 2012 a survey by Peking University's Research Center for Contemporary China (RCCC) found that 63% of Chinese people said the United States represented the greatest danger to China (Japan was next with 17%), and 74% saw the United States as either a rival or an enemy to their country.[57] Almost half of the population believed that the United States was actively trying to prevent China's rise.[58] Of course, even such an enduring rivalry fluctuates over time. The heated rhetoric of 2020 was a far cry from the calls for cooperation of 2010[59] and the engagement of the 1980s.[60] State accusations of "hostility" are also not just limited to the United States, however, often arising against whomever Beijing is facing a territorial or diplomatic dispute with. Japan is the obvious target, given its history, but other recent campaigns have focused on countries ranging from Philippines to Vietnam, from India to Australia.

This suggests that if the CCP wants foreign pressure to backfire, it should only pass on to its public pressure that comes from a geopolitical rival—ideally the United States—especially when tensions are high, so it can easily claim that the pressure is driven by hostility. The obvious question is: why can't the CCP manipulate who is a rival? Whoever criticizes China, whether it is a friend or an opponent, why is Beijing not just able to fire up its propaganda machine and bombard its public with accounts of their inherent anti-China hostility?

The problem is that even with a powerful propaganda apparatus, some countries are far more difficult to suddenly portray as hostile than others. While Beijing has sought to calm public sentiment toward Japan in recent years, twentieth-century history means that it would not be difficult for leaders to fire up the hostility again. On the other hand, set against a background of seventy years of stories of a "friendship deeper than the deepest sea, higher than the Himalayas and sweeter than honey,"[61] or even of weeks of positive messages about economic cooperation, a sudden shift in tone is difficult, a message of hostility much harder to make stick. The CCP also needs to think about its other priorities. Suddenly turning against a key ally, calling it hostile, and directing public anger against it could seriously damage the country's vital diplomatic relations, while even lashing out against established rivals like the United States at the time of a major trade deal could have negative economic consequences.

Issue

Whether the pressure is seen as hostile or not may also depend on the human rights issue that is under scrutiny. Some issues addressed by the human rights community are much more closely tied to the nation and its standing and power than others, and it may be far easier for under-pressure regimes to frame criticism on these subjects as hostile.

This is perhaps most obvious for human rights that are related to a country's borders, its separatist movements, or breakaway territories. Some of the human rights violations in these territories will be the same repressions of civil and political liberties faced in the rest of the country, like gay rights, freedom of speech, or child labor. Other violations will be specific to the struggle for autonomy or minority rights in those territories—from the push for democracy in Hong Kong to the treatment of minority rights activists in Tibet and Xinjiang. International pressure on China often focuses on these kinds of territorial matters.

By their nature, separatist movements threaten the integrity of the nation-state. Even movements that mention autonomy or minority issues highlight something about the country, its borders, and the national identity of its people. This is particularly stark for countries like China, countries that contain territories over which sovereignty has been closely contested in recent centuries, from Tibet and Xinjiang in the West to Macau and Hong Kong in the South. And just to make foreign interference even more sensitive, Western countries have played a central role in this contestation, from British rule over Hong Kong to Central Intelligence Agency (CIA) support for Tibetan insurgents in the 1950s.[62]

So when international pressure addresses any human rights that also touch on these issues of territorial integrity, it becomes much easier for the CCP to link this kind of criticism into the nation's integrity, to frame it as a hostile attack on the country that needs to be defended against. It is much harder to do this for criticism on issues concerned with more general nationwide human rights issues like the prevention of domestic violence or the strengthening of the rule of law.[63]

This suggests a somewhat counterintuitive hypothesis: the CCP will be more likely to broadcast news that it is under pressure from the international community when it comes to human rights in Tibet, Xinjiang, and Hong Kong. This is counterintuitive because discussions of human rights in Xinjiang and Tibet are some of the most likely to be censored on social media.[64] We might expect that foreign comments about these topics should also be more likely to be hidden from the public.

Form

The form of the pressure and the way it is presented may also affect this calculation, albeit more indirectly. Some pressure is highly specific—think of Amnesty International reports describing police discrimination against a religious minority in explicit detail, or of a foreign country's diplomats accusing security forces of torturing one of their citizens. This kind of pressure is often novel—what we call the "naming" part of naming and shaming—in that it has not yet made it onto the news. If pressure is of this kind and reveals specific information about acts of discrimination or individuals tortured, it should be far harder for a propaganda machine to make the population ignore the content of the violations and instead think about international competition. As we might expect, information supported by strong, detailed evidence has been shown to be more persuasive[65] even when the source is not especially credible.[66] These are the kinds of information that autocrats are especially keen to stop their public from finding out about.

On the other hand, pressure that merely references generic government failings over human rights—what I call "general" pressure—will be much more weakly tied to the content of individual violations, and therefore much easier to link to international competition. Many instances of international pressure are of this kind, from sanctions to presidential statements and UN resolutions.

One reason some scholars have argued that naming and shaming human rights abuses might be especially effective in authoritarian countries is because few people in these environments have been able to find out about the abuses in other ways.[67] But shaming will not tell people anything new if it is just rehashing broad generalizations that they have heard many times before.

Consider two pieces of criticism of human rights violations in Tibet in 2008. In July 2010, Human Rights Watch issued a report on the crackdown on riots in Lhasa in March 2008, a report that included highly specific accusations, such as how police "were coming from the direction of Jiangsu Lu firing at any Tibetans they saw, and many people had been killed."[68] Compare this to George W. Bush's generic expression of "deep concern" about the same situation in July 2008,[69] a statement that had been repeated numerous times over the previous months. The nature of the new, detailed information about highly specific incidents contained in the Human Rights Watch condemnation is much harder to reduce to international competition. The public will also be less likely to be already aware of this new information, so this kind of pressure may reignite grievances and provide mobilization opportunities for activist groups. General statements of concern like that from President Bush, on the other hand, statements that are very similar to previous statements on human rights in China, provide very little new information, seem distant from the actual use of repression that went on in Tibet in March, and can therefore be much more easily portrayed by the authorities as just another American attempt to have a go at China.

This brings us to one extra category of pressure, what I term "policy" pressure. Some human rights abuses, like torture, are carried out covertly, generally unknown by the population. Others, like capital punishment, are carried out openly and overtly and are generally well known by the population.[70] Policy pressure is pressure that addresses these overt abuses—existing, often unpopular, but widely known government policies, such as the one-child policy in China or the campaign against the Falun Gong.

For these ongoing government policies, the costs to regimes from reporting foreign pressure are likely to be especially low, as illustrated by a survey of Chinese intellectuals in the 1990s. The survey shows that regular listeners to Voice of America—the American radio service in China that heavily covered the Tiananmen massacre—were the most likely to say that they opposed their government's actions in 1989 and the subsequent jailing of political dissidents. This was presumably because they had picked up more information about those repressive actions than nonregular listeners. But listening to Voice of America had no effect on the level of support for the one-child policy, the long-standing directive that limited most Chinese parents to one child. Nonlisteners and listeners alike would have been equally aware of the policy, so it is unlikely that foreign media provided any novel information about the issue beyond what people already knew.[71] A study twenty years later randomly exposed Chinese students in the United States to American news stories about different social and political problems in China. When students were given stories highlighting news of repression in Tibet or economic troubles—topics that are heavily censored in China—they became far more critical of their government's performance. However, when they were given stories about problems surrounding food safety—a serious issue, but one discussed relatively openly since the melamine scandal in 2008—their evaluations of the CCP did not change, and even became more positive for those who already knew something about food safety in China.[72]

So the more specific and novel the human rights violation featured in the international pressure is, the more likely that citizens will focus on this content and downgrade their views about their human rights conditions.[73] In contrast, it is far easier for a regime to obscure the content of human rights violations when reporting general human rights pressure and pressure that focuses on existing government policies. Moreover, given that the public will have already heard about the human rights issues featured, the risk of passing on this pressure is far lower.[74]

Individual Reactions

We have talked so far about the sender of pressure, the topics they put pressure on, and the form in which pressure is delivered. But the impacts of that pressure will also vary considerably depending on who hears it. Take, for example, people's relationship to the victims of human rights abuses themselves. The stronger their ties are to those victims—they may be a member of the same persecuted ethnicity or religion, for example—the more they should support foreign efforts to pressurize the government carrying out that persecution.

For others, the impact of pressure could go either way. For example, we might expect people to react more defensively to human rights pressure if they care in some way about human rights. Those who do not particularly care how their country deals with freedom of speech and political rights may feel that they still need to defend their country against an attack but would presumably be less bothered by news that their country is not performing well on these measures.

But then again, people who care strongly about human rights should, presumably, also be the ones who welcome foreign assistance. We know that people are more comfortable accepting information that fits in with their existing beliefs,[75] so those people who already believe that their country is repressive and hold strong grievances about their government's behavior should be less likely to feel that their nation's standing is under attack if they hear news that others also think so. Pressure should, therefore, be most likely to backfire among those people who already firmly believe that their country respects human rights and, more importantly, among those people who have not made up their mind either way. After all, these are the people who might actually change their mind on an issue, rather than just digging in on their existing views.

If true, this also means that a backfire should also be most likely on those issues on which people have not yet made up their mind. Pressure on firmly held universal norms like norms against slavery or mass murder, or pressure on norms that already face deeply ingrained local opposition, is unlikely to change many people's views either way. Perhaps most likely to have an impact is pressure on complex situations where there is a range of competing norms, like the balance between security and liberty in the war on terror, or on previously neglected issues that many in the public had not considered much before, like transgender rights or internet privacy.

These kinds of characteristics are important considerations to keep in mind when thinking about the impact of pressure, but they are not specific to the hostility hypothesis, and I do not spend much time evaluating whether they hold in this book. The hostility hypothesis predicts that there will be one main characteristic that determines how people react to foreign pressure—how attached they are to their nation.

I should note that this is a subtly different logic to the traditional "rally 'round the flag" story. The traditional rally argument is that external threats unite people and strengthen their attachment to their nation. The hostility argument, on the other hand, does not predict that people will identify more with their nation or become more patriotic after criticism. Instead, it argues that those who already have the strongest attachment, whose sense of self-worth is already most closely linked to their country, will be the most likely to interpret foreign criticism in terms of an attack.[76] The closer the bond people have with their country, the more important that country's performance, honor, and international standing will be for their self-esteem,[77] and the more they will feel like they need to fight back. Those who care little for their nation should care little about criticism of it. One implication of this is that, since members of persecuted groups have been widely shown to have lower national pride,[78] members of these groups may be more likely to react positively to foreign pressure, even if pressure does not explicitly address their own persecution.

It also implies that at times when public nationalism is high—from international tensions and conflicts to war anniversaries and sporting events—international pressure should be more at risk of backfiring. A more general rule is that for countries where there is a strong attachment to the nation among the population, it should be especially easy for the ruling party to weaponize foreign pressure (a theme to which I will return in the concluding chapter).

The Target

For China, it is not just the firm attachment that many citizens have to their nation that is important, but also the form of that attachment. The target of most international human rights pressure is rarely the country as a whole. By its nature, pressure is exerted to try and change something, to push leaders to change their policies on human rights. As such, it normally targets the leaders, the authorities, the people who have the power to do something to improve human rights in their country. For authoritarian countries like China, this target is invariably the regime itself.

The worry, then, for regimes seeking to weaponize foreign pressure and make their citizens fight back against the attack on the nation is that the citizens do not really see the pressure as an attack on their nation—they see it as an attack on their leaders. They ignore the appeal to hostility and focus on the content. The solution for the leaders is to strengthen the tie in their citizens' minds between the government and the country as a whole, or in one-party states like China, the CCP and the state. This policy is a familiar Stalinist one—devote all propaganda efforts toward the doctrine that the leaders and the people are one, that any threat to the leaders is a threat to the people.[79]

As has been well documented, in the years after the Tiananmen Square massacre the CCP instituted a "Patriotic Education" campaign in schools and the media.[80] This campaign was designed not just to instill a sense of patriotism in its population, but also to strengthen the link between the CCP and the nation in the public's imagination, to press home the message that the Communist Party is China, and that a threat to the party leaders is a threat to China.[81] If this propaganda has succeeded, then when people hear about foreign pressure on the government's human rights policies, they should view it as an attack on their country as a whole.

We should note here that the Communist Party as an entity is not the same as the *leaders* of the Communist Party. In 2020, over ninety million people were CCP members, many of whom joined not just for ideological reasons but to help further their career.[82] However, very few of these were policymakers in any form (only 8.4% worked for a party organization or civil service),[83] and only a tiny proportion wield any real power over policy. Some might say this tiny proportion only includes the leader himself, Xi Jinping. And propaganda officials have also sought to closely tie Xi to the Chinese people and the Chinese nation.[84] Xi has become the "Core" of the nation,[85] the "People's Leader,"[86] the "Helmsman of 1.3 billion people's Chinese dream."[87]

But what if the population does not equate the ruling party's leaders with the nation as a whole, or with its people? What if the population sees its leaders as outsiders, as a narrow band of ruling elites who do not represent the people or the country? In these cases, a country's citizens should be far less likely to view foreign criticism of these leaders' policies as criticism of the country as a whole. Since it targets some small group of elites who do not represent them, they can safely dismiss it or engage with the content of the criticism without feeling the need to fight back.

What does this mean in practical terms for human rights pressure in one-party states like China? If corruption is high and leaders look like they are taking money from the citizens, if leaders have given away some of the country's territories to appease foreign opponents, or if leaders are clearly failing to provide for the people, then there may be cracks between the ruling party and the nation. Citizens may see their leaders as individuals acting in their own interest rather than in the interest of the country.

More mundanely, foreign comments themselves could make the ruling party appear less representative of the nation, by explicitly framing foreign human rights pressure as targeting government leaders over their policies on human rights and explicitly not targeting the nation or population as a whole. Pressure that praises the people, expresses solidarity with their cause, or emphasizes the patriotism behind human rights activism may serve to reduce the likelihood that a country's citizens automatically see a foreign attack on their government's specific violations of human rights to be a hostile attack on their whole country.

Implications and Tests

Let's bring all this together. Of course, we cannot test all the aforementioned, but we do now have a number of implications that we can observe and test about the reactions of state media and citizens to international pressure. In Table 2.1 I list only the implications that are a consequence of the hostility hypothesis, and which I will test in the coming chapters. Readers interested only in these implications should note that while I explore the hypotheses in chapters 3 and 4, I will not systematically test them until chapter 5.

Alternative—but Complementary—Explanations

There are two main alternative explanations for how autocrats might deal with foreign pressure, alternatives to weigh against my hypotheses as we go through this book.

Table 2.1 Implications and Tests of Hostility Hypothesis

Implication of Hostility Hypothesis	Tests	Chapter(s)
International pressure on country's human rights will be more likely to backfire:		
When pressure comes from a geopolitical opponent	Analysis of Chinese state media articles about foreign pressure	5
	Online survey experiments with Chinese citizens on response to different kinds of foreign pressure	6
	In-depth interviews with 210 Chinese citizens	7
	Quasi-natural experiment on the impact of the Dalai Lama's meeting with President Obama	8
When there are ongoing geopolitical tensions between the source and the target	Analysis of Chinese state media articles	5
When the pressure addresses human rights issues related to territorial integrity	Analysis of Chinese state media articles	5
	Survey experiments, interviews, and quasi-natural experiment	6, 7, 8
When the pressure addresses existing government policies or general human rights issues (rather than specific abuses)	Analysis of Chinese state media articles	5
When the citizens have strong attachments to their nation	Survey experiments, interviews, and quasi-natural experiment	6, 7, 8
When the pressure seems to target the whole country or its citizens	Survey experiments	6

Informational

The first is the common-sense argument that I have already discussed: encountering foreign human rights pressure makes citizens more concerned with human rights conditions in their country and makes them more likely to support domestic activism over it. If the information seems even vaguely credible, then authoritarian leaders should look to censor the information wherever possible, and not report it in domestic state media reports. The more "sensitive" the issue is, the more likely that the criticism will be censored.

Media Credibility

Recent studies in China have begun to challenge the traditional view that autocrats censor all criticism. One influential article found that the CCP does sometimes allow people to criticize the government on social media, as long as this criticism does not call for protests in the streets.[88] A plausible explanation is that the act of carrying out censorship could itself be damaging for authorities, potentially more damaging than the risk of allowing people to read about low-level criticism on social media.

With the growth of the internet, many citizens of authoritarian countries are already aware of some high-profile news stories, including prominent foreign criticism of human rights in their own country. For the increasing number of Chinese youths fluent in English, for example, there are plentiful sources of foreign news that are not blocked. Even for those without this language ability, virtual private networks allow anyone to jump over the firewall and access Chinese-language foreign news sites. Services like the blocked *New York Times* Chinese-language website receive millions of visits per month, many from within the mainland.[89] Several interviewees featured in chapter 8 who were studying abroad said they had learned of foreign human rights pressure when in China through the *New York Times*, BBC, and other foreign news services. If state media censors or does not mention criticism widely discussed on English-language sites, then it may lose credibility, making it less effective as a trusted propaganda tool. Pre-emptively addressing the issue in state media avoids this risk and allows the CCP to frame the discussion the way it wants.[90]

If so, state media should proactively report on foreign criticism of human rights, but only criticism high profile enough that a sizeable proportion of the population has already encountered it through other sources. If credibility is the only driving force behind state media behavior, we would not expect there to be domestic news stories about minor pieces of criticism barely reported in the international press, even if they are stories that are particularly threatening or hostile.

It should also mean that state media reports of foreign criticism will be heavily influenced by the volume of foreign news stories flooding into the country through the internet. More internet access means more public exposure to foreign news and more need for propaganda officials to be proactive. Note the difference with the hostility theory here. The hostility theory expects that state media decisions will be affected not just by the amount of foreign pressure available to the public, but also by how willing and able the state is to push regime propaganda—in the form of foreign pressure—on to the public. In the next two chapters we will see that since 1949 the CCP has sometimes taken a more relaxed approach to political propaganda work in China. At other times, this ideological guidance has intensified.[91] If we find that at these high-control times—rather than at times when more foreign media stories are leaking through to the public—the regime eagerly broadcasts foreign efforts to put pressure on China over its human rights, then this suggests that propagandists are proactively using that pressure for a strategic purpose. The competing predictions from these accounts are summarized in Table 2.2.

I should stress, however, that these accounts are not mutually exclusive. The goal of this book is not to rule out the other accounts of the Chinese government's behavior but to provide a comprehensive explanation, an explanation that highlights how its behavior is also determined by the desire to use foreign pressure as propaganda.

We can easily imagine a scenario where these accounts all apply: where new information from foreign sources about a regime's human rights abuses is censored by its media when it first comes to light. The regime holds off reporting on the news until the international media coverage is so high that it cannot hide it from domestic audiences—something that could take days or even weeks. At this point, once the abuses have come to light in domestic media, the regime will

Table 2.2 Main Predictions of the Three Theoretical Frameworks

	State Media's Response	Citizens' Response
Informational	Censor all foreign human rights pressure, especially pressure on more "sensitive" topics	All foreign pressure increases people's grievances if they see it as credible
Media credibility	Report foreign pressure if it is prominent in international news or on social media As internet access increases, report more foreign pressure	All foreign pressure has minimal impact on people's grievances
Hostility	Report foreign pressure if it is perceived as hostile—even if the criticism is not prominent in other news sources or is on sensitive topics As control over propaganda increases, report more foreign pressure	Foreign pressure decreases people's grievances if they see it as hostile

continue to report foreign shaming and efforts to pressure it into changing its behavior—but only the efforts that it can easily frame as "hostile."

In the chapters that follow I will explore whether this account does indeed explain how authoritarian regimes like the CCP deal with international pressure over their human rights.

PART II
THE REGIME

3
Pressure as Propaganda
From Mao to Hu

In January 2012, Human Rights Watch (HRW) issued its annual China report. The report delivered sharp rebukes over the arrests of human rights defenders, checks on freedom of religion, and hard-line policies on ethnic minorities through the previous year.[1] But on this occasion the Chinese Communist Party's (CCP's) mouthpiece, the *People's Daily*, did not censor the report, as it had in previous years, or even mention the document's praise for China's rapid economic development. Instead, it devoted a dozen separate articles to HRW's detailed and often passionate criticisms of the state of human rights in the country. One *People's Daily* article on January 27, headlined "How Does Building Houses for Ordinary People Violate Human Rights?," recorded HRW's condemnation of Tibetan authorities' forced relocation policy.[2] It went on to quote the report's observation that "80% of the population of Tibet—including all herdsmen and nomads—were moved elsewhere," before issuing an extensive justification of government housing policy in the autonomous region.[3] The following day another *People's Daily* article focused on the criticism of authorities' use of forced confessions, the failures to respect defendants' rights, and the widespread use of torture. Again, the newspaper quoted the report's quite severe criticism, saying:

> The police dominate the criminal justice system, which relies disproportionately on defendants' confessions. Weak courts and tight limits on the rights of the defence mean that forced confessions under torture remain prevalent and miscarriages of justice frequent.[4]

Why did state media alert citizens to this relatively obscure report? The articles featured not only criticism of government policies on extremely sensitive issues—Tibet and the use of torture—but also criticism that it is hard to imagine many would have heard about through other sources. The HRW report barely received a mention in the international press.

As we will see in the next two chapters, the CCP's newspapers have written about this kind of foreign outrage far more than we might otherwise expect, often using the pressure as a tool to help introduce sensitive news about human rights, like the arrests of dissidents or crackdowns on protests. Leaders wield this

Hostile Forces. Jamie J. Gruffydd-Jones, Oxford University Press. © Oxford University Press 2022.
DOI: 10.1093/oso/9780197643198.003.0003

tool most frequently not just at times of intense high-profile foreign criticism, but also at times when the party's drive and ability to control the information environment in China is especially high.

This chapter, which takes us from the Tibet crackdown in 1959 up to the Tibet crackdown in 2008, and the next, which brings us into the 2020s, highlight how the CCP uses the international community to help frame human rights issues in China.

Before Tiananmen

Between the attempts to abolish the practice of foot-binding in the late nineteenth century (discussed in chapter 6) and the Tiananmen massacre almost one hundred years later, foreign attention toward human rights in China was rare. Despite atrocities throughout the twentieth century, the rights community mainly pushed its head into the country when Tibet was concerned. The first time was in March 1959, when a popular uprising in Lhasa spread into a full-scale revolt against Chinese rule. Mao Zedong's response was swift, and Communist forces crushed the nascent rebellion within a few days, killing thousands of Tibetans and prompting the Dalai Lama to flee to India. The actions sparked condemnation around the world, the news of which Chinese newspapers eagerly fed their readers.

At the time, the CCP had almost complete control over the information that reached its citizens.[5] Newspapers were not just state run but were the state's voice,[6] and by 1959, in the heart of his Great Leap Forward campaign, Mao was using the media as a personal propaganda tool, even penning his own editorials in the *People's Daily*.[7] Given that China was closed off from the outside world at this time, for the public, state-run media was the only way they could find out about what was going on beyond China's borders. Through the 1950s much of this news came in the form of anti-American propaganda, and especially news of its aggressive interventions abroad, from Vietnam to Latin America.[8]

For Mao, foreign condemnation over Tibet fed in nicely to this narrative. The *People's Daily* focused its ire on the "imperialist" United States, where senators had accused Chinese forces of the ethnic cleansing of Tibetan citizens.[9] The paper also lavished attention on the British media, which had led the criticism of the crackdown. A *People's Daily* report on April 8 gave a summary of the denunciations from British newspapers, denunciations of the "violent suppression of the freedoms of powerless people," and "attempts to wipe Tibet off the map."[10] In some ways this response was surprising. Given the rickety media infrastructure at the time, there would have been almost no opportunity for the public to otherwise hear about their authorities' use of repression in Lhasa, over 1,500 miles away from Beijing, never mind foreign disapproval of the actions.

In October of the same year, Ireland and Malaya sponsored a UN General Assembly Draft Resolution calling for "respect for the fundamental human rights of the Tibetan people and for their distinctive cultural and religious life."[11] The document passed with a vote of forty-two to nine, only the Soviet bloc opposing. The Indian delegation abstained, despite pressure from members of Parliament (MPs) at home, as did the United Kingdom, France, and Belgium, perhaps mindful of what support for the resolution might mean for their own colonial behavior. Further similar resolutions were tabled and passed in 1961 and 1965.

The *People's Daily* gave these discussions almost blanket coverage, with over fifty articles about the vote in the week of the 1959 meeting alone. In 1961 the paper told its readers how the General Assembly was "gravely concerned at the continuation of events in Tibet, including the violation of the fundamental human rights of the Tibetan people and the suppression of the distinctive cultural and religious life which they have traditionally enjoyed."[12] The articles all sang an almost identical refrain, attacking the United Nations as a tool for American imperialism and Cold War hostility,[13] and postulating that the sponsoring countries had only done so under orders from the United States.[14] Since Chinese soldiers had fought in Korea against forces under the UN banner a few years earlier, the accusations were not hard to make. In a front-page editorial on October 24, 1959, headlined "Opposing American Intensification of the Cold War," the paper said:

> The United States' conspiracies in the United Nations are just examples of its policies of aggression around the world, especially in the Far East. The United States is madly slandering, attacking, and ceaselessly provoking the Chinese people, which just goes to prove that it still clings to a policy of hostility and aggression towards China.[15]

By the time the third resolution passed in 1965, the story was a clear one: the United States was using the United Nations to take over Chinese territory, just as it had with Taiwan,[16] and was using the process to cover up its own aggression in Vietnam.[17] According to a *People's Daily* commentary on October 17, the resolution "proves that US imperialism is the Chinese people's most ferocious enemy; they are determined to destroy the unity of China's ethnic groups."[18] Conflicts along China's western border in 1962 turned India into enemy number two for the press machine, the UN resolutions now the manifestation of a joint United States and Indian attack on China itself.[19]

After this flurry of action, international attention to Mao's treatment of his citizens died down. Despite the millions killed in the Great Leap Forward and persecuted in the Cultural Revolution, foreign concern over China's rights conditions through the 1960s and 1970s was almost nonexistent.[20] Perversely, it took the end of these campaigns and the opening up of China to attract the gaze of the international community. Amnesty International began its China research program in 1976 and started to write up reports that addressed crackdowns on pro-democracy protests and treatment of political prisoners in the country. Amnesty's reports did not go unnoticed in Beijing, and sensitive to the novel attention, CCP officials resolved to prevent details about any political prisoners from being released to the outside world.[21]

Foreign interest grew into the 1980s as other nongovernment organizations (NGOs) began to focus on China, but in general, as Roberta Cohen demonstrates in her standout study, China was very much still the "human rights exception."[22] The combination of the American wish to keep Beijing as a cog in its anti-Soviet alliance and the recognition that conditions in China were far better than they had been ten years before meant that even while NGO and press attention grew, foreign governments tended to ignore it. And Chinese officials, perhaps confident in the good relationship their country was enjoying with Western countries, had no discernible domestic reaction to the criticism that did take place, reporting almost nothing from abroad in state media. Notably it was at this time, in spite of the limited overseas condemnation of his treatment of human rights, that then-leader Deng Xiaoping chose to adopt several international human rights agreements,[23] signing the UN Convention against Torture and joining the UN Commission for Human Rights.[24]

Tibet, 1987

It again took repression in Tibet to arouse the international community's interest.[25] In September 1987, Chinese forces met pro-independence protests in the region with arrests and violence. The crackdown ushered in, if not a torrent, a small stream of international pressure on Beijing. While the US State Department remained officially noncommittal over the actions, Congress was much more forthcoming in its disapproval. In September the Dalai Lama was invited to Washington to speak,[26] in October the House and the Senate passed a resolution condemning China and linking arms sales to the treatment of Tibet,[27] and then in December a clause that enshrined support for Tibet was entered into the Foreign Relations Authorization Act.[28] As riots and repression in Tibet continued through 1988, condemnation grew from Amnesty International and HRW as well as from the British Parliament, while in June the European Union also invited the Dalai Lama to speak to the European Parliament about the conditions.[29]

In comparison to their response in 1959, Chinese newspapers were subdued. There was a media blackout on the riots in Tibet throughout the whole of September, the *People's Daily* deciding that grape production in the region was more worthy of attention.[30] It was only in October, after state media latched on to the Dalai Lama speech and the US Senate condemnation of the repression, that domestic news began to trickle out on the unrest itself.[31] Despite this, the *People's Daily* ignored most foreign comments about the unrest, with even the Dalai Lama speech in Europe only receiving a short repost.[32] The only real mentions of anything untoward happening in Tibet came through mentions of some suspicious "anti-China" activity in the US Congress. Any avid *People's Daily* reader in 1987 would have been very up to date on the progress of American congressional resolutions but would have had little idea about the details of what had actually been discussed. Articles mainly ignored the reasons for the congressional action, merely mentioning that the resolutions attacking China for repression in Tibet had "passed" and focusing on the $200,000 worth of congressional funding given to the Dalai Lama.[33] In contrast to the rhetoric of the 1960s, there was little outrage, with any comments limited to criticizing the United States for interfering in China's domestic affairs and calling for better bilateral relations.[34]

What explains this restraint? On one side, we need to look at China's geopolitical position at the time. Not only might a more belligerent reaction have risked the burgeoning relationship with Western nations[35] but also the public's perception of the United States was very different from the early 1960s. After Mao's death in 1976, state media had spent years creeping away from the old story of American rivalry and imperialism toward a new narrative of cooperation and friendship.[36] The *People's Daily* certainly devoted plenty of attention to China's diplomatic relations with the United States through the 1980s, but in contrast to the previous decade, barely any of this focused on stories of conflict between the two states.[37] Given the "fragile" but cooperative relations between the two nations at the time,[38] any proclamations of American hostility would have fallen slightly hollow.

Moreover, at this time Deng Xiaoping's government was suffering a post-Mao legitimacy crisis, with growing political instability from protests over corruption, inflation, and democracy.[39] In these pre-Tiananmen, prepatriotic education days, the CCP was subject to rising disquiet from disgruntled nationalists. Widespread anti-Japan demonstrations in 1985 quickly became criticisms of the Communist Party's failure to take a strong line against foreign aggression, criticisms that then morphed into calls for democratization. The nationalist protests were not trying to defend the party against attacks from abroad, rallying the people around the flag, but in some cases were targeting the party itself.[40]

There was also less centrally led ideological propaganda than there had been under Mao. Deng's government had relaxed controls over the country's media, and through the 1980s there was an explosion in new daily newspapers, many with commercial goals that did not necessarily chime with the Communist Party's own interests.[41] For the party, this meant that the whole information environment within China was harder to control—especially information coming in from abroad. But despite the real possibility that news of foreign criticism of the events in Tibet would seep into the rest of the country, the party was much more reluctant to talk to its people about the criticism than in the closed-off days of the 1950s. In those days the media had a unified voice, a unified narrative, and portraying the United States as a hostile actor trying to use Tibetan unrest to divide China was an easy sell. In the late 1980s, propaganda officials faced a more divided media landscape, a more divided message on the United States, and a more divided populous. In this environment, foreign comments were potentially far more dangerous.

Tiananmen, 1989

The Sino-American goodwill did not last through the military crackdown on the streets of Beijing on June 4, 1989. Condemnation from around the world came almost immediately, from the United States[42] to the Philippines[43] and even the Soviet Union.[44] The United States immediately banned weapons sales to China and then, in coordination with the G7 and the European Commission, expanded sanctions. Japan and the World Bank froze loans, the United Kingdom canceled bilateral visits, and France opened its borders to democracy protestors hoping to flee China after the massacre.[45]

The gamut of foreign condemnation gave the Deng regime a dilemma—hide the criticism, as with the riots in Tibet two years earlier, or follow Mao and play it up? To begin with, authorities took the first route and tried to limit public knowledge of the violence in Beijing and elsewhere as much as possible. Passing on stories of foreign accusations, sanctions, and the canceling of economic and diplomatic deals might substantiate rumors and fill in details about what the forces had done on the night of June 4, for those in the population who were unaware.[46] As a result, in the days and weeks following the massacre, state media was very careful about the foreign criticism it reported to the public.

While the criticism arrived almost immediately, it was only four days later, on June 8, that it started to trickle into state-run news. It began with a brief story in the *People's Daily*, noting only that President Bush had suspended a US-China arms deal for "things happening at present."[47] The newspaper was more forthcoming about the news that Professor Fang Lizhi, a leader in the Tiananmen protests, had been given asylum in the US embassy.[48] This story gave state media a chance to portray Fang and his wife Li Shuxian as traitors, fleeing their nation to join anti-Chinese and anti-Communist foreign forces.[49] Whereas articles about foreign criticism that directly attacked the CCP's actions of June 4 would have shone a light on what happened that night, the dispute over Fang allowed the CCP to play the criticism and sanctions as a bilateral dispute between two international competitors, even giving the foreign ministry the opportunity to say that US actions were a "violation of international law."[50]

More than anyone else, state media focused on the Voice of America (VoA).[51] At this time, VoA was perhaps the most widely used foreign news source in China[52] and a crucial way for locals to pick up information about the ongoing events in Beijing.[53] In 1989 around 80% of VoA's Chinese news time was devoted to the Tiananmen movement,[54] and the service may have had up to a hundred million Chinese listeners, using its Mandarin and Cantonese short-wave radio service to reach homes around the country.[55] Many students and urban intellectuals heard about the 1987 unrest in Tibet through the service,[56] and the government explicitly blamed it for spreading news about pro-democracy protests in 1986.[57] In a 1996 survey, 63% of Chinese intellectuals working and studying in the United States said that they had listened to VoA at least once a week when they were in China and the service had given them different interpretations of the stories covered in ordinary Chinese media.[58] As one respondent said, "my experience told me that VoA plus Chinese media equalled the truth."[59]

From June 10, almost a week after the massacre, the *People's Daily* began to report on some of the stories coming out of VoA radio broadcasts, seeking to cast doubt on the station's trustworthiness and motives. One article on June 10, for example, went into some detail on the "rumours," already reported on VoA, that over three thousand people had been killed and that tanks had entered Tiananmen Square, before going on to reject them as deliberate falsehoods.[60] This was a risky strategy, as even with the reach of VoA, repeating such damning stories in national newspapers would ensure that a far larger proportion of the public would learn about them. It seems that the sheer weight of news about the massacres from the VoA and other media outlets, as well as word of mouth, had made the events of June 4 impossible to ignore for state media.

And as time went on and news of the crackdown became more widespread, criticism and sanctions from the United States became a useful brush with which to tarnish VoA, and stories on the two were often entwined, with the station framed as a tool of a hostile opponent that was intent on bringing China down. In the eyes of the *People's Daily,* VoA was "dishonourable,"[61] a "government mouthpiece,"[62] and a tool for the "economic blockade" of China.[63] As the newspaper said when it admonished the US government on June 17:

Why did the turmoil receive such support from the Voice of America and the American government? To put it bluntly, you have never given up your dream of interfering in China's affairs, and your dream of changing the colour of China![64]

We cannot know the consequences of this damage control, although Zhang and Dominick's study suggests that even among liberal Chinese intellectuals living in the United States in the 1990s, VoA was not seen as very objective—respondents scoring its level of "bias" as 3.88 out of the highest score of 5.[65] Even so, the CCP made strenuous efforts to limit Chinese people's access to the station through the decade, aware of the damage that this kind of unfiltered information could do. By 1996 its attempts to "jam" VoA and the less conspicuous BBC radio and Radio Free Asia had become more successful. One such tactic was the use of a "firedragon"—a series of folk songs played on a loop on the frequency of undesirable radio stations so loudly that they drowned out any of the content.[66] These censoring tactics meant that VoA's listenership declined to around 1.3 million by 1998,[67] or just over 0.01% of the population, and when the station finally shut down its China coverage in 2011, it commanded around 2 million listeners a week.[68]

Resolutions and Reports

The events of June 1989 revived the international community's interest in human rights in China, and foreign pressure on the issue continued throughout the early 1990s, especially from the United States and European nations. Despite the need to engage China for its help in ventures like the first Iraq war, NGO and American congressional attention meant that the issue of human rights in the People's Republic remained at the top of many Western countries' agendas.

The aftermath of Tiananmen also brought forward an old foe for CCP leaders—the condemnatory UN human rights resolution. Every year from 1989 to 2001 (except 1998) the UN Commission on Human Rights (UNCHR) tabled high-profile draft resolutions that criticized human rights violations in the country. Despite Chinese protests, two months after the Tiananmen massacre the UN Sub-Commission on Prevention of Discrimination and Protection of Minorities passed, fifteen to nine, a somewhat anaemic resolution stating members' concerns "about the events which took place recently in China and about their consequences in the field of human rights."[69] While mild, the resolution was notable for being the first time a Security Council member had been called up on its human rights in this way.[70]

What Rosemary Foot calls "an indication of the extent to which Beijing abhorred being the subject of a UN condemnatory resolution,"[71] a follow-up UNCHR resolution the next spring faced enormous diplomatic pressure from the Chinese side. The forty-person delegation warned of economic and political reprisals and a "no action" vote on the resolution narrowly passed.[72] But in August 1991 the UN subcommission returned, this time to successfully pass a resolution over the ongoing crackdown in Tibet. The declaration strongly echoed the wording of those resolutions thirty years earlier on Tibet, with its concern at the "violations of fundamental human rights and freedoms which threaten the distinct cultural, religious and national identity of the Tibetan people."[73] This would be the last successful draft resolution on China, as unrelenting threats and inducements from Beijing gradually weakened UNCHR activity through the 1990s. By 2001 many countries had replaced public condemnation with bilateral dialogues, and in 2004 only the United States, under pressure from Congress, was willing to sponsor a resolution. A "no action" resolution voted it down, twenty-eight to sixteen.

One goal of UN resolutions is to shame the target country into improving its behavior.[74] So, as in the 1950s and 1960s under Mao, resolutions posed a dilemma for China's leaders. On the international side, resolutions could damage the country's reputation and cause it to lose foreign investment and aid.[75] But they are one of the most high-profile examples of multiple countries agreeing in a respected international forum that the country does not uphold global norms to protect human rights. So they are also a real problem domestically, as officials need to work much harder to persuade the public that this kind of cross-national disapproval is a hostile attack. But by the mid-1990s the leadership was in a much better position to deal with this kind of pressure than it had been in the 1980s. The patriotic education campaign, showcasing the mantra that love of China meant loyalty to the CCP, was in full swing,[76] and propaganda officials could now more easily bend foreign condemnation of the leadership into an attack on the nation.

Having pushed down heavily on non-state-owned media outlets in the years after the Tiananmen crackdown, Deng Xiaoping's successor Jiang Zemin did start to relax restrictions on commercial newspapers again by the mid-1990s, at least on more "politically safe topics," but at the same time worked hard to centralize control over the media industry, and in particular over the more sensitive human rights–related issues.[77] Authorities were very aware of the need to control foreign criticism on these issues. Through the 1990s and early 2000s the propaganda department's classified journal *Neibu Tongxun* issued regular cautions about the risks of the public finding out about unfiltered Western views on China. Guidelines told newspapers to "be very careful in selecting international news stories for publication in China-wide publications, don't unwittingly promote the incorrect viewpoints of the West . . . [and] don't use our media to promote the views of the West."[78]

In the VoA's heyday in the late 1980s, and in the foreign media spotlight of the early 1990s, when the treatment of human rights in China was on the front page of Western newspapers, details of the ongoing international machinations in the United Nations would have reached a fair number of interested Chinese citizens. But as state control deepened, censorship and propaganda tightened, and overseas media interest faded, the proportion of the public who might have come across news of UN efforts to shame China would have been increasingly limited. Indeed, by the 2000s, news of the resolutions became scarce even in American media. Many newspapers ignored the 2004 UN human rights gathering completely, and those that did chose to relegate the failed China resolution to a sidenote.[79]

But despite authorities' increased vigilance to foreign criticism, the waning international coverage, and therefore the likelihood of people finding out about UN resolutions through other routes, state media still passed on news about the resolutions, almost without exception. The exception is worth noting. It came in 1991, when the Tibet resolution succeeded in the UN subcommission. The *People's Daily* ignored the news, except for one report that mentioned only that a UN "conference" on Tibet was ongoing.[80] The successful resolution in 1989 did receive a strong refutation in state media, but with few rhetorical flourishes or detail on the resolution itself,[81] in contrast to the extensive discussions of the successful UN votes thirty years earlier.

The contrast between propaganda officials' reaction to the failed votes and the successful ones is telling, however, and gives insight into both the damage and the strength that can come from international pressure. Successes tell of an international community coming together to agree that China has violated its norms—but failures tell of China's victory over a hostile opponent. And the failed resolutions of the 1990s were given extensive coverage, although *People's Daily* articles were much more tightly controlled than the free-ranging rebukes under Mao, with minimal detail about the wording of the resolutions themselves or about the conditions in China under scrutiny. Instead, the articles followed a familiar theme, condemning each year's resolution as driven by the United States in a predictable "anti-China attempt,"[82] a pretext by Western countries to drag China down and prevent its global rise.[83] This is perhaps summed up best by Wu Jianmin, the head of China's delegation to the UNCHR in 1996. According to Wu, quoted in the *People's Daily,* by supporting these resolutions the United States was "not concerned with China's human rights, but with its own power and hegemony. It attacks China with all its might."[84]

This rhetorical device not only obscured the actual content of what the United Nations was debating but also framed the resolution as an annual us-versus-them competition, an attack on the nation itself, which China's brave leaders would invariably "foil."[85] As time went on and international coverage of the resolutions diminished, the shock value of having the country's human rights subject to international condemnation also diminished. As the resolutions provided no new information about human rights in China, all that was left was news of yet another attack from the hostile US-led "anti-China forces."[86] By 2001 the *People's Daily* was positively reveling in the news of another failed attempt, claiming:

> The United States and other Western countries' use of human rights as an excuse to impose a hegemonic ideology and power politics has once again been proven bankrupt. These anti-Chinese UNCHR resolutions are not a new thing.

The paper went on:

> The proposal is a ridiculous one that has no facts and is full of contradictions. It is designed to use human rights as an excuse to interfere in China's internal affairs, undermine China's stability, and obstruct China's development and progress.[87]

Of course, the United Nations was not the only source of foreign pressure. In the early 1990s, human rights overshadowed the whole diplomatic relationship between China and the United States. One main area of tension was over China's most favored nation trading status, which came up for renewal every year. Members of Congress repeatedly introduced bills that sought to link the trading status to improvements in China's human rights situation, until President Clinton chose to permanently delink the two in 1994. For Foot, the decision "represented the end of a highly public and contentious dimension to the USA's human rights policy."[88]

But even as international pressure waned, propaganda officials under Jiang Zemin stepped up their coverage. The *People's Daily* focused on pressure from the West that followed a predictable pattern—threats of economic reprisals, sanctions, calls for improvements in China's behavior—especially anything that came from the CCP's recurring enemy, the US Congress. These kinds of pressure rarely risked giving any new information about China's human rights, instead providing a familiar picture of Western countries going on about the same old problems. State media paid little attention to groups like Amnesty International, who were writing about mistreatment of political prisoners and other very specific violations. Coverage of American criticism, on the other hand, was widespread and took a familiar form—angrily refute the claims, then attack the criticizer. The attacks decried US hostility toward China and, in language almost identical to the response to UN resolutions, called out its attempts to "use the human rights issue to vilify China's international image, undermine China's stability, and curb China's development."[89]

By the mid-1990s, state media found a promising counterattack—criticism coming from the United States, with its own poverty, injustice, and discrimination, was hypocritical.[90] In 2001, one *People's Daily* response to another American effort to pressure China to work on human rights was simply: "Americans do not enjoy the basic needs of the right to live, to be free from hunger. . . . [T]here are still a large number of homeless and beggars in American cities."[91] How could the United States point fingers at China when it had these human rights issues of its own to deal with?

One of the most predictable battlegrounds has been over the United States' annual Human Rights Reports. Since 1994, the US State Department has issued a stand-alone report on human rights in China (at the same time as it issues reports about other countries), normally published between February and June every year. The reports on China have rarely held back; the one in 2015, for example, began: "repression and coercion markedly increased during the year against organizations and individuals involved in civil and political rights advocacy and public interest and ethnic minority issues,"[92] and filled the next 140 pages with detailed discussions of abuses and illiberal policies. International media outlets have often taken interest in the reports, although details about the content are often sparse, and coverage of the China report has declined dramatically in recent years. US newspaper articles about the release of the global reports in 2016, for example, gave little attention to China, merely quoting that the report had been issued and noting only that it was critical of Beijing's human rights policies.[93]

As we might expect by now, however, Chinese media has paid a great deal of attention to the dossiers. Indeed, since Xi Jinping came to power in 2012 and stepped up his control over the media environment, domestic coverage has increased, even as overseas publicity has slipped. In the early 1990s, *People's Daily* articles about the reports were extremely detailed, discussing in depth the criticisms and issuing extensive retorts,[94] but by the late 1990s, state newspapers settled into a stock response: the reports were part of a geopolitical fight between the United States and China. Details of the violations condemned inside were written about less and less, to be replaced in 1998 with news of China's own reports on human rights in the United States, often issued the day after the US report.[95] The US report was often featured diametrically opposite to articles about the one on China, making the two reports appear as two sides of the same coin—what the *People's Daily* came to call "tit-for-tat" accusations.[96] Rather than about human rights, the reports became framed in newspapers as a geopolitical game between two states fighting for power, the "stale smell of Cold War thinking, power and hypocrisy."[97] Just to drive home the point, news of the 2015 reports was placed in state-owned tabloid the *Global Times* under a fiery intertwining of the US and Chinese flags[98] and in the *People's Daily* under a somewhat incongruous montage of American fighter jets.[99]

Dilemmas of Human Rights Pressure

Chinese authorities have made strenuous efforts to discourage international pressure over their treatment of human rights yet have often used their state media to report that pressure to the citizens in extensive detail. On some occasions, the criticism has been so globally prominent that authorities have had no choice but to react in some way. The sheer volume of foreign news filtering into the country after the violence around Tiananmen Square in 1989, for example, meant that hiding the condemnation from the public was almost impossible.

But at the same time, a greater willingness to play up foreign criticism at home has also coincided with periods of stronger state propaganda and censorship. In the 1950s and '60s, Chinese citizens would have had little way of finding out about events on the Tibetan plateau, but state media under Mao still reacted bullishly to UN criticism of the crackdowns in the region. And then even as the media environment opened up in the 1980s and international attention began to grow again over human rights in Tibet, state newspapers were nonetheless much less willing to discuss foreign pressure from the CCP's new allies in the West.

The aftermath of the Tiananmen crackdown highlighted the danger from this attention, in particular the danger of unfiltered information about human rights coming into the country through radio broadcasts. And by the mid-1990s, a reinvigorated propaganda apparatus went back to the 1960s and became far more aggressive in its treatment of any international criticism. This was even though this criticism, from congressional comments about dissidents to State Department country reports, was featured less and less in foreign newspapers or in the now-stifled shortwave radio broadcasts, so it was increasingly unlikely to reach much of the public. Newspapers like the *People's Daily* became more refined in their reporting, cutting out the details of the human rights abuses that were the target of the criticism, and instead playing up the international confrontation that lay behind it. And as Jiang Zemin was replaced by Hu Jintao, state media settled into its own standard responses to the periodic State Department and congressional human rights outcries, accusing the United States of hypocrisy and hostility, but happily ignoring most of the criticism from other sources.

As we will see in the next chapter, however, this settled pattern was shaken up again in 2008. The sheer scale of international coverage and criticism of the March crackdown in Tibet served as a jolt to the system, pushing the CCP to once again consider how best to deal with foreign pressure on its human rights.

4
Hostile Human Rights
Tibet, Hong Kong, and Beyond

Tibet 2008

On March 14, 2008, rumors of heavy-handed police treatment of monks commemorating the anniversary of the 1959 Tibetan uprising turned peaceful protests into riots. Tibetans from Lhasa to Gansu joined increasingly violent demonstrators, who clashed with security forces, attacked and killed Han civilians, and burned cars and businesses. After a period of initial quiescence, authorities responded with force, sending thousands of armed police and troops into Tibetan areas, issuing curfews and mass arrests.[1] According to Human Rights Watch, the troops used "disproportionate force in breaking up protests, proceeding to large-scale arbitrary arrests, brutalizing detainees, and torturing suspects in custody."[2]

Western media seized on reports of state repression as they leaked out of Tibet on March 14 and 15. Newspaper articles and television reports spoke of the furious protests, and most pointedly the scale and violence of the crackdown. Even the more dispassionate reports such as that from the *New York Times,* which widely quoted Chinese government sources and Han residents about the violence from the demonstrators, also highlighted the vast military presence in the region and drew parallels to the Tiananmen Square crackdown in 1989.[3] Other newspapers like the *Daily Telegraph* disregarded all nuance, leading with headlines like "Tibet Protest Crackdown Claims up to 100 Lives"[4] and "Could Tibet Be Another Tiananmen?"[5] CNN was one of the biggest advocates of the story of Chinese brutality against peaceful protests, its commentator Jack Cafferty calling CCP leaders "goons and thugs"[6] for their response to the riots.

Western and non-Western leaders alike were quick to condemn. UN Secretary General Ban Ki Moon expressed his concern about the level of violence and called for restraint,[7] while Australian Prime Minister Kevin Rudd in a joint meeting with US President George W. Bush said "it's absolutely clear there are human rights abuses going on in Tibet."[8] Calls for restraint were echoed by leaders from Taiwan[9] to India,[10] twenty-six Nobel laureates,[11] and forty Olympic athletes.[12] The European Union paid special attention to the repression, with the presidency's declaration of concern[13] followed by a special EU foreign ministers meeting on the issue.[14] In a parliamentary resolution on April 10, the organization said that it "firmly condemns the brutal repression by the Chinese security forces against Tibetan demonstrators" and "criticizes the often-discriminatory treatment of non-Han Chinese ethnic minorities."[15]

Around the world people protested in front of Chinese embassies[16] and took part in candlelit vigils, even briefly within China itself.[17] The torch relay for the upcoming Beijing Olympic Games provided a perfect opportunity for demonstrators. Over a thousand pro-Tibet protestors created chaos on the London leg by attempting to grab the torch, a feat that was trumped in the Paris stop on April 8, where protestors extinguished the torch five times and managed to injure Jin Jing, a Paralympic fencer who was carrying the flame at the time.[18] There were further protests on the torch route through North America, India, Australia, Japan, and South Korea.[19] Immediately after the violence began in Tibet, calls came for a boycott of the Olympic Games,[20] and March 27 Polish Prime Minister Donald Tusk became the first head of government to announce that he would not attend the Opening Ceremony, closely followed by the Czech leader Vaclav Klaus.[21] The following day German Chancellor Angela Merkel said that she would not attend, amid domestic pressure,[22] while French leader Nicolas Sarkozy suggested that he would not rule out following suit.[23]

At first, the CCP worked hard to prevent news of the unrest in Tibet from reaching the public. In the aftermath of the violence on March 14, YouTube, Yahoo, Google News, BBC, and CNN were blocked;[24] the word "Tibet" was censored on Baidu.cn, the main search engine in China;[25] and internet news sites like Sina.com were banned from carrying *any* news beyond that provided by the state news agency *Xinhua*.[26] *Xinhua* itself carried only one story on the unrest in the first few days after the protests: a five-line note saying that a government representative had answered some questions on fighting in Tibet (which had been organized by the Dalai Lama),[27] while the state China Central Television news service gave only brief clips of rioting Tibetans two days after the unrest began.[28] Coverage of the unrest began on March 18 and 19, finally becoming the main news story on March 22, just over a week after the riots had begun. Foreign journalists were forcibly ejected from Tibet and prevented from reaching Tibetan areas in neighboring provinces. Some were detained and threatened for trying to cover the protests and forced to delete any footage they did have.[29]

Despite the heavy censorship, it appears that by this time many citizens were aware of the violence that had been taking place. Tibetans learned about the protests through mobile phone networks and—just like in 1987—through foreign radio stations.[30] Many in Tibet and through the rest of China found out about the unrest through online forums, despite government attempts to stop them. In the *Tianya* forum, for example, a site with over six million members, netizens used innocent-looking streams about the beauty of Tibet to circumvent the censors.[31]

The dilemma for Hu Jintao was that acknowledging foreign criticism would provide the public with news about the unrest and would potentially frame the subsequent crackdown as a violation of international norms. But as with the Tiananmen response nineteen years before, the quick spread of information and weight of foreign media coverage had already made the unrest and crackdown impossible for state media to ignore. So once the CCP had agreed on a unified response on March 22, foreign interference again became a useful way of channeling what was going on in Tibet. State media stories about the unrest began to be accompanied more and more by stories attacking foreign media coverage[32] and criticism from the West.[33] By April, any discussion of what had happened in mid-March in Lhasa was lost under the sheer volume of news about Western condemnations, protests, threats, and boycotts.

The response to foreign criticism was two-pronged. According to one newspaper editor, the first strategy was to start an "unprecedented, ferocious media war against the biased Western press."[34] Throughout March and April state media piled into any and every mistake made in Western news on the unrest in Tibet, from a poorly cropped picture to a misleading headline.[35] Many of these errors were self-inflicted, such as the BBC use of a picture of Tibetan protestors being beaten in Nepal to illustrate a story about Chinese government repression.[36] Chinese authorities had of course deliberately limited the ability of foreign news organizations to report accurately on the events in Tibet by banning them from the region, naturally increasing the likelihood of inaccurate reports.

Genuine reports of repression of Tibetans were then grouped together with journalistic errors, all portrayed as fabricated rumors from biased Western media.[37] Newspapers tracked down as many sources as possible to suggest that Western reporting was biased—even comments on internet threads.[38] According to the first *Global Times* article to address foreign criticism on March 22, "In the *Times* website on Tibet . . . a man called 'Arabian Users' said 'to say that it seems Han and Tibetans are reluctant to live together is completely wrong. In fact the Han Chinese and Tibetans are like brothers.' "[39] Commentaries accused Western media of having ulterior motives arising from "deep-rooted prejudice against China."[40] Jack Cafferty's "goons and thugs" comments only helped to play into this portrayal, and as such they were jumped upon by domestic media outlets, with ten *Xinhua* headlines alone about the comments in April and May. In a piece on April 17 entitled "Cafferty's 'Violence through Words,' " the *People's Daily* insisted without hyperbole that

> Cafferty's remarks are long beyond freedom of the press and freedom of speech. They are not only an insult to the Chinese people, but also a challenge to the conscience and justice of all mankind, and a blasphemy for the common values of human society.[41]

Cafferty's comments also reinforced the second media message: that China and its hosting of the Olympic Games was under attack. Despite the potential shame that could come from hearing that other countries' leaders did not want to attend the Olympic Games, the media reported heavily on calls to boycott the Opening Ceremony, in particular by French President Sarkozy. The trigger was the attempt by pro-Tibet activists to seize the Olympic torch in Paris from Jin Jing, who became a national heroine of sorts.[42] Foreign pressure on China was an attempt to destroy China's Olympics, and Sarkozy's threat to boycott the Opening Ceremony and the French public's calls to boycott Chinese products were emblazoned in state media throughout April.[43] The *People's Daily* imagined what Western politicians were thinking:

> If we can use the Olympics to help the Dalai Lama achieve his dream of a "Greater Tibet," then we can occupy the moral high ground of "human rights" and "freedom." We can ruin the dreams of the Communist Party, realize our goal of splitting up China, and maybe relive our old dream of invading and dividing the country, even robbing and murdering the people.[44]

The threat to the Olympics from the boycotts and attacks on the torch relay provided a focal point for the public to organize and fight back against. In the aftermath of the Paris incident, a Chinese user of an online message board called for a campaign of resistance against foreign bullying of China, and a movement to boycott French goods grew. By 18, this had built up into full-scale mass protests in front of stores of the French supermarket Carrefour.[45]

The protests were excellent propaganda, whether or not the Communist Party had planned or encouraged them. Chinese citizens' efforts to publicly defend their country and its Olympics against perceived foreign attacks were accompanied by increasingly visible support for the CCP's actions in crushing demonstrations in Tibet. In the first small anti-Carrefour demonstration on April 12 in Beijing, protestors unfurled a banner that read "against separatism, let's protect the Olympic flame."[46] Many people appeared to agree with (and even helped to encourage) the CCP's accusations of Western media bias. In March a Chinese student Rao Jin set up the site "anti-CNN.com," which became an emblem of the people's resistance to perceived Western media bias against China. Authorities were quick to endorse the site.[47] A government-sponsored internet campaign on Sina.com on March 30 against biased foreign coverage had the title "Oppose Splittism, Protect the Torch" and received over five million signatures.[48]

Protecting the Olympics, protesting Western media bias, and opposing independence movements in Tibet all became tied closely together. Some citizens even complained that the authorities had not done enough to crack down on the rioters.[49] Jessica Chen Weiss argues that within China, any protests directly related to Tibet, even pro-government ones, would have been too risky for the CCP to allow.[50] Abroad, however, there were no such risks, and pro-China protests continued in cities from London to Sydney. These youthful protestors, often overseas students, demonstrated against perceived biased Western media coverage, but also the Dalai Lama himself and "splittism" in Tibet, burning Tibetan flags in university campuses and attacking pro-Tibet movements. After the attempted disruption of the Olympic torch relay in London, the protests morphed into a global movement to "protect the torch,"[51] a very visible expression of defensiveness against foreign attacks.

While the devastating earthquake in Sichuan Province in July put a temporary end to hostilities, August's Olympic Games in Beijing provided a perfect venue for worldwide attention on China's human rights. International nongovernmental organization (NGOs) used the Olympic Games to highlight government abuses, from Amnesty International adverts appealing the use of torture[52] to Human Rights Watch stories of the disappearance of protestors.[53] On his visit to China for the Opening Ceremony, George Bush made a highly critical speech about violations of basic human rights in China and the detention of dissidents.[54] Yet this time, in marked contrast to the previous months, and even though the speech and the other stories critical of China's treatment of protestors at the Olympic Games circulated widely internationally, state media chose to ignore it all. The Amnesty International adverts, for example, circulated on online messaging boards and criticized in Foreign Ministry statements, were left out of the domestic press.[55]

This is a pattern around high-profile diplomatic or political events in China, where media attention and foreign criticism gather over China's human rights but are completely left out of domestic media. Whenever Western leaders have visited China, they have often been under pressure in their own countries to bring up the issue of human rights, and their comments on the issue have been closely covered by foreign reporters. Chinese media, on the other hand, has almost invariably chosen to ignore mentions of human rights on these visits. President Bush's comments in 2002 about the absence of political and religious freedoms were cut from the official media coverage of his speech to an audience of Chinese university students.[56] President Clinton visited Tiananmen Square in 1998 and in a press conference with Jiang Zemin criticized the CCP for the massacre there nine years before.[57] None of his comments were reported.

Criticism of China when its leaders visit other countries has seen similar treatment. While Xi Jinping was feted by British government officials on his visit to the United Kingdom in October 2015, he was met with protests from the public[58] and criticism from opposition leaders and media outlets.[59] In 2012 Hu Jintao's visit to India was subject to extensive Tibetan protests, covered heavily in international media.[60] Premier Li Peng on his visit to Europe in 1994 faced demonstrations over his role in the Tiananmen massacre five years earlier[61] and canceled meetings and visits in Germany to avoid further public outcries.[62] In the end he chose to cut back his trip early rather than deal with the unwanted attention.[63] On all these occasions, the Chinese media omitted any mention of the protests, focusing purely on the red-carpet welcome and the business deals made.

As we will see in the next chapter, censorship of foreign criticism at these times reflects the competing pressures on authorities. It suggests that messages of hostility are harder to make when the overall media narrative is one of cooperation and diplomacy. While a picture of international conflict and bullying from the West is sometimes a useful one to put to the public, at other times leaders want to show they are international statesmen, respected members of the international community. Events like the Olympics and bilateral visits are key tools for pushing this narrative—and the China Central Television news channel is rarely free of stories of officials shaking hands with their foreign counterparts over some trade agreement or other.

Dalai Lama, Dissidents, and Lawyers

A common theme in state media coverage of the 2008 Tibet protests was to blame the Dalai Lama and his "clique" for the riots and accuse them of organizing the international reaction. As I discuss in detail in chapter 8, one way in which the international community has expressed displeasure with policies in Tibet and sought to raise visibility over the issue is by setting up meetings between national leaders and the Dalai Lama. These meetings have occurred on a regular basis since 1987 but have declined over recent years, in part due to Chinese economic and diplomatic pressure. One risk for authorities in allowing the media to report on the meetings is that Tibetan activists find out and gain encouragement for their cause. As discussed earlier, the US government's award of the Congressional Gold Medal to the Dalai Lama in 2007, discovered by Tibetan monks through foreign websites and radio broadcasts, was partly responsible for the unrest in 2008.

And in the 1990s, even though international coverage of the meetings was often quite extensive and Tibetans would have been able to find out about them through the Voice of America, they were rarely mentioned in Chinese media. When they were mentioned, as in 1990 following an official meeting between the Dalai Lama and German President Weizsäcker, all the *People's Daily* did was to briefly state that the meeting "hurt the feelings of the Chinese people."[64] As Figure 4.1 shows, all that diffidence changed in 2008 when, despite their declining number, almost all the meetings started to be picked up by state media.

60 HOSTILE FORCES

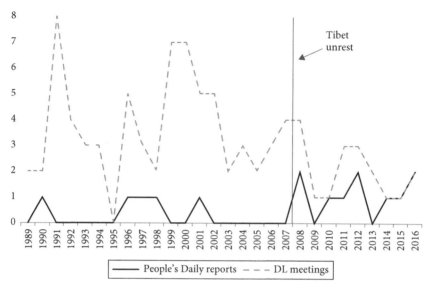

Figure 4.1 Number of Dalai Lama (DL) meetings with foreign heads of state, and number of meetings reported in *People's Daily*, 1989–2016 (number of meetings reported rather than number of articles).

There are two plausible reasons for this change. The first is that Tibetans, the group most likely to mobilize, were generally aware of the meetings in any case, and by 2007 the CCP was seemingly unable to control their access to foreign news about the Dalai Lama. The second is that the aftermath of the Tibet riots had demonstrated that there was some public sympathy for the notion that the Dalai Lama had been responsible for the unrest and was conniving with foreign nations and media to push his independence agenda. As I demonstrate in chapter 8, post-2008, far from being an embarrassment or source of information about China's human rights problems, Western leaders meeting with the Dalai Lama could be used as a propaganda tool to increase public support for the regime.

When Nicolas Sarkozy met the Dalai Lama in Poland in December 2008, state media reported widely on the summit. According to *Xinhua*, the meeting "seriously hurt the national sentiments of the Chinese people,"[65] while the *Global Times* reminisced about the threats that Sarkozy had posed about skipping the Olympics months before, suggesting that we would again see angry protests from the public[66] (and there were indeed renewed online calls for a boycott against Carrefour).[67] When Barack Obama held an open prayer meeting with the Buddhist leader in Washington, DC in February 2015, state media claimed that "Obama is acquiescing to the Dalai Lama's attempt to split Tibet from China"[68] and compared Obama calling the Dalai Lama a "good friend" to the Central Intelligence Agency's (CIA's) funding of Tibetan separatists in the 1950s.[69] But at the same time, and often in the same paragraphs, articles also attempted to play down the diplomatic importance of the meeting—arguing it was low key and brief and was just one part of Obama's meeting with other religious leaders.[70] The need to address two audiences—Tibetan groups and the broader public—helps to explain this somewhat confusing desire to both dismiss and dramatize the meeting.

And foreign pressure over exiled or imprisoned dissidents like the Dalai Lama does bring risks for the CCP. It highlights the justice system's failure to meet international standards and gives a platform for the issue for which the dissident was arrested or exiled in the first place, potentially making the dissident a martyr for their cause. This may be why the international community's protests over imprisoned dissidents were very rarely reported before 2008. High-profile efforts through the 1980s and 1990s to secure pro-democracy activist Wei Jingsheng's release received minimal coverage,[71] for example, and even up to 2007, prominent appeals on behalf of Hu Jia, an activist arrested for petitioning for land rights, were ignored in Chinese media.[72]

Then in 2010, China's most renowned dissident, Liu Xiaobo, was given the Nobel Peace Prize. This was the first time a Chinese citizen had been given a Nobel Prize—albeit a citizen who was resident in a prison in Beijing—and unsurprisingly the news was front page across the globe. The award was quickly condemned by the CCP,[73] which warned of damages to bilateral ties with Norway[74] and, in a flashback to the days of fighting UN resolutions, put hefty diplomatic pressure on other leaders to not attend the ceremony.[75] Domestically, the news of the prize immediately became a top-trending topic on several microblogs[76] and, according to the *China Digital Times,* received a few messages of support amongst *Weibo* users. For some, a Nobel honor for a Chinese human rights stalwart was something to applaud.[77] Some even tried to stage celebrations of the award, celebrations that were quickly shut down by police,[78] and Liu's supporters were arrested across the country.[79] In response to the prize, twenty-three retired Communist Party officials wrote an open letter calling for free speech, a letter again abruptly pulled from internet sites.[80]

In a familiar reaction, the CCP first tried to censor all news of the prize, jamming foreign television services that carried the news and cutting the terms "Liu Xiaobo" and "Nobel Peace Prize" from search engines and social media.[81] According to a leaked document in the *China Digital Times,* the propaganda ministry issued instructions that "Websites are not to create news items or exclusive stories on the Nobel Prize. Exclusive stories that do exist must all be deleted. . . . The *Xinhua* News Agency will shortly circulate copy."[82] This copy, released to state media, was one short article that called the award "blasphemous."[83] This coordination of media lines is what Margaret Roberts calls "flooding," a form of censorship often used around particularly sensitive dates or events that pushes one approved message to prevent the spread of more damaging or sensationalized information.[84]

A few days later the *People's Daily* attacked the award and Liu himself in more aggrieved tones through a series of articles. In one, entitled "Against the Wishes of the Nobel Peace Prize," the paper trawled through an extensive history of the prize and its purported use as a Cold War instrument, linking it variously to the attack on the Olympics in Beijing, the ongoing dispute over censorship with Google, and the conflict over the Diaoyu/Senkaku Islands.[85]

The Nobel Prize highlighted how difficult it was to completely censor coverage of such a high-profile individual. And state media was starting to become more proactive in how it dealt with foreign pressure over activists and dissidents. Let's look at a few examples.

Ilham Tohti

Chinese authorities arrested the well-known Uighur academic Ilham Tohti in early 2014, before sentencing him to life in prison for "separatism."[86] As we saw, prior to 2010, the Propaganda Department had generally suppressed news of this kind of political imprisonment. The arrest and sentencing of Tohti, however, both received quite extensive attention in state media.[87] In contrast to Liu Xiaobo, whose name is still completely censored on the site, news about Tohti's arrest and sentence was also kept available on *Weibo*, although this was limited to state media news stories. Comments on these stories or mentions of Tohti that strayed beyond the official news narrative were deleted. There was plenty of foreign media coverage of Tohti's treatment, and notably the *People's Daily* report on Tohti's arrest explicitly referred to stories about the incident in the *Wall Street Journal* and BBC online (both websites with Chinese editions).[88]

The arrest was met with appeals and condemnation from Amnesty International, the European Union, the United Nations, and the United States,[89] and these appeals formed a large part of the reporting on Tohti in China. Indeed, state media used American pressure as a way of introducing the story. The *People's Daily*'s first news about the arrest led with the headline: "Uighur Scholar Ilham Tohti of China Central Nationalities' University Is Arrested: The United States Puts Pressure on China," and before even setting out the reasons for the arrest, it described the US State Department's "deep concern" over the incident.[90] In response to renewed US pressure over Tohti's life sentence later in the year, *Xinhua* suggested that American concern was proof of the link between the United States and Uighur terrorist groups.[91] In an indication of the sensitivity of the sentencing, the Central Propaganda Department issued instructions for media to stick to *Xinhua* copy.[92]

Xu Zhiyong

Just a week after the arrest of Ilham Tohti, in January 2014, Beijing's First Intermediate People's Court published the news on *Weibo* that Xu Zhiyong, a high-profile human rights activist, had been sentenced to four years imprisonment for what it called an "unlawful gathering."[93] Xu had drawn the ire of the CCP as one of the founders of the "New Citizen" movement, a group that campaigned for the rule of law and against corruption in China.

Xu's name was briefly uncensored in Weibo searches, presumably to allow the public to see the official verdict,[94] and the *People's Daily* issued a cursory note summarizing the sentence.[95] Accompanying articles focused primarily on the critical reaction from Western countries, however. As with Tohti, when the *Global Times* passed on news of Xu's sentence, the first paragraph included a statement that the US State Department was "deeply disappointed."[96] Other articles in the *People's Daily* began with the American response. One took the headline "Supporting Chinese Dissidents: The Western Conspiracy"[97] and sought to tie Western criticism over Xu to an attempt by the West to stifle China's growth.

After the initial relaxation, Xu's name was once again blocked on *Weibo*[98] (and remains blocked years later). The only information available about his case on social media is through state media commentary, which focused heavily on the Western reaction to his sentencing. We cannot read too much into the public posts underneath these stories, in part since they are carefully pruned by the authorities for their own propaganda purposes and appear to be dominated by posts from paid government commentators. Typical examples under these stories were brief exclamations like "Breaking the law should be punished!" or "China needs a stable social environment!"

Nonetheless, different framings of the story do appear to influence the tone of online comments over Xu's sentence, illustrating how authorities have used foreign criticism to co-opt online nationalists into cheerleading their actions. For example, one *Global Times* story about Xu Zhiyong discussed Western intervention but focused primarily on the chaos that activists like Xu would bring to China. While most comments underneath firmly supported this view, a surprising number were quite critical of the sentence, and of the government's actions in arresting him.[99] A story by the same paper a day later focused instead on Western efforts to have Xu and other Chinese dissidents released. Comments under this story were, unsurprisingly, flooded with anti-West sentiment, along the lines of "Anti-Chinese forces in the West are using this to mess up China, and their efforts are totally useless!," with very few expressing any kind of anti-government position.[100]

Human Rights Lawyers

At 4 a.m. on July 9, 2015, Tianjin police arrived at the house of Wang Yu, a lawyer in the Fengrui Law Firm, and took her into custody. The next day, seven more members of Fengrui were detained, and by the end of July, over two hundred lawyers and activists from across the country were under police investigation.[101] Many of the lawyers had been celebrated for taking on the cases of those disadvantaged by government policies, from food safety to minority rights. In the days after the arrests, *Weibo* comments on the lawyers were censored[102] and the only information available online was an official announcement from the Ministry of Public Security stating that police had "smashed a major criminal gang that used the Beijing Fengrui Law Firm as a platform to organize, plot, and hype-up over 40 sensitive incidents and severely disturb social order."[103]

An accompanying *Xinhua* article went into rigorous detail about the lawyers themselves and their supposedly illegal actions.[104] Such proactive state media coverage of the arrests suggests that this high-profile crackdown was at least in part designed to send a message to other "rights defence," or "Weiquan" lawyers, while also ensuring that the narrative of the events was kept tightly controlled. Soon, state media began to feed news of foreign pressure into this narrative. Two days later, *Xinhua* devoted a piece to the US State Department's criticisms of the arrests, calling the words attacks by "Western forces" on China's internal affairs. It continued with a rousing call to arms:

> Eliminating the criminal gang of "rights defence lawyers" is not only necessary to ensure China's security and stability, but also necessary to make Chinese people more confident and united in winning the fight between Chinese and Western ideology. This is a battle for law and order and a battle for humanity, and our fight in the next battle should be no less serious than in the last.[105]

While many on *Weibo* appeared to support this approach, one popular comment is worthy of note. According to the user "Favourite Three Grandfathers": "if it wasn't for the Americans' comments, we wouldn't even know about these [arrests]." This comment encapsulates the fine line the CCP walks when reporting on outside criticism of sensitive human rights issues. Foreign pressure may provoke defensiveness and nationalism but may also inform people about repression they may not otherwise have known about.

After this initial barrage, state media trained their sights on rights lawyers, using international criticism of their arrests to push the claim that the lawyers were merely tools of hostile foreign forces.[106] One example is Pu Zhiqiang, a high-profile Weiquan lawyer and activist who had been arrested in May 2014 for "causing a disturbance" after attending a private meeting to commemorate the Tiananmen Square anniversary and in December 2015 was eventually given a three-year suspended sentence. Perhaps because of the widespread foreign media coverage of Pu's trial, or perhaps because of the wish to send a message to other human rights lawyers, state media devoted numerous articles to the sentencing, mainly on the (lukewarm) criticism of it from the United States and European Union.[107] *Xinhua* took care to repeat the US State Department's assertions that the CCP was "detaining Pu Zhiqiang without trial"[108] and accused Western critics of using Pu as a "hidden way to push their political interests."[109]

Hong Kong

Even before the city returned to Chinese sovereignty in 1997, state media had seized upon international efforts to promote democracy and human rights in Hong Kong. In 1994, for example, when British Governor Chris Patten pushed through proposals for electoral reform, the Chinese government's opposition was vociferous, with articles in the *People's Daily* loudly attacking the British proposals as "lies and deceit"[110] and attempts to "undermine China's unity."[111]

In September 2014, tens of thousands of peaceful demonstrators took to the streets in Hong Kong as part of the "Occupy Central" movement. The movement called for universal suffrage by staging a sit-in in Central—the main financial district on Hong Kong Island—and grew into what was termed the "Umbrella Movement," after the umbrellas that protestors used to protect themselves from police tear gas. The CCP, concerned that they might spread to the mainland, suppressed information about the events. Photo-sharing site Instagram was blocked, and terms linked to the protests were censored on *Weibo*.[112] The narrative was strictly controlled. State television freely showed images of rioting protestors but held back images of tear-gassing police and imposed blackouts on CNN and BBC news coverage.[113]

From the start, Beijing sought to portray the protests as the brainchild of "hostile foreign forces." Mainland media highlighted the financial assistance given by one American NGO, the National Endowment for Democracy, to train democratic political parties in Hong Kong,[114] and stories in Hong Kong's pro-Beijing press referred to ominous American "black hands" stoking the demonstrations.[115] Hong Kong Chief Executive CY Leung announced that "external forces" were behind the movement,[116] while a People's Liberation Army general suggested that Occupy Central was another Western attempt to instigate a "colour revolution."[117] Leaked propaganda directives show that officials called on news websites to "prominently re-post" rumors of shady US involvement.[118]

Perhaps wary of these accusations, the foreign forces themselves were loath to explicitly support the movement or criticize the Hong Kong establishment's attempted crackdown. The British Foreign and Commonwealth Office stayed mainly silent throughout the autumn, only issuing a statement saying, "It is important for Hong Kong to preserve [the rights to demonstrate] and for Hong Kong people to exercise them within the law."[119] US leaders also refrained from explicitly supporting the movement, and President Obama was pushed to publicly deny that the United States had any role in encouraging the protestors in a press conference with Xi Jinping.[120] Other countries were less reserved in their appeals for democracy in Hong Kong, most notably Angela Merkel, who called on Beijing to recognize freedom of speech and democracy in the territory.[121]

Leaders of the Occupy Central movement were equivocal about the role of the international community. Joshua Wong, a student leader of the movement, actively called on Merkel to make pro-democracy statements prior to her visit to Beijing, arguing that domestic pressures could only work if there was also a top-down push on the CCP from the international community. Fellow movement leader and Hong Kong University Professor Benny Tai was more reticent about how the international community could best support the protests. In 2015, he said that the protests certainly sought to attract international attention—but emphasized that the movement needed to be a domestic one.[122] According to Tai, while there could never actually be any evidence of foreign influence over the movement, the accusations alone helped to shift the debate in Hong Kong, forcing activists to deny that they had accepted money or assistance from abroad.[123] This may have been precisely the aim of the government's "hostile forces" rhetoric—to force activists onto the defensive and, by discouraging foreign governments from getting involved, sway international public opinion on the protests.

On the mainland, any British or American concerns that did arise about the handling of the protests became a feature in state media.[124] After a British parliamentary debate criticized the Hong Kong police, Chinese authorities refused to issue a visa to those who spoke at the debate, and their "fact-finding" mission was canceled.[125] But the nationalist *Global Times* reported the debate in extensive detail for its readers, even directing them to the committee's website for further information.[126] An editorial in the paper by John Ross, a British scholar at Beijing's Renmin University, claimed:

> If we turn time back to the 19th century or start of the 20th century, after this kind of parliamentary debate the British might have sent a military expedition

to China.... [W]ith the fall of the empire that the sun never set upon, the British Parliament can no longer use gunboats, and must instead use a "verbal cannon" to interfere in China's internal affairs.[127]

A sign of how propaganda chiefs sought to frame calls for democracy in the territory comes from social media. Almost all the *Weibo* search results for "democracy in Hong Kong" are either news stories about British or American pressure on Chinese authorities or stories about Hong Kong activists' demands for independence. The (uncensored) comments on these articles are in turn overwhelmingly defensive and nationalistic, blasting the protestors and the foreign powers.[128] Anecdotal reports suggest that these views were not unusual, and that there was indeed limited support for Occupy protestors on the mainland. Chinese students interviewed in the *Washington Post*, for example, showed little sympathy with demands for democracy in Hong Kong and support for the government line that the unrest was the fault of radicals and foreign actors.[129]

In the mass protests of 2019, this pattern repeated itself. Some Hong Kong demonstrators waved US flags and chanted pro-America slogans to try and encourage President Trump to increase American pressure against Beijing. Yet while members of Congress made statements of solidarity with the protests, the official US response was as lukewarm as in 2014, with Trump determined not to derail ongoing trade talks.[130] The British government also stayed relatively silent, merely issuing statements expressing concern for the ongoing violence on both sides.[131] But even half-hearted expressions like this were again leapt on by Chinese officials and state media, which accused both administrations of hostility and hypocrisy in not condemning violence from the protestors.[132] In late November 2019, under pressure from Congress, Trump gave in and signed the Hong Kong Human Rights and Democracy Act, an act that links Hong Kong's trade status to its political status and threatens legal sanctions for human rights violations. The signature was roundly celebrated by protestors on the streets of Hong Kong[133] but was castigated by mainland media. Multiple *People's Daily* and *Xinhua* articles attacked the legislation for its "hypocrisy and cold-bloodedness,"[134] its "sinister intentions,"[135] and as a "weapon for waging wars."[136]

With the world's attention on the protests, such a harsh state media reaction might not come as a surprise. However, as we will see further in the following chapter, arguably more incendiary statements from non-Western sources have generally been ignored. When Malaysian Prime Minister Mahathir bin Mohamad called on 2019's Chief Executive Carrie Lam to resign,[137] for example, the comments were completely absent from mainland news websites.

Controlling the Narrative

Since 2008, whenever Western countries have decided to make even bland statements of concern about human rights in China, state media has been notably quick to pounce. One reason for this increased attention to critical Western comments has been the internet, and its availability through the 2000s has amplified people's ability to find out about foreign criticism of human rights. The sheer volume of stories potentially now available to any citizen with access to a virtual private network (VPN) clearly affects how state media deals with those stories. Looking just at political prisoners in China, for example, coverage of a detainee in Chinese state media is much higher if they have already had some foreign media attention. Using a sample of 1,199 political prisoners released in China since 1987 (from the US Congressional Executive Committee on China's database), we can see that when the *New York Times* writes about a politically motivated arrest or sentencing in China, Chinese newspapers are significantly more liable to then go on and report the news. If the prisoner is featured in the *New York Times*, then the *People's Daily* is 11% more likely to subsequently write about that prisoner, and other media almost 20% more likely to write about the prisoner.[138]

But the growth in internet access does not seem to be the whole story. As discussed, even through the mid-2000s in China, the *People's Daily* barely reported any foreign pressure on the CCP to free its political prisoners. As Figure 4.2 illustrates, this was true for all kinds of human rights pressure, as even with the public's growing access to the internet, the overall proportion of foreign pressure reported by the *People's Daily* actually dropped through the 2000s.[139] It was only after the Tibet unrest in 2008 that the newspaper began to start picking up its coverage.

The unrest accelerated a change in the CCP's approach to sensitive human rights–related events. It is no coincidence that it was in June 2008, just three months after the March riots, that Hu Jintao delivered his first major speech on media policy. His message was a clear one: state media could no longer merely passively react to unexpected events like protests and riots but had to "actively set the agenda."[140] Rather than just treat websites as things to be shut off whenever they became inconvenient, authorities needed to take the initiative and use the internet as a platform to proactively push out the party line.[141]

Under Hu's leadership, China's media was already shifting from a policy of "guiding" public opinion (舆论导向) to "channeling" public opinion (舆论引导). While seemingly subtle, this shift encouraged propaganda officials to focus less on suppression and censorship of bad news and more on actively directing coverage, getting ahead of the story, to ensure that events were framed according to the party's interpretation and agenda.[142] This view was one that Hu had

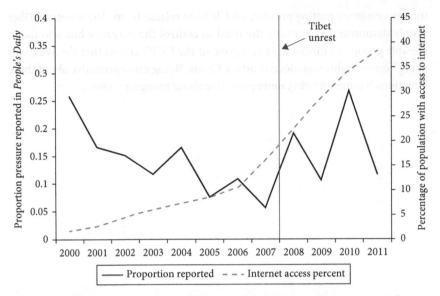

Figure 4.2 Proportion of instances of human rights pressure that are reported in the *People's Daily*, and percentage of Chinese population with access to the internet between 2000 and 2011.
Credit line: World Bank, https://data.worldbank.org/indicator/IT.NET.USER.ZS?locations=CN.

long maintained, but it was made even more urgent by the furor over Tibet.[143] According to *China Media Project*'s Qian Gang and David Bandurski, the CCP regarded its initial response to the unrest—days of total censorship before, belatedly, putting out its own unified version of events—as a failure.[144] The passive reaction allowed international media networks to tell their own story of what was happening, a story that authorities then had to react to. Even before the Nobel Peace Prize for Liu Xiaobo, the events in Tibet highlighted that officials could no longer simply sit on a sensitive news item, which could be picked up by foreign reporters and spread into the social media ether before they could start to bury it. Propagandists needed to be proactive. Follow-up editorials to Hu's speech in the *People's Daily* emphasized that they needed to "touch sensitive issues"[145] and that the newspaper itself should "dare to speak, to speak early."[146]

On the sensitive issue of political prisoners, this newfound enthusiasm is clear. Instead of complete censorship, since Hu's speech, propaganda officials have reacted by talking more openly about arrests or prison sentences, flooding one authoritative story through media outlets[147] while blocking any social media comments that might tell a different story. And foreign pressure has been a vital part of this authoritative story. Indeed, often the only information available on social media about a political prisoner has been state media articles about foreign countries putting pressure on China to release them. The events in Tibet visibly demonstrated not only the need to control the narrative but also that a sizeable group of citizens were receptive to the CCP's claims that the West was using human rights violations to attack China. Being more proactive about these violations has meant being more proactive about foreign pressure.

5
When Does Pressure Become Propaganda?

It was easy to miss Causeway Bay Books, burrowed up a small flight of stairs between a pharmacy and a clothes store. For more than twenty years it had perched in the middle of a busy shopping district in Hong Kong Island's Causeway Bay, making a successful business publishing and selling books about Chinese history and politics.

In late 2015, five staff members of the bookstore completely disappeared. One vanished from his holiday home in Thailand, three fell out of contact while on trips to the mainland, and one went missing from Hong Kong itself. The problem, it appeared, was that Causeway Bay Books had begun to make a lucrative trade in fictional and often salacious stories about Xi Jinping, the leader of the Chinese Communist Party (CCP). In 2015, with its publishing house Mighty Current Publishing, the shop had been putting together a new book on Xi's love life, by all accounts to be called *Xi Jinping and His Lovers*.[1] It may have been this book that crossed the line for Chinese authorities.

The bookseller who vanished from Hong Kong was Lee Bo, a joint Hong Kong and British national. Lee's disappearance was, at the time, a shock to many, because if CCP agents had indeed arrested him inside Hong Kong's territory, then this was an unprecedented (and illegal) abduction of a Hong Kong citizen from outside the agents' jurisdiction. These concerns were hardly eased a week later when pro-Beijing newspapers reported that Lee had faxed his wife a handwritten letter from the other side of the Hong Kong border, saying:

> My visit to the Mainland this time is entirely my personal decision, in order to get an understanding of some personal issues. It is none of anyone's business. I do not understand why it is made into such a big deal.[2]

The incident sparked criticism from Hong Kong's former colonial power. In February 2016 the United Kingdom's Foreign and Commonwealth Office (FCO) issued its annual report on the territory to the British Parliament, calling Lee's disappearance a "serious breach" of the bilateral treaty between the United Kingdom and China on the handover of Hong Kong in 1997.[3] While many observers criticized the FCO report for being too easygoing in its treatment of the crackdown

Hostile Forces. Jamie J. Gruffydd-Jones, Oxford University Press. © Oxford University Press 2022.
DOI: 10.1093/oso/9780197643198.003.0005

on civil liberties in the city,[4] China's governmental-controlled media took a different view. On February 14 several state and commercial newspapers simultaneously printed an article entitled "British Report Fantasizes That They Have Special Rights to Interfere in Hong Kong's Affairs." The article described both Lee Bo's case and the FCO's "serious concerns" in full, including the accusation that Lee had been transferred to the mainland—a transfer that directly contravened Hong Kong laws.[5] Other newspapers called the British criticism "irresponsible" and "unreasonable accusations"[6] and castigated the United Kingdom for trying to claw back some of its imperial control over the territory.[7] At the same time, authorities were careful to make sure that all terms relating to the Causeway Bay booksellers were censored on social media sites, so these state media stories became the only sources of information that were available about the disappearances.

On the face of it, this was a risky strategy on the part of propaganda officials. The articles explicitly informed the public that their ruling party had allegedly violated its firm commitments made in the 1997 handover, abused its own laws in deploying police forces in Hong Kong, and was squeezing the rights and freedoms of Hong Kong citizens. Yet as we have seen, despite having one of the most extensive censorship systems and internet firewalls in the world, the Chinese government has regularly passed these kinds of highly critical and sensitive pieces of information about its human rights situation on for public consumption.

But when are authorities most likely to do this? We know that the Communist Party–run press has also chosen to hide prominent pieces of foreign pressure on human rights from the public, including other criticism from the United Kingdom. As just one example, when Britain's then-prime minister David Cameron publicly criticized the treatment of foreign journalists on the first day of his high-profile 2013 visit to China,[8] the comments were left out of Chinese press discussions of the meeting. And as we saw in the last chapter, while state media has pounced upon comments coming from the United Kingdom about Hong Kong, when the UN Human Rights Committee took a similar line in 2014 and called for universal suffrage in the territory, the appeal was ignored in Chinese newspapers and television and censored in social media.[9]

To understand how regimes like the CCP view foreign pressure, we need to understand the conditions under which they are most likely to proactively tell their citizens about it and when they are most likely to ignore or censor it. This requires a systematic exploration of the decisions made by China's state media. To do so, I gathered together one new database of all instances of human rights pressure on China, along with another new database of all the articles about that pressure in the CCP's primary mouthpiece, the *People's Daily*. As we will see, the kinds of stories reported in the newspaper—and the times they were reported—are precisely what we would expect to see if the CCP was looking to use foreign pressure as a propaganda tool to provoke a defensive reaction in its citizens.

This chapter is the first opportunity to test the implications of the hostility hypothesis. In it I examine directly how the source, the content, and the timing influenced how the CCP Propaganda Department has chosen to deal with foreign pressure.[10]

The Party's Battle Position

According to David Shambaugh, "Virtually every conceivable medium which transmits and conveys information to the people of China falls under the bureaucratic purview of the CCP Propaganda Department."[11] The Propaganda Department decides what news the Chinese people should hear: what should be censored from them and what should be widely circulated. It issues directives to all kinds of media organizations, from social media companies to television directors, informing them which kinds of topics should or should not be covered.

These "prepublication" directives normally take one of four forms: push positive coverage of an issue (the lightest touch); carry only *Xinhua* coverage on the news but allow the newspaper to write its own opinion pieces; carry exclusively *Xinhua* coverage for news and opinion; and then, most severely, completely ban all coverage of an issue.[12] As we saw in the last chapter, breaking human rights stories generally fall into one of the last two categories, with the Propaganda Department since 2008 tending to flood the media with *Xinhua* copy rather than resorting to complete censorship.

The directives are often vague, however, and editors are often forced to guess at how they should deal with a particular breaking news story. Normally this means that journalists self-censor and choose to stay away from potentially sensitive topics.[13] If they miss the mark, however, and write up a piece that crosses the line, the Propaganda Department (or sometimes local officials) will quash the story or even order it to be removed after publication if not spotted in time.[14] Authorities will order internet search engines like Baidu or social media websites like *Weibo* to delete posts on the story and to omit the topic from their search results.[15] There are stories of newspapers being (often literally) pulled from the shelf to contain an aberrant piece, and offending journalists or editors warned—or sometimes fired—over their conduct.[16]

The *People's Daily* (or *Renmin Ribao*, 人民日报) is perhaps the most tightly controlled of all these mediums—a paper that Xi Jinping has called "the Party's battle position"[17]—and the most authoritative media outlet in China. The newspaper is closely overseen by the Propaganda Department, with CCP leaders sometimes writing their own editorials to broadcast the views and position of the central leadership to the people.[18] As such, we can be confident that any news contained within the paper, including foreign criticism, has been approved by the Propaganda Department for dissemination.[19]

74 HOSTILE FORCES

To test how human rights pressure is reported by this "battle position," I first created a database of all foreign attempts to get the Chinese government to improve its behavior over human rights over the period from the country's opening up in 1979 until the end of 2011. The database includes a wide range of tactics, from generic criticism to sanctions, from meetings with dissidents to public appeals for liberalization. This gives us a grand total of 1,337 separate instances of international pressure on human rights in China between 1979 and 2011, shown in Figure 5.1.

This graph demonstrates just how dramatically pressure grew after the Tiananmen massacre in 1989, before gradually waning again from the mid-1990s, and then peaking over the Tibet unrest and Olympic Games in 2008. Of course, this database only provides a limited sample of all the foreign pressure on China, not least because it only contains pressure from English-language sources, and also misses the kinds of low-key appeals from small nongovernmental organizations (NGOs) that would not have been picked up in any media coverage. However, the goal of this chapter is not to calculate an exact figure of the total amount of pressure on China over the years. The goal is to have a relatively unbiased sample of high-profile pressure and to use this sample to see how

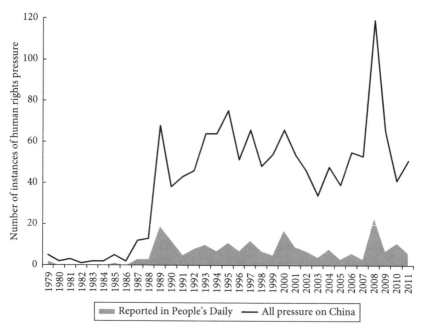

Figure 5.1 Instances of foreign human rights pressure on China, and number of instances of pressure reported in the *People's Daily* newspaper, by year, 1979–2011.

different kinds of pressure are treated by the Chinese media. For those interested, I provide an account of how this sample was put together in Appendix 1.

I then searched for whether each of these instances of pressure was written about in some form in the *People's Daily*.[20] A surprisingly large 228 separate instances (around 17%) were reported over the thirty-three years, with some pieces being featured in over a dozen separate articles. This means that, since Tiananmen, even Chinese citizens who only read the *People's Daily* would be consistently aware of foreign pressure on their country's human rights record, seeing on average nine instances of pressure per year. As Figure 5.1 shows, the amount covered has varied quite considerably over time, however, with the paper reporting on as much as 30% of all pieces of foreign pressure in the years after Tiananmen. By the mid-1990s, it was only featuring half of that amount, however, and was covering as little as 10% by 2007, before returning to almost 30% by 2010.

Which Kinds of Pressure Are More Likely to Be Reported in the *People's Daily*?

As a reminder, the hostility hypothesis predicts that pressure from "hostile" sources, especially at times of bilateral tension; pressure on issues related to the country's territorial integrity; and pressure on existing government policies or general human rights issues are more likely to be actively reported on by state media. The media credibility theory suggests, moreover, that this reporting is also likely to be affected by how much the pressure is covered in international media. I use logistic regressions to examine whether there are indeed particular characteristics of the pressure—who it comes from, what it is about—that affect whether it is featured in the *People's Daily*.[21] All the following results are robust to various analytical tests and control variables.[22]

International Media Coverage

Let's start with the impact of international media coverage. If the "media credibility" argument discussed in chapter 2 is correct, then newspapers—even state-owned ones—may face credibility issues if they choose not to publish widely featured foreign news stories about China. A piece of low-key criticism that is barely reported in foreign press, however, will be much more difficult for even sophisticated internet users to access, and therefore poses much less of a risk to the Propaganda Department.

This means that the more high profile a piece of foreign pressure, the more likely the *People's Daily* should be to write about it. A decent guide for the level of international coverage is whether the pressure is featured in the *New York Times*. And analysis of the database shows that pressure that is reported in the *New York Times* is indeed almost twice as likely to be reported in the *People's Daily* (see Table 5.1; the key regression output is provided in Appendix 1).

This is not a particularly surprising finding. We saw in chapters 3 and 4 how even when the CCP has initially tried to hide all news about a sensitive incident from the public, the extent of global outrage has meant that state media has eventually been forced to address it in some form. Take the case of dissident Liu Xiaobo, who (as noted in chapter 4) won the Nobel Peace Prize. In 2017, Liu died of liver cancer while in Chinese custody. Initially, the Propaganda Department sought to completely shut off all information about his long illness, relatively successfully as it turned out.[23] However, the sheer volume of foreign media coverage of Liu's final few weeks made it impossible to continue to entirely ignore the international reaction. While censorship remained high, the *Global Times* eventually used an editorial to address Liu's death and attack the negative comments raining in from the outside world.[24]

This finding does have an implication for our other tests, however. It means that the *People's Daily* may be more likely to write about certain kinds of pressure—from the United States, for example—for the simple reason that these stories are more high profile than news about pressure from non-Western states. To address this possibility, I also include as a control in my other regressions whether the pressure appeared in the *New York Times*.

The Form of the Pressure

I argued in chapter 2 that the form of the pressure should matter—whether it highlights new, specific abuses or instead talks about well-known human rights issues. To examine this, I split the database into three different kinds: "policy" pressure (addressing widely known existing government policies like the one-child policy, rules on elections in Hong Kong, or laws regulating foreign NGOs), "general" pressure (including resolutions or statements that do not mention specific instances or policies but refer generally to concerns about human rights conditions), and "specific" pressure (referring, as its main topic, to a specific violation of human rights, such as the killing or torture of protestors).[25] Note that while these specific abuses are often previously unreported, I focus just on whether the pressure targets specific abuses, not whether those abuses are new.

The results are clear: pressure that is general in nature is reported over twice as much as pressure that addresses specific human rights violations. Pressure that

Table 5.1 Impact of Different Types of Foreign Human Rights Pressure on Probability That the Pressure Will Be Subsequently Reported in the *People's Daily*, 1979–2011

Type	Pressure Is Reported in NYT	Not Reported in NYT	General Pressure	Specific Pressure	Pressure Is on Existing Policies	Pressure Is on Territorial-Related Issues	Not on Territorial-Related Issues
Probability of being featured in the *People's Daily*	0.24 (0.04)	0.13 (0.01)	0.16 (0.02)	0.07 (0.02)	0.26 (0.04)	0.20 (0.05)	0.12 (0.02)

Rounded to 2 decimal points. Standard errors in parentheses. Full table in Appendix 1.

addresses existing policies is especially well covered, almost four times as likely to be featured in state media as specific pressure (see Table 5.1).

This finding helps explain some otherwise puzzling behavior from officials. As mentioned back in chapter 1, when President Obama called for China to open up its internet at the Asia-Pacific Economic Cooperation (APEC) summit in 2014, government authorities ordered the call to be deleted from all websites.[26] But when Obama's secretary of state Hillary Clinton launched an attack on Beijing's use of censorship at an internet forum in 2010, the Propaganda Department instead issued orders for media to report the speech, using *Xinhua* copy only.[27]

Obama's criticism did come in the midst of a high-profile diplomatic event in Beijing, the kind of event that, as I discuss below, makes it difficult for authorities' ability to play up geopolitical tensions. What is interesting in the Clinton case, however, is that unlike most human rights issues, foreign criticism of press freedom in China is almost always censored.[28] There was something different about Clinton's speech, and it seems that this something was not just the identity of the speaker,[29] but the speech's peculiar content. Of the dozens of high-profile public criticisms of censorship in China made by foreign countries and organizations up until 2012, only five have been printed in the *People's Daily*. These were all about one event—the hack of Google's servers in early 2010 and the company's subsequent decision to refuse to censor its search results in China. While Clinton's speech addressed a range of concerns around internet censorship, the repost in domestic media focused purely on her condemnation of the hacking and censorship of Google.[30] This was not just an everyday critique of internet freedoms, but an attack on an explicit government policy, a policy that would push Google out of the mainland Chinese market.

Or take Amnesty International, which issued hundreds of reports on the state of human rights in China through the 1990s. Yet none of its reports about crackdowns on peaceful protests and arrests of political prisoners were reported in state media. The *People's Daily* only mentioned three Amnesty reports in total through the decade—and two of these were reports that criticized authorities' policies on the use of the death penalty.[31]

Foreign countries' headline-grabbing broadsides about the state of human rights in China are also a popular feature in the *People's Daily*. The US State Department's annual country reports on human rights that we talked about in chapter 3 are a prime example. While every year they include over one hundred pages of rich analysis of human rights violations in China, in recent times foreign media articles have only mentioned the report's headline, the same every year: human rights in China remain poorly respected.[32] And these repetitive headlines are invariably highlighted in state media, with as many as a dozen separate *People's Daily* articles talking about the report in some years.

Criticism that focuses on specific, new human rights violations, on the other hand, is rarely featured. In June 1989, foreign denunciations of the massacres around Tiananmen Square came immediately and were heavily discussed across global media networks. However, since the criticism provided new and precise information about what had happened the previous night in Beijing, none of it was reported. Using the time-series analysis discussed later in this chapter, we can see that in the week after the Tiananmen massacre, foreign pressure was around a sixth as likely to be reported in the *People's Daily* as at any other times, despite the massive increase in outside attention. It was only toward the end of June that newspapers began to properly react to the mass foreign condemnation, by which time news of it had already seeped into the country and the crackdown had become an official "policy."[33]

Foreign criticism also flooded in immediately in the days following the 2008 Tibet riots on March 14. However, once again, authorities were unwilling to let new information about the events reach the public, and in the week after the riots foreign pressure was less than a third as likely to be reported in the *People's Daily* as at other times. The *People's Daily* only began to write about foreign (American and French) condemnation over a week after the demonstrations began, on March 22, just as the CCP publicly acknowledged the existence of the riots and made re-establishing stability in Tibet an official policy.

The Topic of the Pressure

The hostility hypothesis predicts that when pressure comes on issues of territorial integrity, it is more likely to be reported on by state media. For China, this means pressure that mentions, as its main topic, human rights in potentially or historically separatist regions: Tibet, Xinjiang, Inner Mongolia, Hong Kong, or Macau.[34] In China, human rights issues related to these regions are highly sensitive, and social media posts on the regions are—normally—much more likely to be censored.[35] Repnikova quotes one journalist's mantra: "completely avoiding some clearly outlawed topics, such as . . . the issues concerning contentious minorities, like Tibetans and Uyghurs."[36]

But in stark contrast, when foreign human rights pressure comes on these "clearly outlawed topics," it is far *less* likely to be hidden from the public. Western criticism of the unrest in Tibet in 2008, Xinjiang in 2009, and Hong Kong in 2014 was regularly featured in Chinese newspapers and television. In fact, pressure on territorial-related issues is almost twice as likely as pressure on nonterritorial issues to be reported in the *People's Daily* (see Table 5.1).[37]

Where Pressure Comes From

The *People's Daily* was far more likely to write about pressure that originated from the United States than to write about pressure from almost all other sources, as shown in Table 5.2.[38] Pressure from other Western countries was the next most popular (albeit less than half as much). Under the hostility hypothesis, this is not particularly surprising. Western countries are quite easily portrayed as hostile through their histories of imperialism and alliances with the United States but are not direct rivals of China in the same way as the United States.[39] As might be expected by those who have read the last chapter, quite a large proportion of these reports of Western pressure were of British criticism over Hong Kong and of French outcries over Tibet and the Olympics in 2008.

Only UN Human Rights Council/Commission on Human Rights draft resolutions were reported more than pressure from the United States. As chapter 3 showed, these resolutions were often led by the United States and were widely featured in international media (at least in the early 1990s). All apart from one were reported in the *People's Daily*. On the other hand, pressure from the most neutral places—non-Western countries,[40] the United Nations (that was not a draft resolution), and international NGOs—was far less likely to be reported than pressure from any Western sources, a difference that was highly statistically significant. While pressure from these sources was quite rare—non-Western countries only issued a total of fifty-nine pieces of criticism in total in the database—it was still almost never featured in state media.

The Propaganda Department's reaction to foreign pressure over the crackdowns around Tiananmen in 1989, Tibet in 2008, and Ürümqi in 2009 demonstrate how important the source of that pressure is. In 1989, countries from around the world issued strongly worded protests against the violence around Tiananmen Square. But Chinese state media focused almost purely on criticism from the United States, from President Bush's statements about the massacre, to the sanctions applied on China, to the refuge of activist Fang Lizhi in the American embassy in Beijing.[41] Over the next few weeks, practically all the articles published in the *People's Daily* about foreign criticism were about the United States, the one exception being the story of the United Kingdom postponing a bilateral meeting in protest.[42]

In March 2008 criticism also arose across the globe over the events in Tibet, but yet again state media attention stayed mainly on what was being said in America. The *People's Daily* concentrated on US House of Representatives Speaker Nancy Pelosi's stated support for the Dalai Lama,[43] House of Representatives resolutions that criticized CCP actions in Tibet,[44] and CNN and the BBC's purported bias in reporting the crackdown.[45] The United States was joined as a hostile protagonist in the eyes of the media by France, an easy target due to the attacks on

Table 5.2 Impact of Different Sources of Foreign Human Rights Pressure on Probability That the Pressure Will Be Subsequently Reported in the *People's Daily*, 1979–2011

Source	United States	Other Western Countries	Non-Western Countries	United Nations (Draft Resolutions Only)	United Nations (Excluding Draft Resolutions)	International NGOs
Probability of being featured in the *People's Daily*	0.30 (0.03)	0.14 (0.02)	0.03 (0.02)	0.90 (0.11)	0.05 (0.03)	0.05 (0.02)

Rounded to 2 decimal points. Standard errors in parentheses. Full table in Appendix 1.

the Olympic torch relay in Paris. The *People's Daily* was incensed by French President Nicolas Sarkozy's threat to boycott the Olympic Games in Beijing. Yet Sarkozy was not the most outspoken in his comments: Polish leaders were the first to threaten a boycott of the Olympic Games,[46] joined by German Chancellor Angela Merkel[47]—yet neither of these threats were mentioned in the newspaper.

Perhaps chastened by the Chinese public's angry reaction to this criticism, when violence erupted between Han and Uighur groups in the northwestern city of Ürümqi the next summer, the Western reaction was much more equivocal. While some European countries' leaders showed concern and appealed for calm,[48] the most explicit censure came from Islamic sources. The Turkish government,[49] Iranian newspapers,[50] and Azerbaijani politicians[51] all harshly criticized Beijing, with Turkish ministers calling the subsequent crackdown on Uighurs "genocide."[52] The Organization of Islamic States, while choosing not to issue an official resolution condemning the violence, complained vehemently about authorities' "disproportionate use of force."[53] None of these criticisms were reported in state media, however, which, having realized it had a receptive audience the previous year, limited its reports to again attack French and American media for their coverage of the clashes.[54] In each of these cases there was plenty of prominent and angry non-Western criticism, but state media almost exclusively reported pressure from those sources perceived to be hostile toward China.

One especially high-profile case of criticism from non-Western countries came in early 2020. As fears of a second wave of COVID-19 grew through China, the Guangzhou local government put in place strict measures for African nationals, including surveillance, testing, and quarantine. The result was an overflow of discrimination against the migrant community. Landlords rushed to evict African tenants,[55] businesses refused African customers,[56] and there was a dramatic spike in racist and xenophobic posts on *Weibo*.[57] Videos of Africans sleeping on the streets, being accosted by police, and being turned away from shops and hospitals spread quickly through social media in Kenya, Nigeria, Uganda, Ghana, and beyond. These viral videos sparked a public outcry, with Twitter users sharing their outrage under the hashtag #ChinaMustExplain and calling on their own countries' leaders to react. The story became front-page news across the continent, with one dramatic headline in Kenya's popular *Daily Nation* newspaper announcing: "Kenyans in China: Rescue Us from Hell."[58]

The result was an almost unprecedented procession of condemnation from African diplomats and politicians. Chinese ambassadors were summoned (Nigerian House Speaker Femi Gbajabiamila published a video of his own stern admonishments on his Twitter page[59]), a dozen African ambassadors wrote to China's Foreign Ministry demanding action,[60] and the South African Human Rights Commission called for an independent investigation.[61]

The mass condemnation was not just front-page news throughout Africa, but across the world, from the United States to Hong Kong. But while China's Foreign Ministry spokesmen and state media's outward-facing English-language editions offered up an odd mixture of acknowledgment and denial,[62] the domestic Chinese-language media was remarkably silent. Official government websites merely mentioned "some of the problems that African friends have with China's anti-epidemic work,"[63] while the *People's Daily* referred obliquely to "incidents" in Guangzhou and a "meeting" of Chinese ministers with African ambassadors,[64] without ever discussing the ambassadors' criticism itself. In fact, while news of the outrage across Africa was available on some blogs,[65] the only story that mentioned the continent-wide discontent was one *Global Times* story, which noted the existence of some "malicious statements claiming that China discriminates against Africans." But in place of any detail about those statements or recognition of the widespread condemnation from African diplomats, the article instead went on to feature Namibian and Botswanan statements that cast doubt on the accounts of discrimination in Guangzhou.[66]

The media reaction to American comments about the incident was very different. After the US State Department issued a statement calling it an example of Chinese "xenophobia" and "abusive and manipulative behaviour," *Xinhua* and *People's Daily* articles seized on the remarks, calling them "arrogant and provocative."[67] The Propaganda Department settled on a familiar theme: the incident was an attempt by the United States to create unrest and to drive apart the relationship between China and African countries. This theme was repeated widely in diplomatic tweets and state media coverage over the following days.[68]

When Is Foreign Pressure More Likely to Be Reported in the *People's Daily*?

Over the last thirty years, the diplomatic relationship between the United States and China has not always been as tempestuous as it was in early 2020. Periods of relative stability between the two countries have been punctuated with heated military, economic, and political flashpoints. If the relationship between the target and the source of pressure is an important factor, then we would expect American human rights pressure to be reported far more in Chinese media in these periods of hostility. In times of more benign relations, however, the pressure should be reported less often.[69]

To examine this question, I first needed times when the relationship with the United States was particularly hostile. To do so I looked at the twenty-eight days after a major international incident with the United States: including the North Atlantic Treaty Organization (NATO) bombing of the Chinese embassy in Belgrade in 1999; the US spy-plane crash in Hainan in 2001; calls for protests against the Iraq War in 2003; US officials allowing Taiwanese leader Lee Teng-Hui to visit the country in 1995, sparking the Taiwan Straits Crisis; Chinese naval harassment of the US naval ship *Impeccable* in 2009; and the large American weapons sale to Taiwan in 2010.[70]

For more "benign" relations, I looked at the twenty-eight days after an official visit by Chinese leaders or foreign ministers to the United States and the twenty-eight days after a visit by US leaders or foreign ministers to China. Perhaps the main reason for official visits to another country is to improve bilateral relations,[71] and there is evidence that American presidents and secretaries of state choose their destinations based on the strategic interests of the United States at the time.[72] US-China visits often involve trade deals, flattering speeches, and red-carpet welcomes, and so we would expect the Communist Party to try and portray bilateral relations in a positive light to the public around the visits. As we saw in chapter 4, state media often uses such international gatherings to emphasize the statesman-like vision and diplomatic wisdom of Chinese leaders.

However, there may be other reasons newspapers feature more American pressure when relations are poor. American leaders may seek to publicly condemn human rights abuses in China to gain an advantage in ongoing geopolitical disputes, or may hold back in doing so in the lead-up to delicate bilateral meetings. In my analysis I therefore control for the volume of international human rights pressure and the volume of foreign news (in the *New York Times*) about that pressure. Secondly, every spring the CCP holds its annual meetings, known as the "Lianghui" (两会). These are periods where international and domestic scrutiny is high, but also periods when the party is potentially more sensitive to foreign criticism, so I control for this period in my model. Since the amount of domestic unrest might also affect how authorities deal with foreign criticism (and may also make international disputes more likely), I also include controls for the levels of protest and repression over the previous twenty-eight days.[73] Finally, we also need to account for the passing of time since 1979, as since the 1980s both US-China tensions and the public's access to information from abroad have grown.

A time series model with these controls shows that, as predicted, in the twenty-eight days of tension after a geopolitical incident with the United States, the *People's Daily* was significantly more likely to write about foreign human rights pressure on China.[74] In these periods, the paper reported on average almost three times as much foreign pressure as similar twenty-eight-day periods in the rest of the year. Yet this increase seems to be limited to pressure from the United States, which was reported over five times as often at these times. Pressure that did not come from the United States was reported at the same rate as any other times.

The aftermath of the NATO bombing of the Chinese embassy in Belgrade in 1999, which killed two Chinese journalists, illustrates the role of geopolitics in human rights. As we might expect, the incident saw a barrage of anti-American propaganda—and American criticism of China's human rights formed a key part of this propaganda. This included new instances of human rights pressure coming from the United States, like a congressional resolution to commemorate the tenth anniversary of Tiananmen Square[75] (an occasion otherwise rarely discussed in Chinese media), as well as historical efforts to condemn China for its rights situation.[76] The reports were seemingly designed to link the denunciation of the CCP over human rights with the very real attack on Chinese property and civilians. In some *People's Daily* reports this link was made explicit. The article on the Tiananmen Square resolution, published a few weeks after the bombing, reads:

> In the US Congress there are some people, who consider themselves "human rights defenders," who, for their own political ends, or from a hegemonic bullying mentality, have called for "human rights above sovereignty." They fly the flag of so-called "human rights," "democracy," and "freedom" in order to interfere in others' internal affairs and trample upon their sovereignty, in order to impose their social system and values onto other countries and dominate the world. US actions in Yugoslavia fully illustrate this point.[77]

Linking human rights pressure to bombs in Yugoslavia had two effects. It helped to prop up the CCP's narrative that the bombing was a deliberate attack to punish China for its support for Yugoslavia, and it pushed the narrative that American human rights pressure was driven by hostility toward China—hostility exemplified by the attack on the embassy.

On the other hand, in the twenty-eight days after Chinese leaders visited the United States, the *People's Daily* reported far less pressure from the United States—little more than a third as much as normal times, even though American criticism of Chinese human rights violations was 20% higher.[78] This willingness to ignore American barbs over human rights is reflected in generally more positive state media coverage toward the United States, with the *People's Daily* using the term "American friends" (美国朋友) almost twice as much after the visits as at other times.

Blurring this picture a bit is the finding that in the twenty-eight days after American leaders visited China, the *People's Daily* only reported pressure from the United States very slightly less than at other times, and indeed did not use the term "American friends" to any greater extent. For some reason, state media appears to be more inclined to play up positive bilateral relations with the United States in the month after outgoing (but not incoming) visits.[79] Instead, the pacifying effect from these visits seems to be a short one: in fact, if we look only at the seven days after incoming American visits, there was an almost complete absence of stories about pressure from the United States in the *People's Daily* (despite the paper featuring human rights pressure from other non-American sources at the same rate as it had at other periods). Once the Americans had left, state media returned quickly to its normal state.

Another way of glimpsing the impact of geopolitics is to take a longer-term perspective. Over the past forty years, bilateral visits have been sure signs of warming US-China relations, from Richard Nixon's diplomatic venture to China in 1972 to Jiang Zemin's visit to the United States in 1997. On the other hand, both sides have also pulled out of official trips to show their displeasure, from American cancellations of high-level calls on China after the Tiananmen massacre in 1989[80] to Chinese officials' withdrawal from visits to the United States over Taiwan tensions in 1995.[81] Figure 5.2 shows how the geopolitical relationship (as represented by the presence of high-level bilateral meetings in that year) influences how American human rights pressure was dealt with in China. Those years where there were no bilateral meetings have clear spikes in the likelihood of US human rights country reports on China being featured in the *People's Daily*,[82] even though the content of the reports over each of these years was almost identical.

As a further check, we can look at the impact of bilateral US-China human rights dialogues. These dialogues are ways for international actors to push China

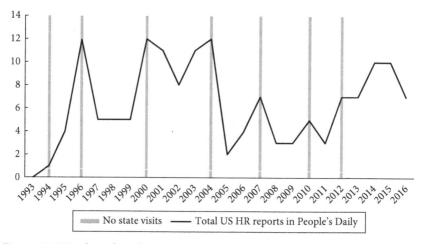

Figure 5.2 Number of articles in *People's Daily* per year about US State Department human rights reports on China, and years where there were no bilateral presidential or foreign minister visits. Individual State Department country reports were first published in 1993.

on human rights in a private arena and were in vogue in Western capitals in the late 1990s and early 2000s.[83] Aware of the popularity of the dialogues, Chinese leaders have periodically canceled them as a way of expressing anger with the more public condemnation (it suspended the US dialogue in 2004 following American sponsorship of a UN resolution targeting China and suspended the UK dialogue in 2012 following David Cameron's meeting with the Dalai Lama). As such, the passage of the US-China dialogues is a reasonable sign that relations between China and the United States are smooth. And in these more benign periods, the twenty-eight days after a US-China dialogue, public human rights pressure from the American side is mentioned less than a tenth as much as at other times.[84]

These results are quite conclusive. But it is not all good news for the argument. I also predicted that when public nationalist sentiment was elevated, foreign criticism might be more effective as a government propaganda tool. In contrast to this prediction, the *People's Daily* was no more likely to report international pressure in the twenty-eight days after nationalist incidents like war anniversaries or in the twenty-eight days following major geopolitical incidents with Japan.[85] This could be because public nationalism has little impact on people's responses to foreign pressure, or it could be that newspapers' attention is primarily directed toward Japan on these days, and their focus is taken up by war memorials and retrospectives. Either way, it appears that public nationalism only leads to more reporting of foreign pressure when nationalism is directed at the source of that pressure.

Alternative Explanations

An increasingly popular take on autocratic politics is that criticism can be quite useful for leaders. One influential recent study shows that the CCP does sometimes allow the public to express criticism of its policies on social media, as long as the criticism does not encourage people to join together in large-scale protests.[86] So why might criticism be useful? One argument is that small public protests or criticism on social media may provide information about public discontent, which can then be dealt with before it spirals into large-scale mobilization.[87] Allowing people to criticize their government may also signal to the public that leaders are willing to listen to their concerns and that their voices are being heard.[88] This does not tell us too much about foreign criticism, however. Leaders are already aware of this criticism before they advertise it, and there is little need for them to signal to foreign critics that they are listening to them.

Perhaps highlighting outside criticism is an underhand way for some elites in the media to subtly criticize the political leadership? If true, we should mainly see reports of foreign criticism when the propaganda chief is from a different political faction to the current leader. For example, in his first term of office, there were reportedly tensions between Xi Jinping and his propaganda chief, Liu Yunshan, an ally of former leader Jiang Zemin.[89] Yet this explanation does not explain the disparaging way in which foreign criticism is reported in the *People's Daily*, nor why it is explicitly framed as an attack on the nation rather than the leader himself. Moreover, the *People's Daily* wrote about foreign pressure quite freely between 1992 and 2002 when Jiang Zemin was in charge, a leader with few obvious conflicts with his propaganda chief, Ding Guangen.

There is one persuasive alternative explanation for these findings: like any newspaper readers, Chinese audiences are drawn in by conflict and drama. They want to read about geopolitical ructions and about attacks on their country from a hostile adversary. Comments from a major rival like the United States on nationalist issues like Tibet or Xinjiang are just much more interesting to readers. Even state-run outlets need to sell papers, and in the commercial world of post-1990s media, they have been pushed in a more and more nationalist direction, to cover stories that play up conflict and geopolitical tensions.[90] The musings of the state-owned (but commercially driven) tabloid the *Global Times* over the last few years are clear signs of this tendency.

The interest factor also means that, as Susan Shirk says, "keeping the Chinese people ignorant of a speech by Taiwan's President, Japan's Prime Minister, or the US Secretary of Defense is no longer possible."[91] The Great Firewall is porous enough that interested citizens will find out about these speeches sooner or later. And if enough interested citizens have already sought out American criticism of China through other routes, then the Propaganda Department will need to get its own account out as quickly as possible.[92]

High-Profile, Commercially Attractive News Is Often Censored

This is a powerful argument but surely cannot be the whole explanation. First, if public interest is what is driving the *People's Daily* to write more about American pressure, then this should also be at least partly picked up by the *New York Times* control, which will overestimate those high-profile and dramatic pieces of pressure coming from the United States. Second, if all that is happening is that state media is reporting comments they believe the people will find interesting, this does not explain why most pieces of foreign pressure—from high-profile condemnation from the United States to accusations of "genocide" from Turkish ministers—are not reported. As shown in the above analysis and in chapter 4, when leaders travel to important foreign partners like the United States, the visit is given exhaustive coverage on state television and newspapers, but discussions of human rights or any protests and criticisms that accompany the trip are blocked almost completely. The difference with the cases Shirk alludes to is the level of sensitivity that human rights criticism brings: unlike a speech on Taiwan or the South China Sea, foreign condemnation of the government's human rights violations does not just risk sparking nationalist sentiment, but also anti-government activity. Even the *Global Times*, which is driven by commercial interests, is state owned and could not report on sensitive topics like human rights in Xinjiang or Tibet without official endorsement.

And the CCP has regularly sought to prevent its citizens from hearing about international pressure on all kinds of "sensitive" issues, even when these issues dominate international media coverage. A good example comes from 2003, when Chinese officials responded slowly to an outbreak of severe acute respiratory syndrome (SARS) in the country, covering up the scale of the outbreak and refusing access to World Health Organization (WHO) officials for over two months. Criticism of the CCP's response rained in from around the globe, with the crisis front-page news from Indonesia to Ireland. CNN[93] and the *Wall Street Journal*[94] published highly critical editorials about the outbreak, and the head of the WHO called out Chinese leaders for their slow reaction.[95] But despite their prominence and public health importance, the criticisms were blocked in domestic media.[96] The comments may well have attracted widespread interest, but that was part of the problem—they would have provided new information to interested citizens about the extent of the crisis and the extent of government mishandling. It was not as if authorities were unaware of the international attention—even while censoring the WHO's criticism, state media was reporting that the organization had "praised China and ASEAN for strengthening cooperation to deal with SARS."[97]

Echoes of the SARS cover-up came in 2008, when infant formula from the Chinese company Sanlu was discovered to contain melamine, a substance that allows substandard milk for babies to pass nutrition tests. Melamine can cause urinary problems and even kidney failure and reportedly led to over three hundred thousand Chinese infants being taken ill.[98] The scandal and its subsequent cover-up by Sanlu and local party officials caused outrage in China and abroad. Criticism came from the United States,[99] the United Nations,[100] and the WHO,[101] among others. The US Food and Drug Administration quarantined Chinese products and warned American customers to avoid Chinese-made formula,[102] while a widely publicized WHO statement called the scandal "deplorable" and called for the Chinese government to improve food safety standards.[103] But again, despite the high-profile nature of the criticism and obvious public interest in the scandal, all these critical foreign comments were ignored in domestic media. Just as with the SARS crisis, the WHO's statement on the scandal was discussed briefly in some outlets but stripped of any mention of untoward behavior. *Xinhua* merely noted that the WHO and China "exchanged opinions on further strengthening food safety cooperation,"[104] while the *Global Times* reported that the organization had "commended the Chinese government for its response to this crisis."[105]

It is worth mentioning here authorities' reaction to foreign criticism of their actions over the COVID-19 outbreak in early 2020. Censorship of the outbreak was immediate, with all comments about the virus blocked from social media up until January 18.[106] Remember Hu Jintao's exhortation for the party to "dare to speak, to speak early"? Over these weeks in early January, the *People's Daily*, the voice of the Communist Party, did not speak at all about the unfolding tragedy. The paper devoted itself to the upcoming annual Lianghui meetings and to a special series about Xi Jinping visiting people's homes.[107]

But as rumors spread in the buildup to Chinese New Year, the censors loosened their grip, and social media lit up with stories, debate, and even criticism of the Wuhan authorities' handling of the outbreak. After Xi Jinping's speech about the virus on January 21, state media belatedly crawled into action, with the *People's Daily* eventually placing the crisis on its front page a few days later.[108] By the beginning of February, the Propaganda Department rumbled back to take hold of the story and to damp down some of the increasingly angry public response. *Weibo* stories were deleted, *Weixin* chat groups were shut down,[109] and a new, centrally coordinated narrative about the crisis was flooded through the press.

Central to this new narrative was what Chenchen Zhang calls "disaster nationalism"[110]: Chinese people were fighting together against a hostile virus and a hostile West, and those who criticized the government for their response were betraying that fight. The reaction to Fang Fang, whose *Wuhan Diary* regurgitated the chaos and despair of the early lockdown, was a perfect example. The *Global Times* called her "a handy tool for the West to sabotage Chinese people's efforts to fight the COVID-19 outbreak,"[111] and she received abuse and death threats.[112]

But unlike the SARS or Sanlu crises, foreign criticism played a part in the COVID-19 story. Of course, at the start, almost all the outside concern, from Africa to Southeast Asia,[113] was indeed withheld from state media. But this time, the short period of loosened control in mid-January meant that most of the population was pretty aware of the origin story of COVID-19. And as the lockdown spring opened into summer, American criticisms of China's response to the virus began to be plastered all over state media. The *People's Daily* did not try to hide the accusations that China—and Communist Party officials' initial cover-up—was responsible for the spread of the virus around the world.[114] The paper repeatedly circled around one theme: America was "passing the buck" ("甩锅"),[115] and around one culprit: US Secretary of State Mike Pompeo. In an echo of 1950s propaganda, a torrent of articles in May and June accused Pompeo of being "disgusting,"[116] "arrogant and absurd,"[117] and the "public enemy of mankind."[118] American attacks were swiftly linked to those domestic critics like Fang Fang. The *Global Times* was particularly unsubtle, noting that

> [Fang Fang's] book comes at a time when the US has been trying to shift blame over its inability to combat the outbreak onto China and has constantly slandered China's efforts in dealing with the pandemic.[119]

Was this narrative successful? Mass censorship of critical social media comments makes it hard to know for sure, but some commentators noted the shift in the tone of the public debate over the virus in China through the spring of 2020.[120] Early calls for freedom of speech[121] were tempered as authorities successfully contained the virus and other nations failed to do the same. By the late spring the online conversation around the outbreak was more nationalistic than condemnatory,[122] with many openly taking the government line that those like Fang Fang were unpatriotic or traitorous for siding with Western critics.[123] In surveys carried out in April 2020, Chinese citizens expressed some of the highest levels of satisfaction with their government's response to the crisis of any country around the world.[124]

Of course, in a time of heavy censorship and reprisals for government criticism,[125] we cannot take these survey responses and online commentary at face value. Future work will be needed to gauge the true impact of the virus, the response, and the propaganda on people's views of their government. What is clear is that in this case, once total censorship had been abandoned, foreign criticism played a key role in building the new narrative.

Low-Profile, Hard-to-Access News Is Often Reported

Look back to chapter 3. In the 1980s, there was a commercial media explosion, with the number of newspapers going from 280 in 1979 to a peak of 2,322 in 1988,[126] yet news of foreign criticism remained relatively limited and civil. Compare this to the 1950s and 1960s. Media was exclusively state run and tightly controlled. Any news contained within was there to serve the party, not the market. But at this time, despite the lack of commercial incentives, and little possibility for interested citizens to find out through other means, newspapers included extensive coverage of foreign condemnation, and especially condemnation that came from the adversary—the United States.

Even after the mass expansion of the internet, there are cases of foreign criticism of human rights in China that are picked up by the *People's Daily* and other state-run media outlets but hardly mentioned in mainstream international media—cases that most citizens would be unlikely to otherwise read anything about. The British government's 2016 Hong Kong report, for example, barely received any global press attention,[127] meaning that it would have been extremely difficult for the public to find out about the report, short of scouring the UK Foreign Office website. But unlike its reaction to the WHO reports on SARS and the Sanlu scandal, state media ignored the explicit praise for Hong Kong's political and economic conditions written in the opening paragraphs of the report. Instead, it brought only the criticism to its public's attention—criticism that came from a former colonial power, that addressed an issue closely tied to China's territorial integrity, and that talked about the CCP's existing political policies in Hong Kong.

State media has not just reported unheralded criticism from old adversaries like the American and British governments. In recent years, newspapers have started to highlight criticism from places where there is little obvious commercial interest. In February 2015, the international NGO Human Rights Watch (HRW) issued its annual report about the state of human rights in China in 2014. The report criticized many aspects of the CCP's performance on human rights, from its actions in Tibet to its lack of progress on women's rights.[128] Despite these criticisms, and the fact that international coverage of its release was sparse at best, the report was featured widely in state media. The *People's Daily* only discussed the part that criticized Chinese policies in Tibet, issuing a detailed rebuttal that described China's developmental successes and investment in the region,[129] while *Xinhua* focused only on the section that addressed CCP's approach to judicial reform and policies on the rule of law.[130] Other articles attacked HRW directly, accused it of producing biased reports, and called it "an excuse for Western countries to impose their hegemony on the world."[131]

As shown in Table 5.1, between 1979 and 2011, criticism from international NGOs was rarely mentioned in the media. Since 2012, however, the CCP has heavily publicized attacks on its behavior from rights advocacy groups like HRW. This approach to international NGOs is a new one in China and is one worth noting. After the role that civil society played in driving the Arab Spring in 2011, authoritarian states around the world became increasingly paranoid about foreign NGOs. Many issued laws that restricted NGO funding and curtailed their activities. China was no exception, and the CCP began to accuse these groups of seeking regime change, both on the mainland and in Hong Kong, and in 2017 pushed through a law that placed foreign NGOs under tight state control.

While Chinese media had ignored HRW reports for years, after the Arab Spring, state-owned newspapers began to publicly call the group out as an American proxy trying to constrain China's rise. Although most citizens would have been unlikely to encounter HRW publications by their own devices, by 2012 the organization's annual reports were splashed all over state media. Figure 5.3

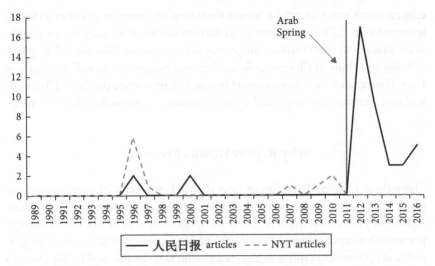

Figure 5.3 Articles about Human Rights Watch reports on China in the *New York Times* and the *People's Daily* (人民日报), by year, 1989–2016.

shows the jump in the number of HRW annual reports on China featured in the *People's Daily* after the Arab Spring—a jump that occurred in spite of the fact that none of these reports were featured in major newspapers like the *New York Times*. This is quite a puzzle, because it means that it was only when the Communist Party leaders started to believe that international NGOs like HRW were dangerous, hostile groups intent on sparking unrest in China that they chose to pass their words on to the public. Only if we see hostile words themselves as being a potential propaganda boost for the CCP can we explain this puzzle.

Obscure foreign media criticism has also been a source of propaganda. In November 2015, French journalist Ursula Gauthier wrote a piece for the magazine *L'Obs* that criticized the CCP's hardline policies toward the Uighur ethnic minority in Xinjiang. Gauthier, who was based in Beijing, argued that the Chinese government had to take its own share of responsibility for the level of violence in the region.[132] The government responded as expected, revoking Gauthier's visa to China and attacking her in state media. The attacks extensively quoted Gauthier's criticism of Beijing's policies in Xinjiang,[133] calling her article "extreme" and "prejudiced."[134]

The original piece by Gauthier barely caused a stir in international media circles, and it was only after her visa was not renewed and the attacks in Chinese media began that international media attention turned to the issue (leading to further foreign criticisms of press freedom in China[135] and further Chinese rebuttals[136]). In this case foreign media attention to Gauthier's criticism and its consequences came *after* the Chinese media reports, suggesting either a clumsy attempt by the CCP to pre-empt other foreign stories about the issue or a deliberate strategy to use Gauthier for propaganda purposes. Like the HRW piece, this was a critique of Chinese policies in its restive regions, as well as a critique from France, a country portrayed as hostile to China since the 2008 Tibet riots and the Carrefour boycott. Gauthier was therefore a reasonably risk-free target.

Why Report Hostile Pressure?

These three chapters have shown how the CCP allows its citizens to find out about information from abroad that questions the country's respect for human rights. They have shown that the party allows its citizens to find out about foreign pressure that appears most hostile to the nation—pressure that comes from geopolitical opponents at times of high tension on well-known and highly charged nationalist issues: in other words, pressure that highlights international competition above real-life injustice. For traditional accounts of authoritarian politics, where autocrats abhor all criticism and seek to hide news of their abuses from their people, this is puzzling behavior. Also puzzling is that the decision to publish foreign criticism does not seem to be purely motivated by the hope of making state media appear more credible or by the need to satisfy the citizens' desire for more salacious geopolitical gossip.

So why would a powerful but hypersensitive authoritarian regime allow its citizens to find out about such potentially damaging information? In the second half of this book I look at the citizens to provide the answer. I show that exposure to foreign pressure—and in particular the pressure that the Communist Party passes on to its people—significantly affects the way those people think about human rights.

PART III
THE CITIZENS

6

Experimental Activism

How International Pressure on Women's Rights Affects Public Attitudes

On the evening of March 6, 2015, a group of young Chinese feminists were working out the final details of their mission to mark the upcoming International Women's Day. The plan was a modest one: go onto buses and subways in cities around China the next morning and hand out leaflets and stickers to raise awareness about sexual harassment. At around 11 p.m. that night, however, police stormed the houses of ten of the organizers and volunteers of the project. They soon released five activists but held the remaining five—Li Tingting, Wei Tingting, Wang Man, Zheng Churan, and Wu Rongrong—without charge. Li Tingting, a twenty-six-year-old Beijing native, was held in her city's Haidian detention center for thirty-seven days and interrogated daily by security agents determined to find the group that was organizing her "subversive" activities. Li recounts how the agents called her "lesbian" and "whore," woke her in the middle of the night to scrub floors, accused her of being a spy for unnamed foreign forces, intimidated her with warnings of ten years in jail, and threatened her parents.[1]

While all news about the activists was censored in China,[2] the arrests sparked a storm of international criticism and media attention. The American ambassador to the United Nations, Samantha Power, questioned China's commitment to women's rights, while former US secretary of state Hillary Clinton called the arrests "inexcusable."[3] Condemnation poured forth from the United Kingdom, Canada, the European Union, and nongovernmental organizations (NGOs) from Japan to India. Finally, after far-reaching public and private attempts to secure their release,[4] on April 13 the activists were finally charged with the nebulous crime of "gathering crowds to disturb order" and allowed to leave on bail.[5]

As we will see, this kind of foreign pressure has a substantial impact on Chinese citizens' views about their government's treatment of women's rights and their willingness to support efforts to improve it. Pressure on women's rights is both an easy and a hard case for this book. It is an easy case because compared to pressure over more immediately emotive abuses like police beatings or torture, it is much simpler to portray foreign pressure over the abstract ideal of women's rights as driven by hostility rather than genuine concern for the victims. It is a hard case

Hostile Forces. Jamie J. Gruffydd-Jones, Oxford University Press. © Oxford University Press 2022.
DOI: 10.1093/oso/9780197643198.003.0006

because it is much more difficult to wave away foreign concerns when you have publicly depicted yourself as an emancipator and a vocal advocate of women's rights, as the Communist Party has done.

The goal of this chapter is to uncover the impact of international pressure on people's views about women's rights in China today, pressure on cases like the arrests of the "feminist five." Using survey experiments, it will show that this impact is dramatically different depending on whether the pressure comes from a geopolitical opponent or a more politically neutral source, whether it explicitly targets Chinese leaders or the country as a whole, whether it touches on territorial issues like Tibet, and what kinds of people read it.[6]

But before we do that, to begin to understand the history of the international community and women's rights in China, we need to go back to the fading days of the Qing Dynasty in the late nineteenth century.

The Movement against Foot-Binding

At this time, young aristocratic women were given the ancient *Analects of Women,* an educational "textbook" from the ninth-century Tang Dynasty, to guide their behavior. One piece of practical advice from the textbook went as follows:

> Keep your daughter indoors as a rule and only rarely should you allow her out: she ought to be under your total command. You should scold her roundly if she is not quick to obey, remind her often of self-discipline and household duties.[7]

And for almost one thousand years, the practice of foot-binding was used to exert this total command. Girls as young as six had their toes tied under their feet and then bound tightly to prevent them from growing. Having three-inch so-called golden lotuses was a sign of status for women, to show that they did not need to engage in manual labor, and the tiny feet became something of a fetish for aristocratic men. By restricting their movement, even to the point of crippling them,[8] foot-binding made sure that women could only work around the house.[9] Despite the ruling Qing Empire's occasional attempts to ban the practice over the previous centuries, by the mid-nineteenth century the tradition had grown to such an extent that it afflicted up to 80% of Chinese women.[10]

It was foot-binding that drew the international community's attention to human rights in China for the first time. In the late nineteenth century, just as the practice reached its height, the European nations' semi-colonization brought missionaries and their families into China. Many in the missionary community were shocked by the brutality of the practice, and their outspoken condemnations of foot-binding attracted Christian women in their congregations, even leading some to pledge to not bind the feet of their daughters.[11] The movement developed rapidly, and in 1895 Mrs. Archibald Little, an English woman, helped to set up the Natural Foot Society (天足会), a group that drew both foreign and Chinese campaigners. The society's pleas to Empress Dowager Cixi to ban the practice eventually caught the attention of leading Qing officials in the Bureau of Foreign Affairs, who replied dismissively:

> The usages and customs prevailing in China are different from those of Western countries. . . . Custom has made the practice. Those in high authority cannot but allow the people to do as they are inclined in the matter . . . they cannot be restrained by law.[12]

Among Chinese intellectuals, however, the missionaries found a fertile bed of support. Reformers Kang Youwei and Liang Qichao saw the end of foot-binding as the star turn of their battle for women's liberation and vigorously joined the campaign.[13] Indigenous anti-foot-binding societies sprung up around the country, and gradually the tide of public opinion shifted. In 1902 Empress Dowager Cixi, five years after her officials had stated that foot-binders could not be restrained by law, announced an edict to abolish the practice.[14] When the Qing dynasty itself fell just a few years later, the new Republican government issued a nationwide ban. The tide had turned against foot-binding, and the practice fell out of fashion, eventually dying out. Almost a thousand years of tradition ended in under fifty years.[15]

It is hard to know whether foot-binding would have disappeared in such a dramatic way without the influence of Western missionaries. Many writers have emphasized the vital role that the transnational movement played.[16] What is surprising is that this would happen in the face of gales of anti-foreign sentiment that had been whirling around China since the beginning of the Opium Wars in the 1840s. The zenith of this xenophobia was the Boxer Rebellion—a peasant revolt that gained popular support in northern China for killing missionaries and their Christian followers—just as the missionary-led anti-foot-binding campaign was getting into full swing. Foreign missionaries were playing a dangerous game by launching campaigns against age-old local traditions at this time.

And in some ways, locals' relatively positive reaction to foreign activists appears to challenge this book's thesis: that when the source of pressure appears hostile, people will react angrily and defensively. But there is a crucial missing condition here. For pressure to appear hostile, there needs to be someone able to make a convincing case to the public that it is indeed an attempt to hurt the country and its way of life, rather than a genuine attempt to improve the nation and its people. And the Qing government made little attempt to publicly oppose the anti-foot-binding movement, never mind portray it as led by foreign forces hostile to China. Of course, unlike most of the state-led human rights violations that we discussed in chapters 3 and 4, the human rights violations from foot-binding were built into societal norms and ways of life. Qing leaders themselves had little material interest in ensuring that foot-binding continued.

They were also in no position to frame the pressure as a hostile attack on the Chinese nation. While hatred and suspicion of foreigners were high, so was disapproval of the Qing government—itself a "foreign" power for many due to its origins in Manchuria—and its inability to deal with the challenges from abroad. As Zhao Suisheng points out, Chinese nationalism emerged at this time not as a way of defending the state against occupying Westerners, "but rather as an ethnic state-seeking movement led by the Han majority to overthrow the Qing Dynasty."[17] The Boxer Rebellion was not merely an anti-foreign movement, but a protest at the favorable treatment given to foreigners and foreign missionaries following the Qing's concessions to aggressive outside powers.[18] Other nationalist uprisings like the Xinhai Rebellion in 1911 and the May Fourth Movement in 1919 were similarly directed not at Westerners, but at their government for its failure to stand up to foreign threats.[19] By the early twentieth century, the public no longer believed that their leaders were adequately defending their nation.

In the face of these challenges, the national reform movement led by Liang Qichao and Kang Youwei directed its attention inward, toward how their country could improve and strengthen itself. The modernizing social and economic climate provided new opportunities for women in education, in employment, and through improved transportation. These developments made women less reliant on traditional familial ties, and therefore less vulnerable to pressure from their family to bind their feet.[20]

For Liang and Kang, the liberation of women was a sign of the nation's modernity and strength, a liberation that included not just issues like foot-binding that captured transnational attention, but also more mundane concerns, like improving women's access to education. While foreign Christian organizations undoubtedly sought to assist in this goal, setting up the first women's schools in China in 1842, missionary campaigning was nowhere near the same level as over foot-binding. The improvements in women's education in the late Qing and early Republican era were primarily driven from within.[21] While Margaret Keck and Kathryn Sikkink in their influential book *Activists beyond Borders* credit foreign missionaries with helping to "roll the stone,"[22] the dramatic abolition of foot-binding was just one part of a period of dramatic social reform in many arenas, not least for women.

So in many ways, the foreign missionaries' campaign fell in extraordinarily favorable circumstances.[23] The missionaries embedded their campaign within a popular nationalist domestic movement and faced no real resistance from conservative elites or the government.[24] There was no organized campaign able or willing to frame it as a hostile attack from abroad on Chinese traditions.[25] Instead, the ban on foot-binding was deliberately framed by activists as an assertion of the national identity, a way to modernize and strengthen the country against the rest of the world. And arguably the most important "foreign" aspect of the anti-foot-binding campaign lay here. The nineteenth-century foreign incursions into China generated anti-foreign sentiment, but also the realization that China needed to fight back against these challenges—and that the Qing government was failing in this fight. The fact that foreigners were involved in the movement highlighted to the reformists that this was an issue on which China was falling behind. In 1898 Kang wrote a note to the young emperor Guangxu saying:

> All countries have international relations, and they compare their political institutions with one another; so that if one commits the slightest error, the others ridicule and look down upon it. . . . There is nothing which makes us objects of ridicule so much as foot-binding.[26]

Foreign Pressure, Women's Rights, and the Chinese Communist Party

The Chinese Communist Party (CCP) was born out of the reformist atmosphere of the early twentieth century. Just like Kang Youwei and Liang Qichao, new Communist leaders recognized the importance of women for their own revolution, and "women's liberation" became one of the party's core pledges. After the CCP's victory in the Chinese civil war, its leader Mao Zedong stated:

> In order to build a great socialist society it is of the upmost importance to arouse the broad masses of women to join in productive activity. Men and women must receive equal pay for equal work in production. Genuine equality of the sexes can only be realized in the process of the socialist transformation of society as a whole.[27]

The People's Republic of China Constitution, signed in 1949, explicitly affirmed that women should have the same rights as men; the Marriage Law in 1950 gave women the freedom to marry and divorce; the Election Law of 1953 gave women the right to vote; and laws were instituted to give women the right to possess property.[28] And in stark contrast to one hundred years earlier when 80% of women were hobbled and housebound, by 1957, 90% of women participated in agricultural production.[29] Its role as a champion of women's rights has remained a pillar of the CCP's legitimacy up to the present day.

But the advent of capitalism after 1978 showed that these long-standing inequalities between men and women had not gone away. New businesses, facing the challenges of providing paid maternity leave[30] and more flexible working hours,[31] resorted to giving women lower pay and poorer promotion prospects than their male counterparts.[32] The percentage of women in the labor force, while still relatively high, has dropped by 11% over the last twenty years.[33] The one-child policy, which was instituted in 1981 to prevent families from having more than one child, also brought back relics of male domination supposedly relegated to the country's distant past. In the Qing period the killing of female babies was a common method of fertility control, a way of controlling the gender mix of families.[34] Yet the combination of the one-child policy and the need for male workers in the countryside in the 1980s saw a sudden re-emergence of female infanticide. The shocking nature of these cases and their dramatic reintroduction into society sparked renewed local interest in women's rights, including campaigns from domestic NGOs like the Women's Federation to "protect the legal rights of women and children,"[35] as well as periodic criticism from foreign governments.[36]

Some of the most prominent women's rights activism in China in recent years has come over domestic violence.[37] Take the case of Kim Lee, the American wife of tycoon Li Yang. After their marriage in 2006 Li began to brutally beat his wife, but despite repeated visits to police stations and hospitals, Kim Lee received no help from authorities. In 2011 she eventually resorted to appealing to public sympathy, using her fame to gain attention by posting online pictures of her bruises and her husband's threatening texts.[38] Surveys suggest that at least a quarter of women have experienced similar domestic abuse from their partner,[39] and domestic violence has become a prime target for young feminists, including Li Tingting and the rest of the "feminist five." These same activists launched a "bloodied bride" protest in 2012, venturing onto the pedestrian Qianmen Street in the center of Beijing in bridal gowns and red paint to protest the lack of a law against domestic violence.[40] And the activism has been a success, albeit a gradual one. Twelve years after the Anti-Domestic Violence Network of China first proposed it, in December 2015 a nationwide law against domestic violence was finally passed. The law bans any form of domestic violence and allows courts to issue protection orders to victims.[41]

Of course, domestic violence and unequal pay are problems faced in any industrialized country. What is exceptional in China is where gender inequality meets the deficiency of civil and political rights. Because of the restrictions on freedom of expression and association in China, women's ability to speak out for their rights is severely limited. Kim Lee took her case, with hard evidence of beatings and threats against her life, to the legal system. Police informed her that the evidence was inadmissible and repeatedly told her to deal with it within her own family.[42] Finally, after a public outcry sparked by her social media campaign and an eighteen-month legal battle, the court ruled in favor of Lee. It granted her a divorce, compensation, and a restraining order against her husband.[43] But even with a law against domestic violence, women's legal routes are often blocked. Hong Fincher argues that what the law is supposed to do often does not translate into how the police and courts work in practice.[44] According to feminist activist Lü Pin, courts simply refuse to accept cases of domestic violence unless the accused admits to the abuse, often making the burden of evidence too high—especially for those without an American passport and a celebrity husband.[45]

In 1995, at the Fourth World Conference on Women in Beijing, then-first lady Hillary Clinton stated in her keynote speech that "it is time for us to say here in Beijing, and the world to hear, that it is no longer acceptable to discuss women's rights as separate from human rights."[46] The message was lost on the authorities, who, concerned that women's rights protests were taking international attention away from the conference, had built a huge security net around the main event and banished the mainly female NGO delegates to a separate conference in a town outside of Beijing.[47] They arrested journalists for filming demonstrations and reportedly banned delegates from the main conference. Police interference was so intense that conveners of the NGO forum threatened to boycott the event if surveillance of their activities continued.[48] In her speech, Clinton took aim at the security measures, saying:

> It is indefensible that many women in non-governmental organizations who wished to participate in this conference have not been able to attend—or have been prohibited from fully taking part.... Let me be clear. Freedom means the right of people to assemble, organize and debate openly.

And in recent years international attention has mainly focused on this kind of suppression of women's civil society, most vociferously over the arrests of the "feminist five." Looking back at this case even with the benefit of hindsight, it is still hard to know the exact impact that the international campaign had on securing the women's eventual release. Other activists credited the private efforts of those such as the deputy secretary of the United Nations, Jan Eliasson, in persuading Beijing to free the women.[49] After their release on bail, the five wrote to UN Secretary General Ban Ki-Moon, calling for the organization to continue to pressure authorities to make their release unconditional.[50] Others argued, however, that the very fact that it had happily detained the women without charge in the face of widespread international pressure showed where the CCP's priorities lay: maintaining the party's international image was a long way behind ensuring that feminists stayed in line.[51]

The five were in detention for over a month, and authorities faced constant, highly publicized international condemnation and appeals for their release. In contrast to the accounts featured in chapters 3 and 4, however, the Chinese press stayed silent. The usual suspects—*Xinhua*, the *People's Daily*, and the *Global Times*—ignored the pressure and indeed omitted all news of the detentions from their pages. It was only a few days before authorities released the activists on bail (and soon after Hillary Clinton and US Secretary of State John Kerry made public calls for their release) that Chinese media finally—briefly—addressed the furor. On April 9 one article appeared in the *Global Times*, mentioning the detention of the activists and the subsequent Western media coverage, focusing on Hillary Clinton's comments on Twitter. According to the article:

> Hillary Clinton called the incident a "human rights violation" on the 6th [of April], and demanded that the five be released immediately. Hillary's interventionist tone is typical of Western public opinion, and just adds to the chorus of accusations.[52]

While the *Global Times* has shown more willingness to publish controversial stories than its sister publication the *People's Daily*, the sheer scale of censorship over the arrests over the previous month makes it hard to believe that the article did not receive central approval. It is possible that Clinton and Kerry's public statements were the sparks that made the furor over the arrests so prominent that authorities felt the need to publicly address them. But through the whole of the preceding month there was very similar—and very highly publicized—condemnation of the arrests, condemnation that was all censored in China. The scale of the suppression of this news meant that even some Chinese feminists had not heard about the detentions.[53] And it is this censorship that is perhaps the most puzzling aspect of the case, given state media's widespread coverage of foreign pressure over other political prisoners in 2014 and 2015.

The CCP's historic commitment to women's rights and the wider sympathy the activism could have attracted among the population certainly make crackdowns on feminist protest a more sensitive topic for the censors. But such high levels of censorship may have also arisen because, just like foot-binding a hundred years before, the issues the feminists were fighting for were less politically sensitive than those fought for by the other political prisoners. Unlike Ilham Tohti and the human rights lawyers, the feminist five were calling for reforms on issues like harassment on public transport and domestic violence, hardly reforms that posed a threat to the nominally pro-women's rights Communist Party. It is hard to see how (beyond dissuading future activism) continuing to hold the five in detention would bring any notable benefits to the CCP. Without these benefits, the CCP had fewer incentives to keep Li Tingting and her colleagues in jail, and so would have been far more susceptible to the embarrassment dealt by the mass campaign for their release. It is a classic case of when top-down international shaming should be most effective, and so it was perhaps not unexpected that the activists were released relatively quickly. As such, authorities had no burning need to rally public support in favor of the arrests—and so no need to highlight foreign pressure.

This all suggests that authorities are more likely to release political prisoners like the feminist five on bail if they have not talked about those prisoners extensively in state media. We can examine whether this is true by looking at the database on Chinese political prisoners held by the US Congressional Executive Committee on China. For many of those prisoners, even those arrested decades ago, there is no evidence to say whether they have been released or not. But if we limit ourselves only to those 1,199 political prisoners in the database whom we know have been released one way or another, we can compare those who were released on bail and not sentenced in court to those who were not released on bail, sentenced, and then released at the end of their sentence. And prisoners are around half as likely to be released on bail and not taken to trial if their arrest is written about in the *People's Daily*. While this is not a rigorous statistical test, it does suggest that authorities are more willing to release activists like the feminist five on bail if they have decided to hide their arrests from the public.

For the feminist five, most of the pressure had come from organizations like the European Union and the United Nations, not organizations that would have seemed overly hostile. If this book is to be believed, perhaps the most plausible reason for why Hillary Clinton's criticism was the only one to be brought up by state media is that for many she was an emblem of American hostility toward China. For many years "希拉里" (Xi-La-Li) was a target for the ire of the media, having been outspoken on Communist Party actions back to her forthright speech at the 1995 World Conference on Women. She had repeatedly and publicly accused the CCP of violating human rights and as secretary of state was vocal in opposition to Chinese actions in the South China Sea.[54] For state media, especially nationalist outlets like the *Global Times*, 希拉里 embodied Western attempts to use human rights to stymie China's growth. As such, we should not be surprised that hers were the only critiques of the arrests that they featured.

More evidence that it was the intervention of Clinton that sparked a media response came later in the year. In September, Xi Jinping hosted the UN Women's Conference in New York to celebrate the twentieth anniversary of the 1995 Beijing conference. The irony of hosting a celebration of women's rights when five women's rights activists were still officially on bail in China was not lost on Clinton, who posted the following on Twitter:

Xi hosting a meeting on women's rights at the UN while persecuting feminists? Shameless. #Freethe20

Clinton's tweet was seized upon immediately. Eliding that the tweet was an attack on Xi Jinping, state media called her "alarmed and jealous," saying that Clinton was attacking the country to gain attention for her presidential campaign.[55] On the surface, for China's embattled feminists, support from an American presidential candidate might be a boost for their ambitions to mobilize support for women's rights. And some activists did welcome the comments, saying that they captured the frustration many felt with the lack of progress since 1995.[56] But others saw Clinton's interventions as state media intended. A typical *Weibo* response went along the lines of

Hillary is a fanatic for opposing China, regardless of what the matter is she can turn it against you.[57]

Pen Xiaohui, a professor in sexology at East China Normal University, suggested that Clinton's remarks were not particularly helpful for the feminist movement. She responded to the tweet on *Weibo*:

Last year after President Xi spoke at the UN Women's Summit, Hillary immediately attacked China's policies on women. The political motives behind this make one pause to consider. A society in which men and women are equal is of course the direction to which mankind needs to strive, but China cannot allow a foreign politician who views China with hostility to meddle in this undertaking.[58]

Testing the Impact of Pressure on Chinese Citizens

While we cannot be sure of the extent to which foreign pressure had any concrete impact on authorities' decision to release the feminist five, the widespread condemnation would undoubtedly have caused the leadership embarrassment on the international stage. In a top-down sense then, there were certainly some benefits from worldwide attention on women's rights in 2015. But this book is not about how foreign pressure factors into leaders' geopolitical considerations. It is about how calls for the release of activists and for better women's rights in China affect the citizens, their beliefs about women's rights in their country, and their support for women's rights activism. At the end of the nineteenth century, the transnational campaign to push society and the weak Qing government to abolish foot-binding was generally welcomed by Chinese citizens. How would campaigns for women's rights fare under a powerful, nationalist, one-party state?

To examine this question, I used two experiments embedded in national online surveys on attitudes to women's rights.[59] Of course, your typical online citizen—or "netizen"—is not the same as your typical citizen. The online samples used in the survey were richer, more well educated, and more urban than the overall population, but they were drawn from almost all provinces and walks of life and were deliberately selected to match the age and gender distribution of the overall population. Perhaps more importantly, the online population (around 50% of the total population at the time of the surveys)[60] is arguably the most likely to pick up on foreign comments about China, and some have argued that among the middle class in China, any political and civil society participation is now most likely to be online.[61] So while the surveys may not reflect the response of every citizen, they do pick up most of those who would be likely to react in some way to foreign pressure.

Source of Pressure

The first step was to examine whether the source of criticism matters. In early 2016 I gave a survey to 1,200 Chinese netizens, randomly assigning them to one of three groups: a "control" group who were just told to answer some questions and two "treatment" groups who were first asked to read a simple short paragraph, with only the source varied, as follows:[62]

> Yesterday a (United States/African Union) spokeswoman criticized China's women's rights conditions. She said: "The Chinese government must improve the rights of women in China."

To see how even the most minimal prompt about foreign pressure on women's rights could affect people's views, I deliberately stripped out any extraneous details about the issue being criticized and the Chinese response. This kind of brief condemnatory statement is often how human rights pressure is presented in international and Chinese media. In its criticism of human rights in China in December 2016, for example, the European Union was reported only as being "'extremely troubled' by the human rights situation in China" in the *Reuters* headline[63] and merely as having "accused China over its human rights" in the *Global Times*.[64]

To see how the perceived hostility of the source of pressure toward China would matter, I chose two sources that were at opposite ends in their levels of geopolitical opposition with China. The CCP portrays the United States as a major geopolitical rival[65] and, as we have seen, since 1989 has repeatedly called it out for its hostility in criticizing China's human rights. The African Union is

108   HOSTILE FORCES

more of a geopolitical ally. Since the Maoist period, Beijing has portrayed itself as the leader of the developing world, and the *People's Daily* has described the relationship with African countries as "friendly" and "a community of mutual support."[66] As we saw in the previous chapter, criticism from African countries—like in early 2020 over racial discrimination in Guangzhou—is generally censored or minimized in the Chinese press.

I also wanted to gauge the differences in people's response to foreign pressure if they were even more aware of their national identity. To test this, half of the respondents, when they read the sentence about pressure, also saw a small Chinese flag in the top left-hand corner of their screen. Even subliminal exposure to national symbols like flags has been shown to accentuate people's attachment to their nation[67] and influence their attitudes about political matters.[68]

As Figure 6.1 shows, this short note about pressure significantly affected survey respondents' concerns about the state of women's rights in China—but the source of that pressure was crucial. While pressure from the African Union had no impact, people who read about pressure from the United States were 6.6 percentage points less likely to say women's rights were not good enough in

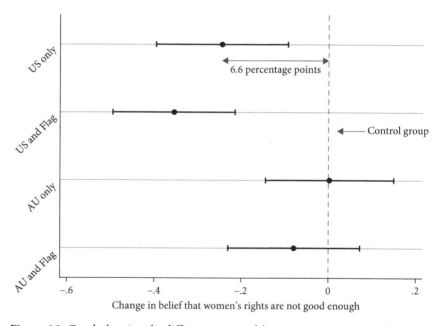

Figure 6.1 Graph showing the difference in people's grievances over women's rights after reading a short sentence about foreign pressure (and being given a small Chinese flag in the corner), compared to the control. This graph has been normalized with 0 as the control, so that a lower score means the fewer grievances people have compared to the control. Lines represent 95% confidence intervals.

their country[69] and 7.7 percentage points less willing to say they would sign a petition to improve women's rights (in comparison to the control group, who received no pressure). To put this into some perspective, women were around 12 percentage points more likely than men to say women's rights were not good enough, so this is a relatively large difference.

Real-Life News

By virtue of its minimalist design, this experiment is quite limited in what it can tell us about how people respond to foreign pressure. To solve some of these concerns, we need a second, more realistic, test. So in early 2018 I gathered a (new) online sample of 1,211 Chinese people from around the country, again representative by age and gender.

To make things a bit more realistic, I provided survey participants with two stories that closely resemble media reports of a genuine incident, the closure of the Zhongze center in 2016, in the format and language of a *Xinhua* news story. In early 2016 the Beijing Zhongze Women's Legal Counselling and Service Centre, run by Guo Jianmei, closed under "pressure" from the Beijing Municipal Public Security Bureau.[70] The high-profile legal aid NGO had symbolized the growth in women's rights in China since the 1990s, and its closure drew international condemnation, including another tweet from Hillary Clinton, saying: "Women's rights are human rights. This center should remain—I stand with Guo."[71] The *Global Times* introduced news of the closure of the center (already featured in Western media) by referencing Hillary Clinton's messages of criticism, suggesting that "it is possible that Clinton was using this women's rights-related affair to promote her campaign for the upcoming Democratic primary."[72]

The two stories are translated into English in Figure 6.2. As you can see, the first provides a simple story about the closure of a fictional women's rights center, the "China United Women's Foundation," that has been featured in international news. The second introduces this very same information through the lens of US pressure, calling for the center to be reopened and criticizing women's rights in China. I also randomly provided a third story, which just mentions the "China United Women's Foundation" in the context of women's issues in China but does not say anything about the closure of the center. The reason for this is that we also want to see whether just "naming" news about the closure, without any accompanying "shaming," has any effect on people's views about women's rights.

What we care about here is not just people's self-reported attitudes about women's rights, but how these attitudes affect their behaviors in ways that might get the government's attention. The CCP spends enormous resources attempting to understand public opinion, through its own "opinion mining" surveys and

Women's Rights Centre Closed Down	US Criticises China's Closure of Women's Rights Centre
Xinhua, Beijing, 13 February Yesterday foreign news media reported that a women's rights centre, China United Women's Foundation, was closed by Chinese authorities as part of growing official regulation of NGO groups. The foundation promoted gender equality in education and the workplace.	Xinhua, Beijing, 13 February The United States has strongly condemned yesterday's closure of a women's rights centre, China United Women's Foundation, by Chinese authorities as part of growing official regulation of NGO groups, as reported by foreign media. The foundation promoted gender equality in education and the workplace. A US official criticised the respect for women's rights in China, saying that the country must improve its treatment of women, and called on China to reopen the centre.

Figure 6.2 Translated control and translated basic "shaming" treatment. Created by the author.

monitoring of social media, and does tilt its policies in response to public outcries, even on sensitive issues like human rights.[73] In 2018, for example, an online commotion over *Weibo*'s decision to remove topics with "gay themes" from its social media platform led to the *People's Daily* publishing an official opinion piece calling for respect for sexual orientation, which in turn caused *Weibo* to reverse its decision.[74] If public outcries like this influence government policy in China, then whether these outcries come as a result of disingenuous cheerleading[75] or genuine firmly held beliefs does not really matter. Publicly disavowing an activist group to demonstrate your patriotism will have just the same effect as doing so because you genuinely disagree with the group.

To see whether people are willing to back up their views, I provided them with a screenshot of a generic *Weibo* post (Figure 6.3) that purports to be from a women's rights activist group calling for the Zhongze center to be reopened and for women's rights to be improved in China. I gave them the option to "like" the post, as they would do on *Weibo*.[76] I also asked respondents to vote for one of four organizations to receive a $150 donation: a women's rights group, an animal rights group, a police group, or a group dedicated to protecting China's maritime claims in the South China Sea.

#Reopen China United Women's Foundation# China's women's rights activists call for the China United Women's Foundation to be reopened and for steps to be taken to improve women's rights in China!

Figure 6.3 Respondents could choose to "like" this (translated) *Weibo* post, attributed to "All-Country Women United."

Earlier in this chapter we talked about how Qing reformers like Kang Youwei pushed for the abolition of foot-binding by saying that countries "compare their political institutions with one another."[77] Do these comparisons, raising people's awareness of their nation's performance against others, really make pressure more effective? One common way by which the international community currently puts pressure on countries to improve their human rights has been through the explicit use of these kinds of cross-national comparisons, by ranking their performance on human rights. The World Economic Forum, for example, provides a highly publicized annual index of gender equality in 144 countries, which in 2017 placed China down in 100th place.[78]

Political scientists Judith Kelley and Beth Simmons, like Kang Youwei before them, argue that doing badly in cross-national comparisons like human rights rankings puts social pressure on states to liberalize. Government elites feel shamed by their peers in other countries, and citizens are "incensed,"[79] pressing leaders to change their policies. In other words, rankings should provide a particularly effective form of transnational shaming. Perhaps recognizing this, in 2014 the CCP Propaganda Department explicitly called for domestic media to censor news that China was ranked 175 out of 180 in the year's Press Freedom Index.[80]

While I cannot speak about government leaders, I can test whether citizens do indeed respond as Kelley and Simmons expect or whether highlighting the nation's standing against rival states instead makes citizens more likely to view that issue in terms of geopolitics and makes them fight to defend their nation. The first experiment used a small flag to make respondents more aware of their national identity, but that hardly reflects this kind of real-life comparison. I therefore randomly allocated to respondents one extra piece of information, informing them that "in the World Economic Forum's 2017 global ranking on gender equality, women's rights in China were rated as worse than international competitors that include the US, Russia, and Vietnam."[81]

For those people who just read a passage about generic women's rights organizations in China, support for women's rights activism was mixed: 40.4% agreed that respect for women's rights was not good enough in China, while 50.2% chose to donate to women's rights groups. Reading about foreign media reports of authorities' closure of a women's rights center slightly increased respondents' concerns about women's rights and willingness to donate to the organizations, however (47.7% of these believed that women's rights were not good enough and 53.3% were willing to donate[82]). Many openly disapproved of the closure, with 67.5% "liking" the activist group's *Weibo* post calling for the reopening of the center and general improvements in women's rights.

What had a significant impact was American pressure. When the same news story about the closure of the center was framed in terms of American pressure on China to reopen, respondents were 9.5 percentage points less willing to "like" the *Weibo* post and 12.4 percentage points less likely to choose a women's rights group for donations, both statistically significant decreases. Interestingly enough, also telling people about their country's poor comparative ranking in gender equality had no impact on their support for women's rights activism.

Pressure on Issues Related to Separatist Regions Increases the Backfire

One thing we have not addressed so far is the impact of pressure that targets human rights issues related to territorial integrity. To avoid asking respondents to discuss the treatment of China's minority groups in separatist areas directly, I made one minor adjustment: I (randomly) tweaked the name of the fictional women's rights center closed down by the CCP. For some, it was "China United Women's Foundation"; for others, "Tibet United Women's Foundation." Perhaps surprisingly, in the absence of any American criticism, respondents were slightly more willing to support women's rights activists when the center was called the "Tibet United Women's Foundation" than when it was generically Chinese. However, when people read about US pressure over the closure, they were 6.3 percentage points less likely to like *Weibo* posts and 10.5 percentage points less likely to donate to women's rights activists when the group was Tibetan (than when it was just Chinese).

Targeting the Leaders Only Removes the Backfire

What if American pressure explicitly targets the ruling elites rather than the public? Let's go back to the first study. For those groups that read about American or African Union pressure earlier in the survey, at the end I included a further sentence that directed the aforementioned pressure explicitly at government leaders. It read: "The spokeswoman continued: 'Rather than the Chinese people, it is the government leaders that have not ensured women's rights are good enough in recent years.'" As Figure 6.4 shows, this extra prompt caused the counterproductive effects of US pressure to vanish, and for those presented with a Chinese flag, it even had a positive impact, with respondents 5.7 percentage points more likely than those who received no pressure to say that women's rights were not good enough in China.

We see something similar in the second study. This time, some respondents were randomly given a news story that sought to distinguish even more clearly the target of the pressure, telling them instead that according to American officials,

EXPERIMENTAL ACTIVISM 113

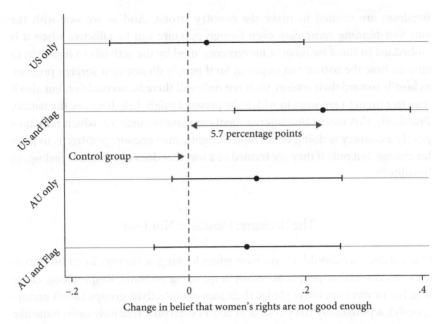

Figure 6.4 Graph showing the change in people's grievances over women's rights after reading a short sentence about foreign pressure that addresses Chinese leaders only (and being given a small Chinese flag in the corner), compared to the control. This graph has been normalized with 0 as the control, so that a higher score means the more grievances people have compared to the control. Lines represent 95% confidence intervals.

it was only the top leaders who had not done enough to improve women's rights, but also emphasizing that the Chinese people did respect those rights.[83] Again, this targeting eliminated the backfire. And when these respondents were also told that their country had a poor comparative ranking in gender equality, they were no more willing to donate money, but were more likely to "like" the pro-women's rights *Weibo* post than the control group—albeit to a nonsignificant level.[84]

We expected that targeting elite leaders but praising the people might minimize any backfire from American pressure. But why might prompts that also highlight the nation reverse that backfire? In one sense this is not a surprise. One of the main ways that activists push for democracy or human rights is by appealing to the public's patriotic sympathies. From 1919 to 1989, major anti-government protests in China were sparked by nationalist movements.[85] Those agitating for change have explicitly emphasized their attachment to their nation, highlighting the ways in which democracy, human rights, and individual freedoms are needed to make the country strong. And as we saw with the anti-foot-binding campaign, even foreign pressure can be effective when it is embedded in these nationalist movements, used by the activists to highlight to citizens how the nation can improve. So if people do not view foreign pressure as hostile toward their nation, then not only will there be no backfire, but also it may free them to see ways in which the pressure might help improve the nation. Practically, this means that international comparative indexes, which rank how poorly a country is doing on its human rights, may encourage citizens to push for change, but only if they are framed in a way that does not promote feelings of hostility.[86]

The Backfire: Hostility, Not Fear

One concern we should always have when looking at surveys in authoritarian societies is whether people are really responding honestly. Respondents chose whether or not to publicly pledge their support to activist groups (albeit anonymously), a potentially risky course of action even on a relatively open issue like women's rights.

But in these experiments, people's fear of being politically censured did not appear to have a big impact on their responses, with almost 70% of respondents willing to like the *Weibo* post in the control group, and even more after reading perhaps the most "sensitive" kind of pressure, pressure that explicitly targeted the regime. We would also expect that people would be more likely to choose the "no answer" option if concerned about revealing their true views, but reading about American pressure did not make them any more likely to do so.

To see what is really going on, let's look at whom respondents chose to (hypothetically) donate to in the second study. While American pressure had no effect on donations to animal rights or police groups, it did greatly increase donations to a maritime defense group in the South China Sea (a focus of US-China military rivalry)—but only if the pressure targeted the nation as a whole.[87] American pressure appeared to make already patriotic citizens view the news story as an issue of geopolitics, a hostile attack that needed to be fought back against, rather than an issue of injustice or inequality. Indeed, when I added to the news story a standard response from the CCP saying precisely this, that the United States was using human rights to threaten China's stability, respondents' willingness to like the *Weibo* post was 8.2 percentage points lower. Interestingly, those respondents who instead received an extra sentence saying the CCP had instructed the United States not to interfere in China's affairs were *more* willing to like the *Weibo* post.[88]

When asked to pick a picture to describe the news story, after reading about American pressure, respondents were over twice as likely to choose a picture symbolizing US-China competition[89] than the nonpressure group. This increase was significantly smaller when the pressure targeted leaders only. On the other hand, these respondents were no more likely to choose a "Love China" picture and no more likely to say that they identified as Chinese citizens, suggesting that the backfire was not caused by people becoming more patriotic and "rallying 'round the flag" in reaction to the threat of outside attacks.[90]

Patriotic—but Liberal—Citizens React the Most Negatively

Instead, in both experiments, the backfire from reading about US pressure was significantly stronger for people who were already highly patriotic. It was also much stronger for respondents who did not trust Washington's policies toward China—who already thought the United States was more hostile. Interestingly enough, though, the backfire was also stronger for those who had the most *positive* views about the United States as a country. It was their beliefs about the hostility of the actor issuing the pressure (not their beliefs about the country as a whole) that made them act defensively.

And while those most negatively affected by the pressure were more patriotic, they were not devout conservatives, but liberal, urban, and well educated. They were equally likely to be women and equally likely to be young. These are groups we might expect to be more concerned about improving women's rights and that in the control were indeed significantly more likely to believe that women's rights are *not* good enough in China. In the first study, if we split people's responses into whether they think women's rights are "good enough" versus "not good enough," we find that American pressure does not just harden the views of those who are already quite satisfied with the treatment of women's rights in China but shifts people from holding some kind of grievance about women's rights to being satisfied.[91]

These results are surprising on the face of it. They suggest that the people who feel threatened by foreign pressure over women's rights are those who already value those rights in some form. If they do not care at all about women's rights, then they simply may not care when those rights are criticized. But the results are also concerning. They mean that it is not just conservatives or chauvinists who get defensive over pressure on women's rights, but also those people who might otherwise support those who complain about the absence of laws against domestic violence or the arrests of feminist activists.

What Can Experimental Evidence Tell Us?

In China, the promotion of women's rights is something that international actors have historically had some success with. These efforts arose once again over the arrests of feminist activists in March 2015. By most accounts, public condemnation and private entreaties embarrassed authorities into releasing the activists one month after their arrest. But the experiments presented here show that the kind of public statements from the United States (from Hillary Clinton and John Kerry, for example) that were mentioned in Chinese media may make people—even younger, liberal women—less willing to show their support for the activists. American pressure pushes people to see news stories about crackdowns on women's rights organizations as stories of conflict between China and the United States rather than about gender equality, especially if the pressure references a region like Tibet, closely tied to issues of territorial integrity. Just "naming" news about the incident, on the other hand (without any pressure on the CCP to change its behavior), does not backfire but mildly increases people's concerns about women's rights.

The experimental evidence also suggests that statements about women's rights from more neutral sources (in this case from non-Western countries) or that explicitly target only the country's leaders are unlikely to spark this kind of backfire. Practically speaking, however, this kind of pressure is unlikely to be reported in the media, so it is unlikely to have a particularly large impact on the general population. The last chapter showed how non-Western pressure is rarely covered, and according to Daniela Stockmann, local journalists say that they are not able to report on stories that contain criticism of Chinese leaders.[92] There are numerous examples of foreign efforts to exclusively target top leaders over their behavior that have been then censored in domestic media.[93] In late May 2020, for example, former British governor of Hong Kong Chris Patten criticized Beijing over its security laws in Hong Kong[94] and then in a separate interview a few days later called Xi Jinping an "old-fashioned dictator" and a "lout."[95] While his first statement was given plenty of coverage in state newspapers,[96] the arguably more explosive comments about Xi Jinping were ignored.

This taps into a problem inherent to the stylized experimental surveys used in this chapter. To what extent can we use these quite specific experimental findings to tell us something about how Chinese citizens react in the real world? In the first place, we might question whether pressure on gender inequality and the closure of a women's rights center would evoke the same kind of reaction as pressure on other issues. What about issues where there is clear evidence to support the foreign criticism, like environmental degradation, or highly charged emotive issues, like forced sterilization or human trafficking? It may be that when people read about pressure over their government's use of physical violence, their visceral reaction may overwhelm any defensive response to imagined foreign hostility toward their country. The ethical problems of carrying out surveys in an authoritarian country on sensitive issues like torture or police abuse means that at present it is not possible to conclusively say anything about public views on these topics. Even so, we should do more to explore whether the findings from this chapter apply beyond just women's rights.

Secondly, how do we know that respondents are genuinely considering the foreign pressure, then updating their existing opinions about women's rights, and not just automatically forming ad hoc opinions in response to being asked about an issue they had not thought about much beforehand?[97] It does appear that people were not just developing opinions about women's rights on the spot—pressure was just as likely to backfire for young, educated women, the demographic in the control groups who felt most strongly about equal rights. But even so, there is still a suspicion that this is all a little abstract. People are reacting to a brief piece of text by filling in a number or "yes/no" to a few preset questions on one idiosyncratic topic. To understand how people respond to foreign pressure, we need to listen to what people themselves say about pressure, why they think it affects them negatively, and how they believe it might be more constructive.

7
People on the Street

Xiao Bei[1] is a recent graduate from the local university, looking for work in a large urban sprawl in eastern China. She is young, well educated, and nonplussed when I tell her the news[2] that the US government had taken China to task over its deteriorating respect for women's rights.

> There are some places where women are treated a bit worse, but these are smaller towns in the countryside, where there are many old traditions, for example that women need to be married at sixteen and the like. But in bigger cities this isn't really a problem. Women have a lot more freedom than maybe they used to.

Xiao Bei's tone shows a measure of pride: "I think men look at women with respect in China." Why, then, would the United States criticize China over its treatment of women? "China and America have never got on well, so this kind of statement is normal. America is just used to putting down China, deliberately attacking us," she notes.

Xiao Bei was defensive about her country and its gender equality, and she expressed her defensiveness calmly and thoughtfully. Not everyone we interviewed reacted like Xiao Bei, however. Some were visibly angry in hearing that countries had criticized China, others shrugged off the comments, and some even vehemently nodded their agreement. What explains this range of reactions? Is there some kind of pattern to the different ways in which ordinary Chinese people think about foreign attempts to condemn, persuade, and coerce their leaders to change their policies? Does it depend on the kind of policy or the kind of issue being criticized?

This chapter shows that citizens do react defensively to foreign pressure, and as we saw in the last chapter, this defensiveness is indeed related to the source and topic of pressure. But the goal is not just to test the implications of the hostility hypothesis. It is also to try and understand the ways through which citizens think about international pressure. And this chapter shows, importantly, that people's reaction to pressure is heavily influenced by what they feel that pressure was saying about their nation and its standing in the world.

In the spring of 2016, my research assistants and I interviewed 170 Chinese citizens in a medium-sized city in eastern China. We approached interviewees

Hostile Forces. Jamie J. Gruffydd-Jones, Oxford University Press. © Oxford University Press 2022.
DOI: 10.1093/oso/9780197643198.003.0007

at random in as many public places as we could find, from coffee shops to restaurants, university campuses to housing complexes, as well as on the street.[3] While the researchers and I made every attempt to approach people in as random a fashion as possible, this sample is, of course, far from representative of the population. For one, it overestimates those people who would visit public places like coffee shops and parks (maybe those who have more leisure time or money), and while the respondents originated from various parts of China, they were all living in one affluent large city. But even with these limitations, our interviewees' words should tell us something about how ordinary people react to foreign pressure. We approached people from as wide a range of backgrounds as possible, with a good distribution of ages, genders, and occupations, from students to retirees, accountants to taxi drivers.

Almost all our interviewees said categorically that they were proud of their country, and around a third said that they thought China was the best country in the world. When asked about the ways in which it could be improved, by far the most popular response was to reduce pollution, with the desire for better health services a distant second (remember that this was early 2016). Notably, almost a tenth of the sample openly said that they thought the most pressing improvement was the need for democracy and individual freedoms, the third most popular response.

For a hundred of these interviewees, we talked about their attitudes to international pressure on women's rights. But we also wanted to see whether these attitudes might apply to other issues, and especially issues that are quite different to women's rights but have still received a fair amount of attention from the international community. So we asked thirty more respondents about their reactions to international pressure over the use of ivory in Chinese medicine, a practice that dates back over two thousand years.[4] In recent times transnational campaigns have targeted the trade in China, including *Wildaid*'s use of huge billboards in underground stations featuring ex-footballer David Beckham, Prince William, and the basketball star Yao Ming.[5] These campaigns have, apparently, been quite successful, with the Chinese government announcing a ban on trade in ivory in early 2017 (soon after this book's interviews were carried out).[6]

The use of ivory in medicine is clearly harmful for the preservation of endangered species, but efforts by foreign nongovernmental organizations (NGOs) to have it banned risk accusations of interfering in traditional local practices. A similar conflict between tradition and conservation has arisen in Japan, with international organizations calling for the country to ban whaling facing off against local nationalist groups railing against foreign meddling in Japanese culture.[7] In China, the ivory trade is a low-salience issue, however, an issue about which most people do not hold very strong opinions. And unlike Japan, there have been no prominent nationalist groups agitating against the ban. While the

Chinese Communist Party (CCP) has often promoted the benefits of traditional Chinese medicine, it has also not shown much interest in taking a nationalist stand against international anti-ivory campaigns.

Finally, we asked forty people for their thoughts on foreign pressure over air pollution in China's cities. China has been subject to intense international attention over its urban air quality,[8] and starting in 2008 the US embassy began hourly tweets giving a reading of the air pollution levels in Beijing.[9] But unlike over the use of ivory, Chinese citizens generally hold robust existing opinions about the state of their air, and have clear evidence of pollution just by looking up at the sky. According to a Pew survey in 2015, 76% of Chinese people viewed air pollution as a "big problem" in the country.[10] One goal in the interviews was to see how these strong beliefs influenced people's response to foreign pressure.

One important reason for choosing these issues is that they are all topics on which members of the public could reasonably freely express their opinions. It would not have been ethical to expose interviewees to questions on sensitive issues like religious rights or local democracy. Given this, how can we know that people's reactions on these issues do indeed extend to civil and political rights? To provide some initial answers, my research assistants and I interviewed thirty-one Chinese students and university staff recently arrived in the United States about international pressure over China's human rights, just after the start of their autumn term in 2016. Naturally this was far from a random sample, involving a narrow range of university students and staff, many of whom had already experienced some exposure to life in the United States. But again, despite these biases, our hope was that the interviews would help tell us whether people's reactions to pressure on women's rights are unique or whether they share something in common with pressure on other human rights.

Awareness of International Pressure

Most interviewees were well aware of the outside world's interest in China. In fact, three-quarters of our domestic interviewees said that they had run into some Western criticism of their country in the past. Some said they had read stories about American opposition to island building in the South China Sea, others pointed to television reports of rude behavior by Chinese tourists, and just over half explicitly highlighted criticism of human rights or democracy in their country. While a very small number (around 5%) admitted that they had heard about these comments by escaping the Great Firewall,[11] most said that they had heard news about foreign comments through newspapers and television, with the remainder finding out through social media.

Almost all the overseas students and university workers in the United States said they knew about foreign efforts to put pressure on China over human rights, even from their time in China. Many said they had heard about the pressure through English-language websites not banned within the People's Republic of China (mainly the BBC, at the time). A few noted that Chinese television sometimes broadcast foreign criticism of China, criticism that was also often left uncensored on social media. Qing Yan, nineteen, said that she believed this was done strategically: "Chinese propaganda tells us America says this, but it's just meant to let the government give a counterargument."

In general, interviewees were very well informed about the struggles facing women's rights and gender equality in their country, not least structural issues like job opportunities and marital expectations, especially in rural areas. Many talked at length about the historical problems faced by women, as well as the improvements that had been made over recent years. Unsurprisingly, the most passionate were young women, those who may expect to be most affected by these structural problems in the future. Around a third of the interviewees (within China) had heard some international comments over women's rights in their country, from Hillary Clinton's recent tweets to long-standing outcries over the one-child policy.

Not many knew about the problems surrounding the use of ivory in Chinese traditional medicine or its link to the world's dwindling elephant population. However, once told about the issue, many people quickly formed strong views, developing almost instantaneous opinions about whether ivory trading should be banned.[12] Despite *Wildaid* billboards plastered throughout the city, the majority said that they were not aware of global campaigns against the use of ivory in China. Of the third who said they were, most talked about its impact on the elephant population in Africa, and some did explicitly mention the *Wildaid* campaign.

Unlike ivory use, most interviewees already strongly believed that air pollution was a serious problem. Even those who said that the environment in China had improved in recent years still rated it as a major challenge for the country, and some stated unequivocally that reducing air pollution should be China's number one priority. Again, around a third said that they had heard foreign condemnation of environmental conditions in China, especially condemnation over Beijing's Olympics in 2008 and the Asia-Pacific Economic Cooperation (APEC) summit in 2014.

Sources of Pressure

We randomly allocated to all interviewees a short paragraph to read, a paragraph that summarized some recent international pressure on China over one of these issues: gender discrimination and domestic violence, the use of ivory in traditional medicine, the levels of air pollution in China's cities, or civil liberties (for those in the United States only). We again randomly switched the source of pressure between the United States and the African Union, and to see whether including a multilateral organization with a "stake" in the resolution of the issue might make people look upon it more positively, we also used the UN Human Rights Council for women's rights and the UN Environment Program for air pollution (which we used instead of the African Union for this topic).

And just like the respondents in the survey experiments, the source of criticism had a big impact on people's views. Interviewees who read a passage from the United States were far less likely to agree with pressure on women's rights in China than those who read a passage from the United Nations or the African Union, as shown in Table 7.1. This difference was even more pronounced for pressure over the use of ivory. The exception was air pollution, where most people said that foreign pressure was justified, regardless of where it came from.[13]

While we did ask some specific questions about their reactions to the prompts, our main goal was to get people to talk freely about their thoughts. And the source of pressure quite visibly affected how interviewees talked about these issues. A common reaction from people who read about American criticism of women's rights was to immediately refute the idea that women were treated badly. Many of these were older, like shopkeeper Liu, fifty-two, who responded to the question with irritation in his voice:

> Women's position in society is very high at the moment in China; it is ridiculous to say that they are badly treated. The women I know are very fairly treated; in China the environment for them is really good.

Table 7.1 Percentage of Interviewees (in China) Who Said That Foreign Pressure on a Given Issue Is "Justified" When Asked

Source	Topic		
	Women's Rights	Ivory Use	Air Pollution
United States	37%	19%	60%
African Union	63%	71%	—
UN agency	67%	—	80%
Number of interviewees	100	30	40

Topics and sources of pressure were randomly allocated.

Bo, a taxi driver from the countryside, dismissed American criticism with a wave of his hand: "These comments are so one-sided. It makes me annoyed, because in China we do have gender equality; the criticism is just not true. In all [the areas mentioned in the criticism] China is so much better than all our neighboring countries; the law protects them here."

This kind of immediate dismissal did not just apply to women's rights. Dong, a retired schoolteacher, said that he could not accept efforts by the United States to stop Chinese people from using ivory in traditional medicine: "Foreign countries should look after their own problems, they don't understand what Chinese culture is like, and they shouldn't try and interfere with Chinese culture. Chinese medicine works, and they should use the medicines that work, not listen to other countries that don't understand." It is interesting to note that, while the sample is small, the reaction to American criticism over the issue of ivory in Chinese medicine was certainly the most belligerent, seeing few of the nuanced counterarguments some people used when discussing women's rights. While the threat to traditional practices may be responsible, it is also hard to develop nuanced counterarguments when you have not thought much about an issue beforehand. Reading about pressure from the United States, the most obvious concern for many people was not that their country was failing to protect an important value that they held dear, but merely the fact that a geopolitical competitor was putting their country under pressure.

Chinese university students and staff recently arrived in the United States were, overall, less obviously angered by American criticism on China's human rights. Some older interviewees, however, like Yu, in her seventies, were adamant: "These comments are not justified, because human rights in America are even more serious than in China! Chinese people have human rights; there is no need to talk nonsense. People live well—how do you know there are no human rights?" Others were simply tired of these kinds of comments. According to Huang, twenty-three, "America has no reason to do this. Every time it seems to be the same kind of criticism, it completely loses its meaning." Zi Wei, twenty-two, had the same problem with foreign attention on Tibet: "I've seen a lot of this; I've started to become numb. Because of these separatists in Tibet, the US will get involved, and China will talk about Tibet creating problems. I think we need security in China, to make sure Tibet does not separate."

Many respondents were more circumspect in their reactions, however. Yes, the American criticism did touch on real problems, but still, things were far better than they used to be, far better than they might be, or far better than they were in other countries. On women's rights, we saw these kinds of responses more from younger female interviewees. Yi, an aspiring entrepreneur, said that she believed it was easier for young women to get by in China today: "I know things used to be worse, but I don't think the Americans really understand China now, because women have so many educational and work opportunities. The pressure on them to find work is lower, and they can work in many areas that we cannot, like in the service industry, or administration, or other nine-to-five jobs." Tao, a first-year student in the local university, was upbeat: "Women are treated reasonably well in China today, but of course there can be improvements. In coastal cities, in developed regions, there isn't really a problem with domestic violence. Perhaps in more inland areas domestic violence is more of a problem—but overall this has been getting better all the time."

Overseas students were also more likely to respond in this more nuanced manner. After hearing about news of US pressure on human rights in Tibet, Mike, eighteen, argued that it was an overreaction: "Native people in Tibet enjoy more freedom than people in mainland China. The Chinese government is serious about racial problems, so locals enjoy higher privileges in Tibet. There are times when police cannot do anything about the locals, so it can get messy sometimes, and there might be some human rights issues, but it is not that serious." Min, twenty-six, said that Western support for Tibetans was misplaced: "We have given minorities a lot of help; we have not been bad to them. Tibet was a feudal society without freedom, and China freed them, supported their education, medical care, health. We have absolutely not been bad to them."

Min said that she had become more patriotic since coming to the United States. "Before, I used to believe that America was better than China. While some people write on the internet that China is perfect and democratic, I know we all have our own problems. . . . But China is a younger, newer country than the United States, and has just started to become part of the new international society." This feeling of growing patriotism after moving abroad was mentioned by several overseas students. Zhao, twenty-one, said that he had become prouder of his country after hearing far-fetched criticisms of China in America. Yet even though there were some claims about China from Western newspapers that he strongly disagreed with, Zhao accepted that human rights violations did go on in China, a position shared by many of the overseas students we interviewed. Encountering stories of human rights violations through his academic studies had convinced him that this was indeed something that needed to be addressed.

When the criticism did not come from the United States, interviewees were notably less defensive. Many stated their dismay over problems in China but often tempered these concerns with hope for the future. After hearing about the African Union's criticism of women's rights, for example, Gong Ting, fifty-nine, said that domestic violence was a structural issue within Chinese society: "Of course this is a problem. We need to give women more legal power. Actually, many women who have suffered domestic violence don't want to get divorced, because maybe they are economically reliant on their husband. So it is very hard for them to be completely equal because of their economic situation. There do need to be improvements, especially in legal protections, because to ensure we have equal treatment we need to have the law on our side."

After reading about condemnation from the United Nations, Jin, thirty-one, a university graduate who had moved to the city five years earlier, said that she had confidence conditions would improve: "[Women's rights] need to get better, especially when applying for jobs. I think there is certainly some prejudice against women. In some jobs there is even prejudice against men. But society is always taking forward steps, and I believe women and men will soon both be able to have the same chances in finding work." Some were more resigned, like Sun Li, a twenty-six-year-old information technology worker: "Things do need to improve, especially with domestic violence; there are real problems and it's not acceptable for women to suffer from these old views, that a man can hit his wife and it's fine. But this is something that women around the world face, and probably everywhere needs to improve, not just China—so I think it's a normal criticism, if a bit one-sided."

On the more niche issue of the use of ivory in traditional medicine, interviewees were far more likely to use the comments from the African Union to inform their views. Xiao Wu, a university student studying English, summed this up well, saying: "I don't really know too much about how ivory is used, but if this kind of material hurts the environment, then we should really not use it, and replace it with things that don't hurt wild animals as much."

Air pollution was a different story, however. People happily accepted criticism from both the UN Environment Program and the United States and agreed that China did need to improve its air pollution. Some even commented favorably on the tone of the criticism, even though it was almost identical to the criticism that others had heard about women's rights and Chinese medicine. Dou Dou, a twenty-eight-year-old visiting her hometown from Shanghai, nodded in response to the comments: "This problem does need to be solved. The smog in the cities was not always this bad, but recently it has appeared on a few days. There are just too many factories at the moment and people using too much coal—we need to find alternatives to this kind of energy." When asked whether this should happen even if it affected the economy, she replied: "Yes. After all, people still need to live here, and it is worth a short-term economic decline to help save the environment in the long run. We should look at economic development from the long term."

Very few of the interviewees said that they believed China should neglect the environment and only privilege economic development. Some, like Hao Wang, forty-one, accepted the criticisms but were more philosophical about the state of China's air: "Sacrificing the environment is a necessary process: which developed country has not done so? We missed the Industrial Revolution, and have arrived late, but happily this means we can draw on others' experiences and find a way to achieve a balance between development and the environment." It is hard to say whether foreign criticism made any difference to these beliefs, but their existing grievances about air pollution meant that people were far happier to accept pressure on their nation from outsiders, even hostile ones like the United States.

Perceived Hostility

So what explains this wide variety in reactions? Anger certainly played a role. On women's rights, some of our interviewees were evidently irritated when they read that the United States had criticized China. Take Wang, a forty-year-old businessman: "Women are treated better in China than anywhere around—these words are completely false. The United States just wants to target China for anything it can, to try and bring China down. Chinese women have nothing to do with them—they should look after their own women. It makes me angry." Even those who agreed that women's rights needed to be improved said that they found the criticism one-sided and politically driven. As Xiao Dong, a postgraduate researcher in his mid-twenties, said: "These politicians don't care about women in China; they're always using human rights as an excuse to attack China, to try and poison international public opinion. It's just politicians being politicians; they always behave like this. I'm bored of it to be honest."

Overseas interviewees agreed. Huang said that the United States was using human rights to target China: "I always hear that America is criticizing China but treating other countries with tolerance. At the moment with Trump, he is always condemning China; it seems unfair. Because of Sino-US relations, the US needs to compete with China, and so to increase its competitiveness it feels it has to criticize China." Mike agreed, in part: "I think the US does care to some extent, but I do think there is a deeper interest-driven motivation. There might be some issues in Tibet, but I think the US is criticizing China because it wants to exert some influence."

Some overseas students explicitly linked supposed American hostility to their own beliefs about human rights in China. According to Wei Tai, fifty-three: "This criticism of China is driven by prejudice. I believe that China does have areas it needs to improve, but we are definitely not as bad as America says." Feng Shuo, thirty-three, said that as far as he was concerned, "I don't think the US actually cares about human rights, but rather is using this issue as political fuel on the international stage to attack China." He went on to insist that "China doesn't have issues with free speech, because we can speak freely. So other countries cannot criticize China on such matters."

These comments were not just limited to human rights. Upon hearing that the United States had called on China to ban the ivory trade, Liu Jin, a factory worker, said that it was doing so "to attack the Communist Party," while Li, a software engineer, said that the United States "did not care about animals. As China's economy is developing and China is getting stronger, they're using it to cause trouble, so that every country focuses on China." Student Zhao was more equivocal: "Criticism is fine; every country needs it. I don't like the attitude in these comments though; they seem to hold some prejudice against China."

Interviewees were not just concerned with American hostility, but also its hypocrisy. On women's rights, one popular response was that the United States should at the least deal with its own discrimination—especially its racial divisions—before pointing fingers at China. Qing Yan argued that American hypocrisy made it a poor arbiter: "When politics and human rights are mixed, it's complicated, so you have to look at the ultimate purpose of the news source. Is this propaganda, or is it looking to reveal the truth? If we are talking about the criticism itself—this is justified, because China does oppress its people. But, when this criticism comes from America, this is not reasonable, because America has its own issues. America has race issues, as well as a hypocritical government—Hillary [Clinton] supports the Iraq War and then says that China shouldn't do XYZ."

The African Union did not receive the same kind of vitriol as the United States, but nor did people see it as a particularly acceptable source of pressure on women's rights. None of our interviewees questioned the African Union's motives, but many dismissed its authority. Several people claimed that the organization did not know what it was talking about, and others dismissed the comments as hypocritical and hard to understand from a continent with its own problems in gender equality. Wei, a nineteen-year-old student at the local university, summed up the sentiment: "I don't think they really understand China. Aren't women badly treated in Africa? I'm not too sure why they would criticize women's rights in China—I think maybe they don't realize how women are treated here. I mean there are problems for some women in our country, but I'm sure it is much worse in Africa."

If people see the African Union as just as hypocritical on women's rights, then hypocrisy is unlikely to be the reason for their defensive reaction to American criticism. Many were just as irritated with the African Union's attempts to criticize China as they were with the United States'. What was different was the content of their irritation. It was notable how those who said that criticism from the United States was unjustified also said that they thought the country was trying to use the issue to attack China. On the other hand, only one interviewee said that they believed the African Union was using women's rights to try and attack China, and not one brought up anything to do with international competition when talking about how they personally felt about the pressure. While interviewees were hardly positive toward the African Union, there was a notable lack of defensiveness in their responses, certainly in comparison to the language used in response to the United States.

On the issue of ivory, interviewees were far more well disposed toward comments from the African Union, with most saying they believed the African Union cared about the use of ivory in China (when asked). Many agreed that its criticism was justified, with one respondent, Ya Fang, a fifty-two-year-old housewife, saying explicitly that her views about the use of ivory depended on the relationship between African countries and China: "It is hard to say whether these comments about China are justified or not. If I were to make a concrete judgment, I would need to go onto the internet and check, because I don't really know much about the relationship between Africa and China. If it really is a friendly country [sic] towards China, then I can accept the criticism, and say that yes [ivory use] is a problem. But if the relationship with China is not very friendly, then I would be much more suspicious."

Interviewees were also quite positive about the United Nations. For women's rights, for example, many people shared the view that the role of the organization was to improve conditions for women around the world. According to retiree Jing: "They have to care about women and whether they are being discriminated against. They do this in every country, so I don't think China is any exception." Only three interviewees said that they thought the United Nations was a proxy of the United States, with many more saying that it had a duty and responsibility to improve women's rights around the world.

The important point here is that when interviewees believed that criticism was driven by hostility toward China, they were more likely to then go on and say positive things about their country. Of course, in interviews like this, it is often hard to determine the causal direction of people's reasoning. It may be that interviewees are falling back on their existing opinions about a certain issue, like the use of ivory, in order to discern the motives of the criticizer, rather than the other way around. Or to put it another way, people may decide that American criticism of the state of human rights in China is constructive only when they are themselves already really concerned about the state of human rights. Look at interviewees' responses to pressure on air pollution in China. While some were suspicious of the United States, overall people were far more disposed to view its comments as benign or helpful rather than attempts to bring down China—in stark contrast to their reactions to US pressure on other issues. Xue Feng, a geology student, said that the comments "showed that developed countries' governments were being responsible, to protect the world's environment," while estate agent Wen Hao pointed to the possibility that "China's environment might affect the United States, so of course they want to help."

Interviewees are almost certainly doing both—basing their views about the criticizer's motives on their own opinions about the issue and basing their opinions about the issue on their views about the criticizer's motives—and it is hard to disentangle this causal chain. What is clear is that people's belief that the United States is driven by hostility toward China is closely linked to how defensive they are in response to pressure.

Acceptable Pressure

So what kind of foreign pressure would be acceptable? Many interviewees parroted the government line: other countries should mind their own business. Those who had read about pressure from the United States were particularly insistent on this point. Li Ling, a coffee shop barista, typified the belligerence: "Foreigners have no right to interfere in China's internal affairs, we don't need it, this is a social issue of China, and we can only rely on ourselves to deal with it." Mo, nineteen, agreed: "They should sort out their own problems first, and not point their fingers at other countries."

Some were more pragmatic. Qing, visiting family in the city, said that he thought that China should accept outsiders' opinions, but that on women's rights, any efforts by foreigners would just not be effective: "International comments on these kinds of issues are not very helpful, because in those more backward areas, where there are real problems with women's rights, nobody is going to hear the sound of foreign comments."

Some echoed a traditional *People's Daily* line, that international busybodies should first have a deep understanding of China's situation, history, and social context. Han, thirty, said that at the least foreign countries should recognize that China was still emerging as an industrialized power. "If [criticism] is onesided and does not understand China's situation, then I cannot accept it. They can make comments about China and point out problems, but it is not acceptable to put pressure on us when they don't understand our country. We are going through the same development period they went through, and they had the same problems." Andy, twenty-two, studying in the United States, also argued that judgments about China needed to be placed into context: "China's human rights situation has some bad aspects, but right now, it fits China, because more freedom in politics requires a more central role for the middle class, so that political decisions are more stable. But if China liberalizes too quickly, this will be bad for China. America's criticism is good for itself, but not necessarily good for China's domestic problems."

Many people seemed sure that if outsiders did not just target China alone and instead looked to work together with China to solve the problem, then the people would be more open to their comments. According to Jian Min, an academic: "Only if what they say is objective and is not just attacking China can

I accept it. If every country also faced up to the fact that their people own ivory, and did not just put the blame on China, then every country should be able to accept this criticism together and work together to find an answer." Yan Yan, twenty-two, believed that women's rights was a global issue and should be treated as such: "The United Nations should help to improve women's rights all over the world, not just in China. There are problems with old traditions here, but I think that the Chinese people have worked hard to improve gender equality in recent years and can help other countries in the world."

Interestingly, people's opinions about the usefulness of foreign pressure on China varied dramatically according to the passage they were given. After reading passages that put pressure on China on women's rights, many said that they were strongly opposed to any kind of foreign pressure, on any issues, and that no foreign actor had any right to intervene. However, when given examples of pressure on air pollution in China, respondents became far more positive (and eloquent) about the role that international efforts could play—and not just over air pollution. Zhou, the owner of a noodle restaurant, saw quiet diplomacy as the way forward: "They should use a friendly attitude to put forward suggestions, not demand that China takes certain steps to make changes, or use sanctions, or push China to change its whole political system to be like America. Encouraging advice for step-by-step changes would be the most useful." Xiang, a recent geology graduate, agreed: "If they truly understand China's national situation and put forward intelligent opinions from this detailed knowledge, then I can accept their comments, even if they criticize China. If they do this, they can cooperate with our officials to give them ideas about how to improve. What annoys me are these exaggerated claims about how bad China is."

Responding to International Pressure

The goal of these interviews was to delve deeper into the ways in which ordinary citizens react to international pressure. We found that a crucial factor in whether our interviewees responded positively or negatively was whether they saw the pressure as hostile to their country. Those respondents who spoke about their nation, spoke about defending their nation, and worried about its international standing invariably responded negatively to being told about foreign pressure. In many cases, the fact that pressure came from the United States was enough to make the specter of international competition more salient than the injustices or damages that come from the issue itself. For some members of the public, pressure made them defensive, irritated, and belligerent. Others reacted by recognizing that there were problems but sought to justify why things were not as bad as the criticism implied.[14]

The interviews also highlight something that we have not explored since Chapter 2—that people's existing opinions about the issue being criticized can be extremely important. When interviewees heard about foreign criticism on a topic on which they did not have strong previous opinions, the use of ivory in medicine, they appeared to be influenced more by whether they thought the source of criticism was hostile toward their country. When they discussed a topic they already believed to be a problem in their country, air pollution, on the other hand, they were receptive to all kinds of international pressure, even when it came from a source that was apparently hostile.

And on the face of it, people's reactions on *Weibo* to foreign criticism of air pollution have not contained the same defensiveness. In November 2010, for example, the US embassy announced on Twitter that pollution in Beijing was not just its normal "bad" or "hazardous" but had reached the level of "crazy bad." While state media managed to ignore the vast coverage given to the tweet for months, it was shared almost immediately across social media inside and outside of China.[15] *Weibo* comments did not exhibit the anger at American interference that we saw in earlier chapters over human rights, however. Instead, the vast majority were supportive, repeating the tweet's sentiment about the poor air quality in Beijing.

In 2012, angered by the US embassy in Beijing's hourly Air Quality Index (AQI) readings, the *Global Times* accused the United States of "selfishness" and attempting to "stimulate Chinese public sentiment"[16]; and called on the embassy to stop issuing the information. But again, in stark contrast to the reactions to criticism on human rights, social media reactions to this anti-American campaign were generally unsympathetic. Comments under the *Global Times* story on *Weibo* were notable in the way they ignored the story's anti-American narrative, instead agreeing with the embassy: China's air quality did need to improve.[17] It seems that, as one netizen pointed out to the newspaper, anti-foreign propaganda is just not very credible when the evidence to the contrary is right there in front of you:

Do you think people are blind? How many blue-sky days has Beijing had lately? Do you think ordinary people will only believe your statements?[18]

Listening to how people talk about pressure on their country shines a light on why these kinds of criticisms might or might not damage their support for domestic activism. But even then, these kinds of interviews and surveys cannot fully recreate how Chinese citizens hear about pressure in real life. We were still approaching people in the street, still prompting them about foreign pressure, and still recording their immediate responses to those prompts.

Pressure on China's human rights and system of government is normally encountered by the public over a long period of time. Whether they hear it through state media, internet news sites, or social media, their response is going to be heavily influenced by how it is framed.[19] They will not form opinions immediately after hearing about the pressure but gradually, over time, after having seen a few stories, read about others' reactions on social media, and discussed it with their friends and colleagues.

So how do people react to pressure in the "real world": a world where they are not explicitly told about a piece of foreign criticism and then immediately asked for their opinions on it? How do they react when they encounter pressure in their daily lives, as just one of a million pieces of information about politics and current affairs?

8
Pressure in Real Time
Meeting the Dalai Lama

International Pressure in Real Time

In authoritarian states, members of the public pick up information about their world through walls of censorship and state media obfuscation, through a mass of propaganda and cacophony of competing news. The question, then, is whether Chinese citizens spend time processing the kind of international pressure discussed in the previous chapters and whether pressure filtered through the Chinese Communist Party's (CCP's) censorship and propaganda system affects people's views about human rights and democracy in the same way.

To answer this, we need to examine a real-time front-page incident of human rights pressure on China, and we need to compare Chinese people's attitudes after the incident to their attitudes beforehand. An excellent example of this kind of event in recent years is the meetings between the Dalai Lama and foreign leaders—increasingly rare, increasingly high profile, and intimately tied up with human rights and democracy in China. The problem, of course, is that if everyone knows in advance that the meeting will occur, then we are unlikely to see much of an impact on their attitudes when it does happen. So it needs to be something of a surprise, and we also need to have a way of finding out about people's views before and afterward. As it happens, in July 2011, President Obama unexpectedly met the Dalai Lama in the White House precisely when survey research firm *Asian Barometer* was in the middle of carrying out its nationwide survey on the public's political attitudes in China.

From this coincidence we can explore whether the main implication of the hostility theory does indeed apply in real life: does a high-profile incident of American pressure on human rights related to China's territorial integrity bolster Chinese citizens' positive views about their country, its politics, and its human rights? The survey also allows us to explore whether this impact is stronger for those more patriotic citizens. In an ideal world, we would be able to examine all of chapter 2's observable implications—from the source of pressure to the target. In a natural experiment like this we are limited by nature, however, and to test all the implications we will have to hope that other coincidences come up again in the future.[1]

Meeting the Dalai Lama

Meetings between foreign leaders and the Dalai Lama are not always explicit criticisms of human rights but are still widely seen as a clear statement of support for the Dalai Lama and his attempts to achieve recognition for the struggles of the Tibetan people. Human rights in the autonomous region are often discussed in the meetings and quoted widely in the foreign press. The White House statement following the 2014 meeting between President Obama and the Dalai Lama, for example, stated Obama's "strong support for the preservation of Tibet's unique religious, cultural, and linguistic traditions and the protection of human rights for Tibetans in the People's Republic of China."[2] This is certainly how the meetings are portrayed in the Chinese media. The *Global Times* story about the 2011 Obama-Dalai gathering, for example, had the subheading: "Obama meets Dalai Lama, reaffirms opposition to Tibetan independence, and expresses concern about Tibetan human rights."[3]

While the White House has been at pains to say that the meetings were purely to respect the Dalai Lama's standing as a religious leader, official assemblies with dissidents and activists have become a common ingredient of American democracy promotion. In 2007 George W. Bush called presidential meetings with dissidents a central pillar of the American "commitment to promote democracy worldwide,"[4] and throughout the 1980s the US administration heavily publicized its summits with Soviet dissidents as part of its efforts to engender political liberalization.[5] As former dissident Natan Sharansky said, these meetings "had a tremendous influence on our movement, on people around us and on the authorities."[6]

But meeting the Dalai Lama can have consequences for a country's leader. Countries that receive the Buddhist leader in an official capacity find that some of their exports to China fall following the meeting.[7] Some leaders have undoubtedly reacted to this, and the number of leaders willing to meet the Dalai Lama has fallen sharply in recent years. President Obama, for example, chose not to hold a meeting soon after coming to office in 2009, delaying the event until after he took his first official visit to China,[8] while the Mongolian prime minister did not meet the Dalai Lama again after his 2002 welcome, when the CCP blocked the railway link between the countries as punishment.[9] On the other hand, refusing a meeting has often led to the leader being criticized in their own country. In 2009, Republican congressmen and human rights advocates criticized Obama for "currying favour" with the Chinese by delaying the assembly,[10] while Swiss leaders' refusal in 2010 drew condemnation in parliament.[11]

Choosing to brave these costs may in fact have become an effective way of signaling a state's resolve over human rights issues. It sends a costly signal to the Chinese leadership that a leader is serious over their commitment to human rights.[12] The target of the meetings may also be Tibetans, a way to pass on to them international condemnation of the Chinese government's policy in Tibet, to tell them that their struggles are remembered. When Tibetans heard of the Dalai Lama–Obama meeting in 2010, many set off fireworks in celebration.[13] Robert Barnett argues that these kinds of gestures may cause a backlash, however, as Tibetans gain false hope about the type of support the United States is prepared to offer them, and their subsequent enthusiasm only serves to provoke even more government repression.[14]

While we might expect Tibetans to respond positively to the meetings, unfortunately the survey I use was not implemented in Tibet for logistical reasons (although I do examine the effects on Buddhists and Tibetan minority provinces in the rest of the country). What I can examine is the impact of these meetings on the general public throughout the rest of China—the focus of this book, of course. One crucial factor for our purposes is that, as chapter 4 shows, these meetings are often heavily advertised by Chinese media. Of the thirty-one overseas Chinese students and university workers interviewed in the United States for chapter 7, twenty-three said that while they were in China they had heard about the meetings between the Dalai Lama and American presidents, with many learning about the meetings through state media.

President Obama and the Dalai Lama

After initially postponing a meeting in 2009, Barack Obama eventually agreed to meet the Dalai Lama in February 2010, drawing a predictably angry reaction from China. He chose to meet the leader again in July the following year, when the Dalai Lama was taking part in an eleven-day Buddhist ritual in Washington, DC. The president had stayed cool over whether the meeting would occur, but on the night of Friday, July 15 (Saturday morning in China), the White House announced they would meet the following day. The two met for a private forty-five-minute discussion in the Map Room, which occurred around 11:30 p.m. Chinese time—enough time to reach the Chinese newspapers the next morning.

A White House statement issued following the meeting said that while Obama did not support Tibetan independence, he "reiterated his strong support for the preservation of the unique religious, cultural, and linguistic traditions of Tibet and the Tibetan people throughout the world. He underscored the importance of the protection of human rights of Tibetans in China."[15] Media reports quoted the Dalai Lama as saying that Obama expressed his concern about human rights and religious freedoms, as well as his "genuine concern about suffering in Tibet and other places."[16] These comments hit the international press from Pakistan[17] to Ireland[18] the following day.

The Chinese government appeared to be somewhat caught off guard, only having time that day to issue a diplomatic warning for Obama to cancel the meeting.[19] This warning was repeated in one brief story in the *Global Times*, which decried the planned gathering.[20] But the next morning, state media returned in force. The *People's Daily* issued a strongly worded editorial denouncing the meeting, accusing Obama of attempting to split the country up. The paper focused its attacks on the criticism of political and religious freedoms in Tibet, saying that "these American officials ignore the social progress in Tibet but instead call the human rights situation in Tibet 'evil,' and accuse the Chinese government of restricting Tibetan language education, and strictly controlling Tibetan Buddhism."[21] The government then used an accompanying feature-length article—the top front-page story on July 17—to elaborate on the policies that they had put in place in Tibet for economic and political development.[22]

A common Propaganda Department reaction to these meetings is to "flood" copy through media outlets to ensure that they push out a unified message,[23] and newspapers dedicated a series of articles to the meeting over July 17 and 18. The *Global Times* headline on July 17 noted that Obama had met the Dalai Lama over his "concern for human rights in Tibet." The story reported the White House press release in detail, including both Obama's opposition to Tibetan independence and his call for "attention to the human rights situation in Tibet."[24] The paper repeatedly returned to the refrain that "Western anti-China forces"[25] were using the Dalai Lama as a political tool in order to embarrass China and that the meeting was designed to bring down China's "sovereignty and territorial integrity."[26] The rhetoric evoked a clear message: the meeting was an attack on China. Articles played up the discussions of political and religious rights and explicitly framed them as a plot by America and the Dalai Lama to split up China for their own political ends. The *Global Times* commissioned a (highly unrepresentative) online survey on the morning of July 17, asking for its readers' opinions about the meeting; 77% said that they were "angry."[27]

The last-minute announcement of the meeting meant that Chinese citizens had little prior knowledge that it would occur. Trends of Google searches (Figure 8.1) show that there were few searches for the "Dalai Lama" until July 16, with interest peaking between July 17 and 19. We can only read so much into this trend, since Google is banned in China, but it does demonstrate that even for citizens willing to breach the internet firewall, there was no awareness of the meeting before July 16, and that interest was high (on July 18 there were almost twice as many searches for the Dalai Lama as for Hu Jintao, the leader at the time[28]).

The unexpected meeting serves as a useful quasi-natural experiment. This is because, completely unrelated to the meeting, over the month of July 2011 the *Asian Barometer* firm was right in the middle of administering its nationwide survey on the Chinese people's beliefs about democracy and human rights. The

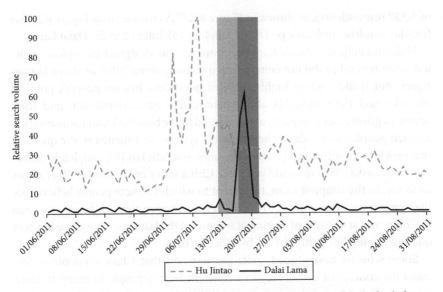

Figure 8.1 Google searches for "Dalai Lama" and "Hu Jintao" in China. Shaded area denotes the period analyzed in this study, with the lighter gray the five days before the meeting and the dark gray the five days after the meeting. The y-axis represents a topic's relative search volume on a given day, on a scale of 0 to 100. This does not tell us about the absolute numbers of searches, but a score of fifty would represent twice the search volume of a score of twenty-five.

firm administered this survey face to face to a random selection of 3,473 adults across the country, weighted to reflect the country's demographics and to ensure full coverage of minority and rural populations in all regions of mainland China except Tibet, Qinghai, Inner Mongolia, and Xinjiang.[29] The timing of the survey gives us a perfect opportunity to examine how a meeting between the American president and the Dalai Lama affects beliefs about democracy and human rights in China.

Since the survey's roll-out was presumably not affected by the Dalai Lama's travel plans in North America, the July 17 meeting date serves as a kind of experimental "treatment," whereby those interviewed just before the date should be almost identical to those interviewed just after the date. The main difference between the two groups is that the post–July 17 group has had the chance to hear or read about any major news that passed through on July 17—and particularly the top story, the meeting in Washington, DC. To minimize the influence of any other events, I examine just those respondents interviewed in the five days before July 17 and compare them to the respondents in the five days after (a total of 1,539 respondents), as shown in Figure 8.2.[30] As we see from Figure 8.2, this five-day window covers the period of people's peak interest in the Dalai Lama.

Unfortunately, the *Asian Barometer* survey was designed to explore political attitudes and so did not contain any questions about Tibet or about human rights. But it did contain highly detailed questionnaires on people's political attitudes and their thoughts about democracy, authoritarianism, and their country's government. In particular, I wanted to see how the Dalai Lama meeting affected people's views about their political system. So I turned to the question that provides a scale from 1 (completely undemocratic) to 10 (completely democratic) and asks, "Where would you place China today on this scale?" This allows us to see, in the simplest form, the extent to which Chinese people believe that their country is democratic. 2011 was a relatively open time for survey research in China, and at the time of writing, it was one of the last times that these kinds of questions could be openly put out by a foreign firm.

Some scholars have argued, quite persuasively, that Chinese people understand the concept of democracy in a different way to people in many Western countries.[31] Public opinion surveys show that the majority see democracy not as a means by which the people choose their leaders (as it is commonly thought of in the West) but instead as an ability to hold government accountable, or as how well government policies reflect public opinion.[32] Lu Jie and Shi Tianjian have found that Chinese citizens generally conceive of democracy as "taking the majority's view into consideration" rather than "majority rule through popular vote." They argue that the government's use of its propaganda apparatus and education system to define democracy in this way has been the major factor in making Chinese citizens believe that their country is democratically ruled.[33] And as we might expect if this were true, support for democracy in the *Asian Barometer* survey was indeed high, with 83.16% of respondents agreeing that "democracy is always preferable to any other kind of government."

But even so, if Chinese people believe that their system is "democratic," then at the minimum what this shows is that they are satisfied that their political system is accountable and responsive to its citizens. Our goal is to find out whether American leaders' meetings with the Dalai Lama would affect this sense of

Figure 8.2 The quasi-natural experiment compares the "control" group of those survey respondents who were interviewed in the five days before the meeting to the "treatment" group of those interviewed in the five days after the meeting

satisfaction. To turn back to our theory's implications, pressure comes from a geopolitical opponent and comes on an issue intimately linked to China's territorial integrity. My expectation, then, is that if people feel that meetings with the Dalai Lama are an attempt to attack China, its political system, and its international standing, then to fight back they may deliberately bolster their positive views about their country and its political system. This will make them more likely to believe that their country is democratic, particularly if they feel a strong sense of attachment to that country.

We should note that this is not a strictly controlled experiment, so there are some demographic differences between the "control group" (interviewed before the meeting) and the "treatment group" (interviewed after the meeting), differences that may affect people's views about democracy. To account for this, in my regression equation I control for respondents' gender, age, education, interest in politics and foreign news, and religion and whether they were urban or rural (and just for safety also use entropy balancing to match the groups as closely as possible[34]). And since differences in responses after the meeting may be explained by the possibility that the survey was carried out at different times in different settings, with substantial differences between richer coastal and poorer inland provinces, I control for the level of provincial purchasing power parity in mid-2011. I also control for whether the province contains a Tibetan minority of over 1% (Sichuan, Gansu, and Yunnan) and report provincial fixed effects.

With these differences accounted for, those in the treatment group interviewed after the meeting should be as similar as possible to those in the control group interviewed before the meeting. To double-check that the groups are closely comparable in their views and knowledge about politics, I also look at their responses to two placebo questions: How democratic is Japan? How democratic is India? The "before" group gave almost identical answers to the "after" group to these questions, suggesting that their level of general knowledge and attitudes toward politics and foreign news is about the same. We are ready to test the hypotheses with ordered logistic and ordinary least squared models.[35]

The Meeting and Chinese Citizens' Perceptions of Democracy

The July 2011 meeting between President Obama and the Dalai Lama made the Chinese public significantly more likely to believe that their country was democratic. As Table 8.1 shows, in the five days following the meeting, people's rating of how democratic China was rose, on average, from 6.64 to 7.2 out of 10.[36] It also shows that, as predicted, this effect only really applied to those more patriotic citizens. For those who said they were "very proud" of their country, the

Table 8.1 People's Ratings of the Level of Democracy in China on a 1-to-10 Scale (1 = Completely Undemocratic, 10 = Completely Democratic) before and after the Dalai Lama–Obama Meeting

	All	High National Pride	Lower National Pride
Perceived level of democracy: five days before meeting	6.64 (0.079)	6.77 (0.096)	6.38 (0.133)
Perceived level of democracy: five days after meeting	7.20 (0.106)	7.67 (0.132)	6.49 (0.177)
Number of survey respondents	1,221	770	451

"High National Pride" denotes people who said that they were the highest level of "very proud" to be Chinese on a 1-to-4 scale. "Lower National Pride" denotes the people who said they were "somewhat proud," "not very proud," or "not proud at all." Standard errors are in parentheses.

meeting made them see China as being 9 percentage points more democratic. In fact, every increase in national pride on the 1-to-4 scale increases the effect of the Dalai Lama meeting on the belief that China is a democracy by about 4.2 percentage points.[37]

To get a better sense of what this means, it may help to split the 1-to-10 scale into two: those who say that China is more of an autocracy (who scored the country as 1 to 5 on the scale) and those who say it is more of a democracy (who scored it as 6 to 10 on the scale). Doing this shows that the Dalai Lama–Obama meeting did not just strengthen the views of people who already thought China was democratic, but also shifted them across the dividing line—from believing China was more of an autocracy to believing it was more of a democracy. Most notably, the meeting made those with high national pride 11.4 percentage points more likely to believe their country was democratic in some form, a sizeable increase.

What we are especially interested in here is how foreign pressure affects people's desire for political change. For there to be a popular will to reform the system of government, citizens need to not just believe that their country is undemocratic, but also *want* it to be democratic. When we analyze the subgroup of people who say in the survey that they prefer a democratic system of governance, we find that the percentage of these who say that they believe China is undemocratic (5 or below on the scale) drops by almost half, from 9.83% to 4.95%. This is quite a dramatic fall in the number of people who say that their desire for democracy is not being met.

Responses to other questions back this up. The meeting makes Chinese citizens significantly more likely to believe that their political system deserves their support, that it is capable of solving the country's problems, and that they are satisfied with the level of democracy in their country.[38] Is the effect only limited to those who see democracy as the ability of the state to provide for its citizens? What about those who see democracy as about Western concepts of checks and balances? Luckily, the *Asian Barometer* directly asks people what they feel is the most essential feature of democracy. And while the Dalai Lama meeting does increase perceptions of democracy among the third of people who see it primarily as a tool for narrowing income inequality, it also does the same for the (richer, more urban) third who believe that it is more about whether the people can choose their leaders.

And the effect was not just limited to democracy. After the meeting, survey respondents became far more positive about their country as a whole. Respondents became 6 percentage points more likely to believe that they had freedom of speech, 4 percentage points more likely to say that their fellow citizens had necessities like food and shelter, 5 percentage points more likely to say that corruption was not widespread, and 4 percentage points more likely to say that the economy was doing well. News of the meeting significantly improved people's opinions about the job their government was doing for their country.

Other Explanations for the Dalai Lama Effect

This is not a laboratory experiment, and we cannot manipulate people's conditions. So we need to think about what else might explain this change in people's beliefs. In the first place, since the CCP portrays the Dalai Lama as trying to engineer the breakup of China, a meeting with the president of the United States may appear to be a direct threat to their country's territory. In places from the United States to Spain, existential threats like wars or terrorist attacks have been shown to "rally" people around their leaders, increasing their attachment to the nation and trust in political institutions,[39] and leading to greater support for authoritarian values and distrust of democracy.[40] The problem is that (as we saw in chapter 6) in the case of this meeting, neither of these rally effects occurs. Following the meeting, respondents became no more attached to their nation and, if anything, valued democracy more. In fact, in the five days following the meeting, they became significantly more likely to believe that democracy is the most preferable form of government (an increase from 81.5% to 88.6% of the respondents) and significantly more likely to say they want democracy in the future.

But maybe the Dalai Lama meeting made people more worried about the consequences of giving their regime a negative review? In a similar natural experiment, Jiang Junyang and Yang Dali find that a 2006 purge of corrupt officials in Shanghai made residents more likely to say that they support the central government—something Jiang and Yang put down to people becoming more scared about admitting their true beliefs after hearing about the purge.[41] It is conceivable that the Dalai Lama meeting has a similar effect, making people more aware of restrictions around freedom of speech in China, and in turn making them less willing to say anything critical of their government. Again, however, this does not appear to be the case. Respondents interviewed after the meeting were no more likely to choose to abstain from replying to questions about democracy and were also no less likely to admit that they had previously been involved in collective action after the meeting—behavior that is arguably even more risky.[42]

Even if fear was not responsible, the social pressures of the survey might have made people give responses that did not reflect their true beliefs. On July 17, state media reports of the Dalai Lama–Obama meeting were accompanied by news stories featuring glowing portrayals of the prosperity of Tibet.[43] Rather than the meeting itself, it may have been these pieces of propaganda that pushed people to feel more positively about their political system. The barrage of propaganda may have also made citizens more likely to feel the need to keep in tune with the media commentators and "cheerlead" to the interviewer positive views about their country, views that they might not actually believe.[44] But "positive" propaganda was not unique to the day of the Dalai Lama meeting, and indeed some of the positive stories on that day pale in comparison to other days that same month. To take an example at random, on July 9, front-page *People's Daily* stories included praise for China's military progress[45] and news of excellent gross domestic product growth,[46] positive propaganda that, as Figure 8.3 shows, had little effect on perceptions of democracy.

Perhaps the big question here is, how do we know that it was the Dalai Lama meeting that sparked these changes? Over the ten days that we studied, there were certainly other news stories. In fact, while the meeting was the main story in Chinese media on July 17 and 18, there was another major news event—a story about bomb-and-knife attacks in Hotan, Xinjiang, on July 18, a story that may have also influenced people's views of democracy. How can we separate these two things out? Well, the attacks did not reach the newspapers until July 19,[47] and full discussions in newspapers and news websites did not come out until July 20 and 21. So to show that the meeting was the critical incident, we can examine when the main change in people's attitudes happened—was it as early as July 17, or was it not until July 20?

To test this, I conducted twenty different "placebo" experiments just like the one earlier—with each regression having a different treatment cutoff date in July.

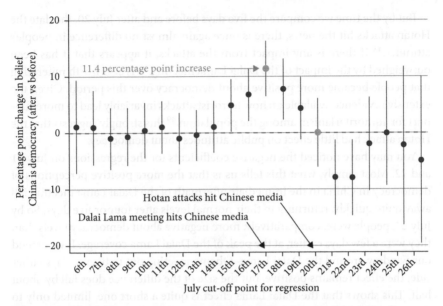

Figure 8.3 Results for twenty-one regressions over five days on either side of twenty-one different dates in July, on a binary measure of whether China is democratic or not (for those with high national pride). Lines represent 95% confidence intervals. At the start of the month and toward the end, there were fewer interviews carried out, giving a larger standard error for these dates.

We can then compare the results for each cutoff date to see when the impact on people's perceptions of democracy on their country is strongest. We start with July 6, comparing the five days before (July 1 to 5) with the five days after (July 6 to 10), then do the same every day, through the actual date of the meeting on July 17, and end with the five days before July 26 (July 21 to 25) compared to the five days after (July 26 to 30). This also allows us to see whether there is really something special about July 17. If the meeting is the most important event, there should be a clear peak on this date.

And this peak is exactly what we see. Figure 8.3 gives the results of daily regressions for our key group, those with above-average national pride. Essentially what this graph shows is the change in people's beliefs about whether China is democratic or not after a given date. We see that in the early days of July, in the lead-up to the meeting, those interviewed before and after each date have almost identical attitudes. It is only when the regressions start to include some days after the meeting that the difference between before and after begins to rise, finally peaking up to an 11.4-percentage-point jump in beliefs that China is democratic between the five days before and after July 17.

But by the time we compare the five days before and after July 20, the date the Hotan attacks hit the news, there is once again almost no difference in people's attitudes.[48] If there is any impact from the attacks, it appears that it has been outweighed by the impact of the Dalai Lama meeting. It is also worth reiterating that people became more positive about democracy over this period. Given the extensive evidence available on how terrorist attacks invariably lead to more support for authoritarianism among the population,[49] this strongly suggests that the Hotan attack had little effect on public attitudes about democracy.

You may have noticed the negative coefficients for the regressions on July 21 and 22. Most simply, what this tells us is that the more positive perceptions of democracy in China in the immediate aftermath of the Dalai Lama meeting fell away quite quickly, returning to their normal levels after four or five days. So by July 23, people were, comparatively, more negative about democracy levels than they were a few days earlier, at the peak of the Dalai Lama coverage. If we extend our window around the Dalai Lama–Obama meeting out to twenty days either side, the effect remains positive, but the size of the difference does fall by about half. This shows that the Dalai Lama effect is quite a short one, limited only to that time when the meeting was front-page news.

Fighting Back

When American leaders meet the Dalai Lama, reports of the meeting make the Chinese public significantly more likely to believe that their country is democratically run. This gives us vital real-world evidence that Chinese citizens fight back against foreign human rights pressure. It also tells us that this defensiveness extends even more broadly than the issue of political rights and that it bolsters all aspects of people's image of their nation: from the economy and access to food to levels of corruption and freedom of speech.

This conclusion is complicated somewhat by the fact that among the Chinese public, there are different conceptions of what democracy actually is, conceptions that do not always match those in the West. For some citizens, the meeting made them care more about whether their government was able to respond to and look after its people, but also believe that it was doing a better job in performing this "guardianship" role. For others, the meeting made them more likely to value a "Western" conception of checks and balances on their government, but still made them more likely to believe that the CCP fulfilled these criteria. However they define democracy, what we can say is that hearing about the international human rights community's pressure on their country does appear to reduce the grievances that they hold with their political system.

The sensitivity of the subject matter precludes asking people within China about their views of democracy and about the Dalai Lama's meetings with foreign leaders. However, at the end of chapter 7's interviews with overseas students and university workers, I also asked the interviewees about their views of meetings between the Tibetan leader and the American president. The majority (twenty-two) said that they disapproved of the meeting, with only six saying that the meetings should go ahead. The overwhelming reason for their disapproval was that any meeting would signal support for Tibetan independence, something interviewees were vehemently opposed to. Those who disapproved were particularly scathing of American motives in staging the meeting, saying that they saw the decision to be a result of geopolitical hostility rather than human rights concerns.

Bao, fifty-three, summed up the disapproval: "They should not meet. America admits that there is one China, and Tibet is a part of China, so they should not meet with a person who wants to engage in political separatism." Liu Fei, a graduate student, agreed: "American presidents often meet with foreign countries' leaders, but the Dalai Lama is not a foreign country's leader. If the United States meets with him then it is showing support for Tibetan independence." Ping Wei, thirty-three, brought up the popular opinion that any meeting would subvert the CCP's ability to properly represent the whole country: "It is done as a political tactic; Obama wants to use Tibet and its religion to try to split China apart. I was very angry [when I heard they had met]—because the US did not meet him with China's consent; it just met with the Dalai Lama. You need to get permission from China's leaders to meet with a figure like him. This person does not represent China's interests, but represents Tibet's interests."

So what does this tell us about whether a country's leader should meet with the Dalai Lama—or indeed any dissidents or activists from an authoritarian country? Meetings with the Dalai Lama help to focus international and domestic attention on Tibet, potentially pressuring the CCP to put in place steps to improve political and religious freedoms in the country while providing much-needed moral support to Tibetan groups. An examination of whether these positive effects do in fact occur is beyond the scope of this book. All this chapter shows is that the meetings can have an important impact on the wider public's grievances over their political system.

I should note that while Dalai Lama meetings are excellent examples of high-profile diplomatic pressure, we may not necessarily see the same results with other dissidents. While Chinese media articles have suggested that the West is trying to use political prisoners and dissidents to bring down the country,[50] the campaign against the Dalai Lama is quite unique. The sheer scale and intensity of his vilification, from school textbooks to television documentaries,[51] means that even your most high-profile dissident is unlikely to compare.

PART IV
THE IMPLICATIONS

9
Implications for China and Beyond

Over the last three decades the Chinese Communist Party (CCP) has fought back against pressure from the international human rights community. The CCP has rewarded its partners, coerced its opponents, molded the agendas of international organizations, and launched worldwide publicity campaigns. And for many, China's growing economic power has given its leaders enough leverage to successfully butter up or break its critics overseas.[1]

In this book I argue that resistance does not just come on the international stage, however. I show how regimes like the CCP can use foreign human rights pressure to stifle popular opposition to human rights violations at home, by framing those violations as issues of international competition, rather than ones of domestic injustice. When citizens believe that their nation's standing is under attack, then they will look to fight back against those attacks, taking steps that will make them more content with the conditions in their country. They will then be less likely to support any efforts to improve those conditions, efforts that range from demanding legal reform to protesting the arrests of dissidents.

Since the 1950s, state media has widely advertised outside criticism of human rights violations in China, especially at times when party control over the media has been at its strictest. And the criticism—framed as an attempt by foreign powers to attack China and restrain its growth—has been put to good use. When the CCP has announced news about human rights to the public, such as the arrests of dissidents or barriers on free speech, it has often introduced it through the lens of foreign pressure. But as analysis of reporting by government mouthpiece the *People's Daily* shows, this is not the case for all kinds of foreign pressure. State media is far more likely to write about pressure that comes from a "hostile" source (like the United States), especially when there is tension between the two sides and when the pressure is about China's territorial issues like Tibet or Hong Kong, existing policies like the one-child policy, or general critiques of "bad human rights in China" that the public is already aware of. These stories are often played up in state-owned newspapers and television channels for the entire public to see, even when the same stories are barely featured in international news coverage. But foreign pressure that provides detailed information about new human rights abuses and comes on issues unrelated to territorial matters, pressure that comes from non-Western sources or at times when bilateral tensions with the United States are low, is far more likely to be censored and hidden from the public.

Hostile Forces. Jamie J. Gruffydd-Jones, Oxford University Press. © Oxford University Press 2022.
DOI: 10.1093/oso/9780197643198.003.0009

So why do propaganda officials choose to pass on this sensitive information? It may be that certain kinds of foreign pressure are just not damaging enough for the Chinese government to feel like it needs to resort to censorship, rather than being proactively used as propaganda. Yet survey experiments on women's rights—an issue on which foreign activism has historically drawn positive reactions in China—show that when Chinese citizens are exposed to pressure from a geopolitical rival, the United States, they do indeed become significantly more satisfied with the state of women's rights in China, and less willing to take action to support activists looking to improve these rights. American efforts even turn more liberal people away from expressing support. But the experiments also show that when the pressure comes from a neutral source or when it only targets elites, the backfire effect is eliminated and may even be reversed.

The backfire is not just limited to hypothetical examples in survey experiments, and nor does it just apply to women's rights. A quasi-natural experiment around President Obama's 2011 meeting with the Dalai Lama shows in real time how an instance of front-page news about American human rights pressure made Chinese people significantly more likely to say that their country was ruled democratically. Extensive face-to-face interviews with ordinary members of the public show that these kinds of defensive reactions are closely linked to the belief that the US government is hostile toward China and wants to use human rights to prevent the country's rise. Yet people's previous beliefs also play an important role. Interviewees were far more accepting of foreign condemnation on the issue of air pollution, an issue on which they had already formed strong grievances.

How do authoritarian leaders know what this influence will be? Perhaps most likely is a process of trial and error, with authorities gradually realizing the kinds of pressure most likely to be useful. Through the 1990s, for example, we saw a shift in state media rhetoric in dealing with UN draft resolutions and congressional human rights reports. In-depth discussion of the details of foreign comments were gradually minimized and replaced with broader accusations of American hypocrisy and hostility. Then after the public outcry against the Dalai Lama and perceived French attacks on the Beijing Olympics in 2008, we saw a surge in state media coverage of foreign leaders' meetings with the Dalai Lama and criticism from French sources.

On the other hand, trial and error also means that some damaging information slips through the cracks. There are numerous examples of even *Xinhua* articles being retracted following directives from the Propaganda Department.[2] One directive (leaked to the *China Digital Times* website), for example, noted that a *Xinhua* article attacking Taiwanese leader Tsai Ing Wen was "having a bad influence on public opinion" and called for it to be deleted when social media commentators used the article to criticize Communist Party leaders.[3] Another directive called back a *Global Times* piece that scorned one of the Hong Kong booksellers, Lam Wing-Kee, and his public retraction of a forced confession he had made in custody. The problem, perhaps, was that by rebutting Lam's claims, the paper gave a full airing to his accusations of kidnapping and torture.[4] If we remember back to chapter 2, this is the key dilemma that state media faces when dealing with international pressure. If there is not enough in a news story about foreign criticism of human rights in China to boil up a stew of nationalism and defensiveness, then all it might be doing is relaying information to the public about a sensitive human rights issue.

One example of this came in 2015, after an open letter from eleven overseas Chinese university students called for the CCP to put on trial those responsible for the Tiananmen massacres in 1989. This obscure letter was seized upon by the *Global Times*, which published a vehement editorial in both its Chinese- and English-language editions. The article reported the letter's content in detail, including the fact that "the post-1980s and post-1990s generations on the mainland have been fooled, and [the authors] couldn't find out the 'truth' of the 1989 Tiananmen incident until they moved abroad to study, where they have unlimited access to the Internet."[5] The article claimed that the writers of the letter had become "new targets of overseas hostile forces." However, as reported in the watchdog website *China Digital Times*, the editorial itself was removed by censors just days later.[6] One of the signatories of the petition, Gu Yi, said that the *Global Times* had unwittingly played into the students' hands by bringing publicity to the letter within China, saying, "The *Global Times* attacking our letter was [the letter's] best advertisement."[7]

The dilemma for *Global Times* editors is the temptation to use the letter to foster a defensive reaction in their readers, hoping that they will be angry about how the students had been taken hostage by foreign forces hoping to attack China. In this case, however, the letter was written by native Chinese students, hardly a "hostile" group like the US government or a suspicious foreign nongovernmental organization (NGO). Moreover, the letter did not just blithely repeat previous criticism of general human rights conditions or pressure to change an existing government policy, but provided potentially new information to the public about how their compatriots overseas view the events of 1989. Passing on this information appears to be a mistake that even a nationalist outlet like the *Global Times* would be unlikely to make again.

Beyond China

China is run by a powerful authoritarian regime, which has leaned heavily on nationalist rhetoric and accusations that Western concerns about human rights are driven by hostility. It is, perhaps, something of an easy case. Maybe it is a unique case. So can it tell us anything about other countries and whether international pressure on human rights would also backfire beyond China? If so, where?

Let's look back at the theory in chapter 2. The psychological tendencies discussed in the first half of the chapter, not least the way that people seek to fight back against information they believe is threatening to their group, are universal ones. There is no evidence that these tendencies are particularly specific to any culture, nor that they only exist in highly nationalist states. This means that international pressure has the potential to backfire for any person, on any issue, in any country. In this book alone we have seen that the backfire is not just limited to conservative regime supporters digging in on their deeply entrenched views. In chapter 6, for example, the most prone to fight back against American pressure over women's rights were the most highly educated and internationalist citizens. In chapter 7, people reacted the most negatively to pressure on an issue they knew very little about: the use of ivory in Chinese medicine. And there is evidence of international pressure backfiring across the world. After being told about international legal investigations into their country, citizens from places as diverse as the United States and Kyrgyzstan became less supportive of international law.[8] Even Sweden, neither a superpower nor a former colony, saw something of a wave of public nationalism in reaction to criticism of its relaxed coronavirus strategy.[9]

Throughout this book I have highlighted certain conditions that are needed for the CCP leadership to be able to effectively weaponize foreign human rights pressure—the source, the issue, the target, and timing. But these considerations can also tell us something about the places where under-pressure leaders will be able to do this most successfully. Think back to the argument: pressure will backfire if it taps more strongly into people's motivation to defend their nation above any other competing motivations, motivations that range from their desire to form accurate opinions about the state of human rights to their need to protect their partisan political group. At the national level, this means that in the simplest terms, a backfire will depend on the target government's ability to be able to effectively frame international pressure as a hostile foreign attack on the nation, rather than as a genuine attempt to improve human rights or as a partisan political issue.

The ability to do this will first depend on whether a government is willing to frame pressure in this way. In chapter 6 we talked about how the Qing government chose not to publicly denounce the foot-binding activists, and how the CCP held back from launching a mass propaganda attack on the campaign to release the feminist five. In these cases, the rulers had little pressing need to devote costly resources to opposing these relatively low-key movements.

A leader's willingness to weaponize foreign pressure may also depend on their country's geopolitical relationship with the United States. Just like the Chinese leadership would tone down its rhetoric about the United States around the time of official bilateral visits, some countries are less willing to risk their good relations with the United States by launching a propaganda campaign against it. As Anja Jetschke notes about the Philippines, for example, attempts to stir up anticolonial nationalism against the United States have historically caused offense and risked a valued alliance.[10] Of course, even this kind of alliance might not be enough. If the regime is under pressure from the United States over an issue that it feels is essential for its survival at home, then it may still be in its interests to make the United States appear like a hostile enemy. In the Philippines in 2016, for example, despite their alliance, American criticism of President Duterte's violent anti-drug crackdown led Duterte to publicly berate the United States over its "imperialist" attitude.[11]

If we assume that a government does decide to weaponize foreign pressure, then its ability to successfully frame that pressure as hostile depends on two main conditions.

Resonance of the "Hostile" Narrative

The first condition is something that we have been talking about throughout this book: any story that foreign human rights pressure is really a hostile attack on the nation needs to be a convincing one. And this story may be much more convincing in some countries than others.

Take a country with a long history of foreign invasion, a country where any Western pressure on its leaders to change their behavior feels suspiciously like neocolonialism. Or take a country that has been subject to what it sees as neverending, unfair victimization by the international community, especially over what it sees as its rightful territory. One of the reasons that human rights pressure over Tibet and Hong Kong evokes such a defensive reaction is because historical Western interference in these territories, as well as repeated criticism of human rights and democracy, means that the picture of hostility is such an easy one to draw.

Israel is a place where the "hostile" narrative is, arguably, especially resonant. The sheer volume of international criticism of their country has led many Israelis to view international law—and indeed the human rights system in general—as antagonistic, biased, and even a threat to the nation (a portrayal encouraged by Israeli politicians from all sides).[12] And this narrative appears to have an impact. As we saw in the first half of the book, when pressure starts to repeat the same old lines of attack on the same old topics, it becomes less informative and starts to appear more hostile. One recent study found, for instance, that international sanctions over Palestine ended up increasing Israeli citizens' backing for more hardline policies in the territory.[13] Another showed that when Israelis were told that their government's crackdowns on peaceful protestors violated international law, they became *more* supportive of their ruling party.[14]

As we saw in chapter 6, pressure is also most likely to backfire in countries where the link between the ruling party and the nation is strong, countries where an attack on the rulers is quite easily framed as an attack on the nation as a whole. Some countries have stronger links than others. The link will be stronger, for example, when there is a historical bond between the leadership and the birth of the nation, in places where the ruling party was responsible for securing independence or winning a revolutionary war. In places where the leadership is seen as illegitimate or alien, or failing to adequately protect its citizens, this kind of link is much harder to forge. Part of what might have made it difficult for the Qing government to organize a nationalist response to the anti-foot-binding movement was the fact that they themselves were seen as outsiders, and that they were failing to defend the nation against foreign forces.

It was also relatively easy for Chinese citizens to identify and sympathize with the victims of foot-binding: women who were members of their families and local communities. This suggests that foreign pressure is more likely to appear hostile when a country's citizens do not identify very strongly with the people whose human rights are being violated. We might see this more in countries where the state chooses to persecute members of a small, far-away, and ethnically distinct ethnic or cultural minority. Arguably one reason that pressure on Tibet and Xinjiang evokes defensive reactions is not just to do with territorial integrity, but because many citizens feel less affinity with Tibetans and Uighurs on the other side of the country than they might with Han in their local communities.

The backfire will also be stronger when there are no political identities that are more salient than the national identity. Think about countries without any powerful opposition groups, deep religious fault lines, or ethnic political divides. The evidence suggests that in these kinds of one-party states, mass campaigns to try and frame the ruling party and its leaders as the personification of the nation— like China's patriotic education campaign—are especially common.[15]

Control Over the Narrative

Patriotic campaigns are common in one-party states because there are often few opposition voices to challenge them, especially when the ruling party also has control over the media. This brings us the second condition for a successful backfire—the ability to effectively control the narrative, to make sure that the "hostile" narrative is the main one the citizens hear. Regimes like the CCP, with a powerful internet firewall and control over the press, can ensure that the message gets through without any opposition. These regimes can also ensure that their citizens mainly hear pressure that is more likely to backfire.[16] In Russia, for example, Vladimir Putin used his control over the media to deploy Western sanctions on firms and government officials over military action in Crimea and Eastern Ukraine in 2014 as a potent propaganda tool.[17] State media played up the sanctions,[18] with Putin calling them "hostile" and responsible for economic woes in the country,[19] a tactic he was particularly fond of around the 2016 legislative elections.[20] As Putin said after his victory, the results were "citizens' reaction to external attempts to pressure Russia, to threats, to sanctions, and to foreign attempts to stir up the situation in our country."[21]

In freer environments, however, citizens are likely to hear more than just pressure from their hostile rivals. Their newspapers may also write about instances of foreign pressure, for example, that come from the United Nations and explicitly target the country's leader over their latest crackdown on protests—pressure that may have very different effects. In these countries, opposition political parties and activist groups also have a platform to promote an alternative narrative, a narrative that may frame the foreign pressure as a genuine human rights concern rather than a hostile attack. If there are partisan political divides, as in democracies or so-called competitive autocracies,[22] then those people who do not support the ruling party may be able to frame foreign pressure as merely an attack on the partisan leadership rather than on the nation as a whole. In this case we may see regime supporters reacting negatively to foreign interference but opponents responding positively.[23]

In India, for example, a country where opposition parties have vocally opposed authorities' human rights violations, one study found that international criticism made people more critical of their country's respect for human rights.[24] Without a pervasive narrative of hostility and discrimination, people are less likely to dismiss the pressure and much more likely to pay attention to what it says. In stark contrast to Israel, when Indian citizens were told that government crackdowns on peaceful protestors violated international law, it reduced their support for the ruling party.[25]

While one of these conditions—a resonant narrative of hostility or firm control over that narrative—may be enough, if both hold then leaders should be able to effectively use international pressure for their own propaganda purposes. This means that a backfire will be especially likely in powerful authoritarian states with weak opposition or activist movements and heavy control over the media, whose ruling party has been instrumental in the fight against foreign invasion or colonialism, or who have faced years of repeated international criticism over the same old issues. A backfire will be least likely in liberal democracies with strong opposition parties, civil society, and free press; where there are weak ties between the ruling party and the nation as a whole; and where the criticism is relatively new.

A proper test of the countries where a backfire is most or least likely really needs a full book treatment. However, we can explore whether we are on the right lines by looking at some carefully chosen cases that meet these conditions in various forms and examining the impact of foreign pressure. I take the United Kingdom and three of its former colonies: Uganda, Zimbabwe, and Hong Kong (see Table 9.1).

None of these countries are as authoritarian as China, but they do vary widely in both the likelihood that a "hostile" narrative will resonate and their ability to control the narrative. At one end we have Uganda, a former British colony, where Yoweri Museveni's ruling National Resistance Movement (NRM) has faced little political opposition since winning a revolutionary war in the 1980s. Then we have Zimbabwe under Robert Mugabe—also a former British colony where the ruling party fought for independence, but which had to deal with a growing political challenge into the twenty-first century. Next we have the former colonizer itself, the United Kingdom, a country with little reason to feel victimized by the international community but with a vibrant political opposition. At the other end, Hong Kong post-1997 is a former British colony, but a former colony with a strong partisan political divide, and where for many in the opposition camp the "hostile" force is not the former colonial power but their rulers in Beijing.

Uganda under Museveni

President Yoweri Museveni has led Uganda since winning a guerrilla campaign in 1986 and has sought to undergird his NRM party with patriotic, nationalist, and anti-colonialist rhetoric.[26] On the other hand, the NRM has become a key partner to Western countries, especially the United States,[27] which has provided extensive development and military assistance to the country.[28] This has made it

Table 9.1 Resonance of the Narrative That the International Human Rights Community Is "Hostile" toward the Country and the Ruling Party's Relative Ability to Control This Narrative in Four Case Studies

	Resonance of Narrative	Control over Narrative
Uganda	High	High
Zimbabwe	High	Medium
United Kingdom	Weak	Weak
Hong Kong	Polarizing	Weak

difficult for Museveni to play up anti-American sentiment, given the risk it could pose to the alliance and the fact that the Ugandan public hold some of the most pro-American attitudes in the world.[29]

The NRM has faced very little political opposition, meaning there are no other established political identities for people to turn to, or indeed powerful parties who can shape a different narrative. On the other hand, Uganda does have a relatively free media environment. While the government has periodically attempted to interfere, there are numerous independent television stations and newspapers, and unlike China or Zimbabwe, the NRM does not restrict its people's access to foreign news.[30]

And there has been Western pressure on Uganda over human rights, not least the 2014 fight over the enactment of an "anti-homosexuality bill," a bill that threatened to punish homosexuality with up to life in prison. The issue was originally thrust forward by local religious groups and then co-opted by Museveni as part of his populist push for electoral votes[31] (in 2013, gay rights were opposed by 96% of the population in Uganda[32]). As soon as the bill was first mooted in 2009, Western activists badgered their governments to put pressure on Kampala to drop the bill. Leaders from the United States to the European Union publicly criticized the bill and threatened sanctions if it was passed.[33]

Sensing an opportunity to reinvigorate his role as a warrior against external colonial interference, with the 2016 presidential elections in sight, Museveni seized upon the issue.[34] Just before the signing of the bill in 2014, then-president Obama threatened that its passage would "complicate our valued relationship with Uganda."[35] Arguably the very reasons Museveni signed the bill may have been these threats—given his rhetoric, he could not afford to be seen as giving in to Western pressure.[36] And indeed, Museveni's spokesman said plainly that the president was signing the bill to "demonstrate Uganda's independence in the face of Western pressure and provocation."[37] The high-profile calls for Western donor countries to cut their aid to Uganda if the bill passed had been featured heavily in the Ugandan press[38] and brought angry retorts even from those who opposed the bill.[39]

Public support for the bill, already high, remained so through 2015,[40] with Museveni receiving a round of applause from officials at its signing.[41] Museveni's own popularity grew noticeably during the furor, while public opinion toward the United States fell.[42] Perhaps most pertinently, despite the discrimination inherent in the bill, Ugandan citizens' beliefs that their country supported equal rights also grew, from 41.7% in 2012 to 44.7% in 2015, with the percentage believing that people are treated equally more than doubling from 9.1% to 20.9%, as shown in Figure 9.1.[43]

The passing of the bill and the spike in support for Museveni demonstrated his ability to successfully weaponize external pressure. The strategy succeeded

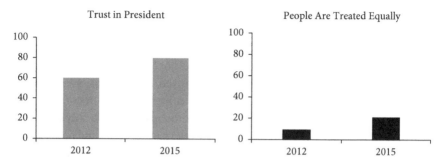

Figure 9.1 Percentage of the Ugandan population who have positive levels of trust in the president, and the percentage who believe that people are treated equally in Uganda.
Credit line: Afrobarometer, 2012 and 2015, https://afrobarometer.org/.

even when it came against a powerful and popular foreign ally and aid donor. But the case also shows the limitations of this strategy. Museveni could only successfully weaponize external pressure when it came on an issue that had been already framed as one of national integrity, as a fight against imperialism, and was an existing government policy on which the public was already firmly on the president's side. As such, any new information about foreign pressure was likely to work in the president's favor, even if it came through independent media sources. This is a tactic that is unlikely to work on less explosively nationalistic issues. For example, when Obama again threatened sanctions on Ugandan officials over their arrests of political prisoners in 2016,[44] the news was not passed on in state-owned newspapers.

This kind of campaign also has international consequences—most notably loss of aid revenue from foreign allies. And later the same year, just before he was to meet with President Obama, Museveni played down the anti-homosexuality bill's importance, and a Ugandan court quietly annulled it.[45] This behavior mirrors the actions of Philippines President Duterte in 2016, who, having publicly railed against American imperialism over his anti-drug campaign,[46] later quietly expressed regret and sought to play down tensions on the international stage.[47] Museveni and Duterte's reactions demonstrate how leaders can both feel the costs of Western pressure and at the same time manipulate it to gain support at home.

Zimbabwe under Mugabe

Robert Mugabe led the ruling Zimbabwe African National Union–Patriotic Front (ZANU-PF) party from independence until 2017 and played heavily on his reputation as the revolutionary leader bringing his country out of colonialism—what Terence Ranger calls an appeal to "patriotic history"—to justify his continued rule.[48] Mugabe used his control over the press to remind his citizens of this history. Zimbabwean authorities have punished journalists that criticized the regime, censored negative news, and jammed foreign media to prevent it from reaching the population. Since only around 20% of the population had any internet access at the end of Mugabe's reign, this meant that the political discourse was very much in his hands.[49] On the other hand, unlike China and Uganda, ZANU-PF was not the only political game in town, as from the late 1990s the Movement for Democratic Change (MDC) emerged as a credible and powerful opposition party. In the 2002 elections the MDC caused a major surprise, winning almost half the seats on offer, and then in 2008 the party won the popular vote and the majority of the seats, sharing power with ZANU-PF under Mugabe's leadership.

Mugabe saw foreign interference, in particular from the former colonial power Britain, as a way of stigmatizing the MDC. The party was just another manifestation of Britain's attempts to take back power in Zimbabwe,[50] and any attempts to condemn Mugabe and his policies were seized upon as evidence of this. Mugabe proclaimed British outcries over land reform in 2001 to be an attempt to recolonize the country,[51] saying to British Prime Minister Tony Blair in an oft-quoted 2002 speech, "Blair, keep your England and let me keep my Zimbabwe."[52]

Condemnation and sanctions on Mugabe's regime grew in the early 2000s, not just from the United Kingdom, but also from the European Union and the United States. The sanctions targeted ZANU-PF leaders for all kinds of authoritarian behavior, from failure to uphold the rule of law to electoral violence. The dilemma for Mugabe and ZANU-PF was that the widespread condemnation and sanctions highlighted to the Zimbabwean public the scale of their violations of human rights and demonstrated just how negatively the international community saw those violations. The existence of a now-influential opposition movement meant that international disapproval could, potentially, be framed as a genuine attempt to improve the lives of Zimbabwe's people.

Initially, the MDC enthusiastically welcomed international sanctions.[53] They provided the movement with legitimacy and gave it much-needed cohesion, emboldening them to take on the regime. When the United States and European Union threatened to impose targeted sanctions on the ZANU-PF leadership in late 2001, MDC leaders advertised them widely, and the threats fed into mass anti-government demonstrations across Zimbabwe. Initially, for MDC politicians and their supporters, the condemnation and sanctions were a clear sign that the international community was on their side and would help them in their push for regime change.[54]

But unlike the leaders of China's anti-foot-binding movement, the MDC did not manage to successfully portray the international campaign as part of a patriotic movement to improve Zimbabwe. One problem was that the various factions within the MDC could not agree on how best to respond to the sanctions, and several of their more prominent politicians publicly announced their opposition.[55] In the face of their reticence, Mugabe confiscated the narrative and from 2002 began to play up the sanctions as a hostile, imperialist attack on Zimbabwe. The strategy is nicely summed up by a (state-run) *Herald* article about British criticism of electoral irregularities in Zimbabwe in 2002, which said, "The British started showing their true colours by advocating sanctions against Zimbabwe for human rights ... [showing] its hidden agenda to topple the present Zimbabwean government.... [T]he victory by Zanu-PF in the just-ended presidential election was indeed a victory over imperialism."[56]

The Western sanctions became a regular sight in state-owned media, and Mugabe fulminated against their use in domestic and international speeches,[57] blaming them for the country's economic decline.[58] The campaign was rolled out in force for the 2013 elections, with sanctions mentioned forty times in the ZANU-PF party manifesto alone,[59] and became almost ubiquitous in newspaper, radio, and television coverage. When anti-government demonstrations erupted again in late 2016, state media accused protestors of being supported by the United States, Britain, and France[60] and, to back up these claims, highlighted how the American ambassador had criticized ZANU-PF's use of force to crush the protests, issuing articles that accused him of hypocrisy, racism, and agitating for regime change.[61]

Mugabe's attempts to play up Western interference also brought him support from fellow African leaders, in particular South Africa's Thabo Mbeki.[62] This meant that pressure on Mugabe over his human rights abuses was arriving only from the West, and not from Zimbabwe's allies. As we saw in China, this made it even easier for Mugabe to portray the sanctions as a hostile, imperialist attempt at regime change, rather than a genuine effort to improve human rights.

The sudden spike in public support for Mugabe and the Zimbabwean political system between 1999 and 2004 shown in Figure 9.2 (trust in the president more than doubles in the Afrobarometer surveys) might seem puzzling.[63] In these years Zimbabwe's economy fell apart, life expectancy dropped dramatically, and political repression increased.[64] Bratton, Chikwana, and Sithole argue that the most likely cause of the public's support was not their misperceptions of economic growth or greater fear of expressing their true opinions, but Mugabe's propaganda network. They show that people's trust in media was one of the biggest predictors of Mugabe's positive ratings at this time.[65] His ability to control the narrative, in particular his control of the media in rural areas, and the weaponizing of foreign pressure in this narrative accentuated his public support.

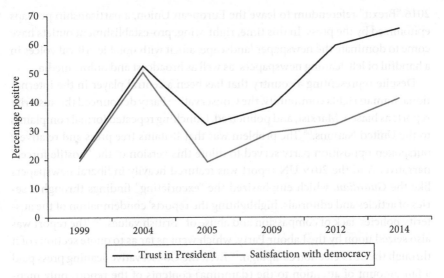

Figure 9.2 Trust in president and satisfaction with democracy in Zimbabwe (percentage that have positive levels of trust and satisfaction, 1999–2014).
Credit line: Afrobarometer, 1999–2014, https://afrobarometer.org/.

United Kingdom under the Conservative Party

The United Kingdom is perhaps the odd one out in these case studies. It has not been colonized for at least nine hundred years and has often been the leader of international opprobrium over human rights, as we saw in the case of Zimbabwe, rather than the subject of it. But after 2010 there was growing international condemnation over the human rights impacts of the British government's austerity measures. The United Nations issued regular high-profile criticisms, with one report from its Special Rapporteur warning starkly that unless British policymakers changed tack, its poorest citizens would soon face a "solitary, poor, nasty, brutish, and short" existence, and that the benefits system had plunged people into "misery and despair."[66]

In Uganda and Zimbabwe, the ruling parties used their control of the media and history of colonialism to grasp hold of the narrative surrounding this kind of criticism. In the United Kingdom, however, the ruling party's ability to either censor the criticism or play it up to evoke a backfire against foreign criticism has been much more limited. The United Kingdom is a liberal democracy with a vibrant parliamentary system. Throughout the Conservative government's post-2010 reign, the main opposition has been the left-leaning Labour Party, a party that put the protection of human rights in the United Kingdom at the center of its election manifestos.[67] And politics has become increasingly partisan since the

2016 "Brexit" referendum to leave the European Union, a partisanship perhaps epitomized by the press. In this time, right-wing, pro-establishment outlets have come to dominate the newspaper landscape, albeit with notable critical voices in a handful of left-leaning newspapers, as well as broadcast and online media.

Despite representing a country that has been a central player in the international human rights community, the Conservative Party denounced the austerity reports as biased, Marxist, and politicized, launching repeated formal complaints to the United Nations.[68] The problem was that Britain's free press and relatively outspoken opposition party served to dilute this version of the "hostile forces" narrative. And the 2019 UN report was featured heavily in liberal newspapers like the *Guardian*, which emphasized the "excoriating" findings through a series of articles and editorials, highlighting the reports' condemnation of the austerity policies' lack of compassion and abuse of "British values."[69] The report was also seized upon by the Labour Party, which went as far as to quote sections of it through the 2019 election campaign.[70] Even the Conservative-leaning press paid a fair amount of attention to the (damning) contents of the report, only mentioning in passing the government's retorts of bias and hostility.[71]

This is not to say that the pro-establishment press has always reacted soberly to international criticism of human rights in the United Kingdom. In 2010 the *Daily Mail* brought the United Nations' review of Britain's human rights to the attention of its readers, calling it "ludicrous" for including condemnation from the representatives of authoritarian regimes like Russia and Belarus.[72] The European Court of Human Rights' occasional rulings against the United Kingdom have seen angry backlashes from the right-wing media, backlashes that played heavily upon the threat to the country's sovereignty from the European Union.[73]

While the UN reports on austerity were high profile for a day or two, compared to the mass international campaigns for human rights in Uganda and Zimbabwe, their significance was quite minor. So unlike Uganda and Zimbabwe, it is hard to see whether limited campaigns like this have any impact. As a result, in April 2020 I carried out a small experiment to explore how people in the United Kingdom do react to foreign criticism, and to see whether it is indeed less likely to backfire. The timing of the study was significant, as it fell right in the middle of the coronavirus outbreak, and just as the first real grumbling of international criticism over the British government's response was beginning. After going into lockdown quite late, the United Kingdom had found itself with the highest death toll in Europe, and by the start of May condemnation began to flood in both at home and around the world.[74]

Just a few days before this wave of foreign condemnation began, I randomly provided half an online sample of 418 British citizens with a generic summary of the British government's actions in dealing to the coronavirus. The other half were also told that foreign politicians had heavily criticized the government's response.[75] Unlike in China, however, telling British citizens that foreign leaders had condemned the United Kingdom made them significantly *more* critical of the British government's response to the virus. Respondents who were just told that their government had taken steps to respond to the virus gave it an average approval rating of 57.3 out of 100. But for those who were also told about foreign criticism of those steps, that approval rating fell almost 9 percentage points to 48.6.[76] On the other hand, the criticism had little impact on people's overall approval of the government's performance, nor their willingness to vote for the Conservatives next time around.

However, things get interesting when we break the results down by how people voted in the elections six months earlier.[77] While the number of respondents falls (not everyone voted), the pattern is clear: the impacts of foreign criticism depend on who you voted for. Criticism still reduces Conservative voters' approval of the response by 5 percentage points, but this is far short of the 11-percentage-point drop for opposition voters. The most striking impact was on people's future voting intentions, however. Here we see that for past opposition voters, the criticism all but eliminated the likelihood they would vote Conservative in the future, the proportion saying they would do so falling from 13% to just 4%. But for those who voted Conservative in the past, foreign criticism firmly solidifies their intention to do so again—up from 82% to almost 98%. While the results are statistically significant, the sample of those who admit they voted Conservative is quite small here (only seventy-five respondents fit this category). So while the pattern is a striking one, the results are somewhat tentative.

So what do these results tell us? They show that in a partisan democracy with a free press, where there is no real history of attacks from the international community, international pressure is unlikely to be seen as hostile, and unlikely to backfire. They show that when people hear about novel condemnation of their government (remember that the survey was implemented before much of the international criticism was reported in British newspapers, and before the pro-establishment press had time to reel out any backlash), they will be much more likely to take it into account in informing their views. And under these kinds of conditions, in this kind of state, partisanship is perhaps more important than nationalism. Unlike in China, British citizens' response was unaffected by their attachment to their nation[78] but was significantly influenced by their political affiliation. There was a backfire of sorts, but it was limited only to ruling party supporters, and it was limited only to those supporters' willingness to go on and vote for their party.

In open partisan environments, then, there appears to be a much more "targeted" backfire, something my coauthor and I also found in the United States. We sought to examine what would happen when Americans read about an international NGO's criticism of their country's criminal justice system while

164   HOSTILE FORCES

Donald Trump was in power. As with the United Kingdom, we found that partisanship was important, and that the pressure had a very different impact on people's views about the issue than it did on their overall attitudes toward their country. While the criticism did make Americans—especially Republicans—more willing to support criminal justice reform, it nevertheless made the same more nationalistic Republican supporters much more positive about the overall state of their country.[79]

Hong Kong, 2014

Finally, we turn back to Hong Kong and the foreign pressure on Hong Kong authorities over the 2014 Umbrella protests. But rather than looking at the mainland, as we did in chapter 4, let's look instead at the reaction in Hong Kong itself.

While Hong Kongers should arguably hold more historical grievances with the West than those on the mainland do, having been colonized by Britain, in recent years anti-British resentment has been overshadowed by partisan political splits between those who are more supportive of Chinese influence in the territory and those who push for more political freedoms and autonomy from Beijing. Figure 9.3 is a stark demonstration of how Hong Kong people's identities have evolved since 1997. It shows how residents have begun to see themselves less and less as Chinese through the 2010s and instead increasingly identify themselves as exclusively "Hong Kongers." What has changed since 2008? Some scholars point to the reduced economic and housing opportunities in Hong Kong in the face of immigration from the mainland,[80] while others lay the blame at the growing political interference from Beijing and its maladroit attempts to impose a Chinese national identity in Hong Kong.[81]

Either way, for many, the main "threat" to their unique identity as Hong Kongers comes not from their former colonizers, but from the mainland.[82] A 2015 survey by the University of Hong Kong's Public Opinion Programme showed that over 80% of respondents who saw themselves as exclusively Hong Kongers believed that Hong Kong's autonomy was under threat, and 65% of these believed that the main threat to that autonomy was the Communist Party.[83]

Politics is increasingly partisan in Hong Kong, divided broadly between the pro-Beijing and the pan-democrat camps. In the 2016 Legislative Council elections, pro-Beijing parties gained around 40% of the popular vote, against 36% for pan-democratic parties and 19% for other localist parties. Despite accusations that Hong Kongers are politically apathetic,[84] this divide spilled over into the Occupy Central demonstrations in late 2014. In September, democracy activists launched a protest in Hong Kong's financial center, a protest that turned into mass unrest—known as the "Umbrella Movement"—after police sprayed

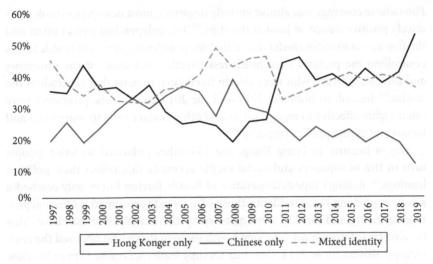

Figure 9.3 How Hong Kong citizens identify, according to six-month survey from Hong Kong University's Public Opinion Programme (results from June included only, excluding "don't knows").

Credit line: Hong Kong University's Public Opinion Programme, https://www.hkupop.hku.hk/chinese/popexpress/ethnic/eidentity/poll/datatables.html.

the activists with tear gas. While public support gradually faded, at its height in October, 37.8% backed the movement against 35.5% who opposed it, seemingly broadly along partisan divides.[85]

Pro-Beijing voices on the mainland and in Hong Kong sought to portray the protestors as manipulated and supported by "hostile" outside forces,[86] with the West as a "black hand" controlling activists to subvert Chinese authority.[87] As discussed in more detail in chapter 4, these accusations served to dampen Western criticism of the behavior of Hong Kong's authorities. Just like on the mainland, pro-Beijing newspapers heavily covered any pressure that did come through, however, accusing Western countries of attempting to recolonize the territory.[88] This theme continued into the following years,[89] with the newspapers calling local activists "race traitors" for attracting international attention and harming Hong Kong's reputation around the world.[90]

The problem for authorities was that Hong Kong enjoyed far more press freedom than the mainland (at least until 2020).[91] The media environment generally reflected the partisan political divides, with some diehard pro-Beijing outlets, but also some newspapers that were highly critical of the establishment. Many independent journalists take this critical role very seriously and until recently were not afraid to take openly anti-government (and anti-Beijing) stances.[92] For the Umbrella protests, except for the CCP mouthpieces *Wen Wei Po* and *Ta Kung*

Pao (whose coverage was almost entirely negative), most newspapers took a relatively positive stance, at least at the start.[93] The independent news outlets and the free access to social media meant that the pro-Beijing stories of hostile forces controlling the protests were much less effective, not least for the protestors and their supporters, who were able to freely turn to news that contradicts the stories.[94] Indeed, in both the 2014 and the 2019 movements, protestors were often highly effective in using Twitter and other social media to share news and tactics and garner public sympathy.[95]

This is because in Hong Kong, just like other polarized societies, people turn to the newspapers and social media accounts that reflect their political leanings.[96] Beijing's repeated narrative of hostile foreign forces only reached a selection of Hong Kong residents, those who already consumed traditional pro-Beijing media and already were quite sympathetic with their narrative. This became clear through my interviews with some of those who opposed the anti-Occupy Movement in 2014. One anti-Occupy leader was quite firm in his view that there had been clear evidence of foreign support for the Occupy protests. Another argued that many in Hong Kong wanted to express their independence from Western imperial powers, and that opposing Western interference was a strong motivating factor for many of those who had joined anti-Occupy protests.

For those on the other side, however, the narrative of Western interference was not only contradicted by what they had read online and in independent newspapers but also appeared to be simply less of a concern. Indeed, as one pro-democracy party leader said, the biggest "threat" to their supporters' identity as Hong Kongers did not come from the United Kingdom but from Beijing. The leaders of the Occupy Movement seemed less worried about Western condemnation of the government than activists were, for example, in Uganda, with some even calling for more foreign pressure on CY Leung, the then-chief executive.[97] These calls grew into the 2019 protests, where many activists and protestors waved American flags, bought advertisements in foreign newspapers, and delivered petitions to consulates calling for them to put pressure on China at international summits.[98]

We cannot show conclusively that international pressure in Hong Kong would not backfire in the same way as the mainland. It is clear, however, that there was a huge partisan divide in how the protest supporters and opponents viewed foreign efforts to intervene, not least because both sides picked up their news—including news about foreign pressure—from highly partisan sources.[99] Both sides were quite happy to celebrate this foreign pressure, as it played nicely into their own narratives and interests. The pro-Beijing camp, already more inclined to view pressure from the United Kingdom and the United States as a threat, saw their newspapers feature stories that played up international interventions and framed them as hostile. The pro-democrats, inclined to see Western pressure as less threatening, were given news that framed it in a much more balanced manner and actively called for more.

Pressure from Above and Below

This is a far too brief comparison, but it does demonstrate the different impacts of foreign pressure around the world. In politically polarized places like Hong Kong and the United Kingdom, the population will find out about foreign pressure from very different sources, and it will affect them in very different ways. What does this tell us? It means that the international community's efforts to put pressure on human rights and democracy risk backfiring a lot less in more politically partisan and free environments—only affecting those people who are already disposed to supporting the government's position and receiving their news from pro-government sources. But on the other hand, the examples reinforce that China is not a unique case. If an under-pressure government wants to weaponize foreign pressure, then when it is able to control the narrative and when that narrative plays into a history of a hostile international community, pressure is highly likely to backfire.

Of course, this brings us back to the question that we have neglected since chapter 1: why should we care about public opinion in these kinds of authoritarian countries? In liberal democracies, many human rights scholars accept that the international community can most effectively improve human rights over the long term when they change governments' "domestic calculations," as Moravscik puts it.[100] The reason that many leaders choose to uphold international norms like the respect for women's rights or the protection of endangered species is because they recognize that they will lose legitimacy among their public if they do not observe those norms.[101]

But one might argue that, by their nature, authoritarian governments do not give their people any opportunity to punish them if they do not respect these norms. And for some of the less well-known issues we have talked about (like the use of ivory), it is only a small activist subset of the population that matters.[102] Whatever the ordinary person on the street thinks, it is these activists who take to social media and to the streets to put pressure on policymakers. Can public opinion on human rights affect government policy in more authoritarian countries and one-party states? If so, when?

Perhaps the most likely means by which members of the public can influence autocrats' actions on human rights is through mass online outcries. In places like China where civil society is heavily suppressed, members of the public are less likely to provide direct material support for the work of NGOs or activist groups.[103] While street protests and petitions do occur on local issues like environmental degradation, factory closures, or housing demolitions, they are far less common on sensitive human rights issues that cross social and political groups.[104] And mass online outcries have seemingly influenced the CCP's policies on issues as sensitive as criminal justice and women's rights. The weight of public opposition expressed through social media sites like *Weibo* and *Weixin* has appeared to spill into media commentary and provide real support for human rights activists seeking to change government policy. Women's rights activists pressed for years for a nationwide law against domestic violence—a law that was finally implemented in 2016—but their efforts arguably could not have succeeded without an extensive online outcry and subsequent mass media attention to the issue throughout 2015 and 2016.

If the public is content with the state of their civil liberties, the extent of gender equality and domestic violence legislation, or the treatment of minority groups, then it is much more difficult for activist groups to pressure the government into change. While a supportive atmosphere may advance the cause of human rights, antagonistic public opinion may hurt their ability to achieve change. This is especially likely on issues that directly affect only a small proportion of the population, such as religious rights for Tibetans, a minority group who may require a broader coalition to make their voices heard. And a broad coalition may be critical in authoritarian regimes, where small groups of activists hold little political influence but where the government may respond to a popular outcry for—at least incremental—change. If foreign pressure damages that broad coalition, then it may damage a route toward liberalization.

I should stress again that this finding absolutely does not seek to challenge the numerous positive stories of human rights pressure making a real impact on state behavior. As I have noted, foreign pressure has certainly appeared to contribute to the release of prisoners like the feminist five,[105] and many activists I spoke to in mainland China and in Hong Kong openly welcomed foreign support for their efforts.[106] Some were very aware that this overseas attention might turn off a few members of the public, but still, for these groups, it was worth it, because the pressure put on government leaders from outside might be more directly effective in bringing genuine policy change.

My own work provides some (limited) support for this. Using the US Congress's database of political prisoners in China, I find that public attention from Amnesty International, the US State Department, and the *New York Times* is not effective in pushing the Communist Party to release its political prisoners early from their sentences. But international publicity does make jailed activists and dissidents significantly more likely to be released on bail and not taken to trial in the first place. In China at least it appears that foreign advocacy is not too effective once prisoners are sentenced but may be very useful in persuading authorities not to sentence them to long prison terms.[107]

And the CCP has employed all its economic and political tools to dissuade foreign states from targeting China in the United Nations,[108] from meeting with the Dalai Lama,[109] and from awarding human rights prizes to its dissidents.[110] This is hardly the behavior of a state that welcomes foreign attention on its human rights, and there are certainly plenty of reasons China would not welcome the attention. It has the potential to tarnish the country's image around the world, embarrass the leaders, damage diplomatic relationships, reduce trade and foreign investment, and, in severe cases, lead to material sanctions.

But we should not forget that none of these negative consequences have stopped the CCP from copiously advertising this pressure to its own public. While human rights condemnation may lead to plenty of diplomatic pain, it may also have very different impacts domestically. And one thing that human rights advocates agree upon is that the best way to squeeze a government is from both sides at once—international pressure from above and domestic pressure from below.[111] This is what is known as the "comprehensive approach," pressure that imposes costs on the elites directly, but also indirectly, by encouraging public support for domestic activism.[112]

This book shows that—in authoritarian states at least—these two tactics may not work together so smoothly. Pressure from above can harm pressure from below. International efforts may reduce the likelihood that members of the public will support the cause of domestic groups looking to fight human rights violations or illiberal policies. In other words, what calls for a "comprehensive approach" miss is that regimes can fight back, manipulating top-down pressure to reduce the effectiveness of bottom-up pressure, so that the international dimensions that push a regime to liberalize may be the very things that make it easier to resist domestic pressures to do so.

In fact, what is most successful from above may even be the most counterproductive from below. Top-down pressure relies on leverage: states will be more likely to change their behavior when they are weak and their accusers are powerful.[113] In the case of China or Russia, human rights pressure that is most successful in pressing leaders to make concessions will come from high-leverage sources like the United States—a geopolitical opponent and precisely the kind of source that appears most hostile and is most likely to reduce public support for human rights activists.

Human Rights Policy

To be most effective, human rights pressure needs to account for these contradictions. To begin with, policymakers should be clear who the targets of their efforts to improve human rights are: whether they are the government elites, the international community, domestic opposition groups, or members of the public. Let's take the example of whether a country's leader should meet with the Dalai Lama. What is the purpose of the meeting? If it is to raise awareness among members of the Chinese public about the lack of political rights in their country, the efforts are clearly failing, as shown in chapter 7. If the goal is to provide moral resources and encouragement to activists in Tibet, then it may have some level of success, even while reducing the overall effectiveness of those protests by cutting public support through the rest of the country.

On the other hand, meeting the Dalai Lama may not be about domestic populations at all. Leaders may be hoping to demonstrate to Beijing their resolve, their commitment to stand up to human rights violations. In this case, external pressure has a very different goal, which is not concerned with the response of Chinese citizens or Tibetan activists but instead designed to make CCP elites think about their country's reputation. But even if this is the goal, policymakers should be aware that their attempts are likely to be played out to the country's domestic audiences. If threats, sanctions, or admonishments are public, then citizens are likely to find out.

So all else being equal, when should the international community publicly pressure China's rulers over their treatment of human rights? China's economic and military power means that its leaders' vulnerability to international pressure is low. This means that on issues that the CCP perceives as being vital to its rule, such as limits on political or civil freedoms, international pressure is unlikely, by itself, to force leaders to change course. If there is any change, it would need to come from a long-term, sustained, bottom-up push from liberal politicians and civil society groups. If this book is correct, then public international pressure could reduce the support that push gets from members of the public.

But there are also cases where the party can make some concessions without seeing them as existential threats to the regime. Changing the law on domestic violence or releasing low-profile women's rights activists, for example, would hardly count as major threats to the CCP's hold on power.[114]

In some of these cases, domestic pressure will be the main driver of change. Longer-term legislative changes like the creation of a law against domestic violence or liberalization of the death penalty have often come out of concerted campaigns from domestic activists, rather than direct pressure on Chinese leaders on the international stage. In these kinds of cases, international shaming may not just be ineffective, but may even risk imperiling popular support for activists. Only when public grievances on the issue are already high, such as over urban air pollution (as shown in chapter 7), will shaming potentially have a positive impact.

And then there are cases that are not existential threats to CCP rule, but where domestic pressure is not the only way that the party will change its behavior. An example of this kind of case might include the decision to release the feminist five in 2015. By itself, the international embarrassment for the CCP was apparently strong enough to ensure that authorities released the activists. Since the party did not face any real domestic costs from releasing five feminist activists on bail, leaders had no need to drum up the public's support for continuing to incarcerate them. And perhaps for this reason, all the foreign criticism, threats, and heartfelt appeals were barely mentioned by state media, and the activists were quietly released from detention. It is on these kinds of cases—cases that only need short-term and low-cost concessions—that high and sustained levels of public international pressure appear to be most effective in influencing leaders in Beijing.

Think back to the condemnation from African countries of the racial discrimination in Guangzhou in early 2020. The condemnation itself was a rare occurrence, but so was the rapid response from authorities. Just a few weeks after the outcry, Guangzhou officials issued a tranche of new regulations that forbade hotels, malls, and restaurants from refusing service to people based on features like their skin color or race.[115] The policy change does not seem to have come out of any domestic outcry, not least because the criticism was either ignored or censored in the media. The fact that the new regulations were not widely advertised at home but published on Chinese embassy websites across Africa suggests that the swift reaction was designed to minimize the diplomatic fallout.[116] China's relationships with African countries were clearly more important to the central government than permitting local officials to racially discriminate when dealing with the coronavirus. The fact that the pressure came on a localized issue and came primarily from allies meant that it was far less likely to be successfully weaponized as CCP propaganda.

This highlights a second contribution of this book: if the international community does choose to publicly apply pressure on authoritarian regimes, then there are certain kinds of pressure that will be less likely to backfire. First, pressure should be carried out wherever possible by allies, or at least parties perceived to be reasonably neutral. If geopolitical rivals need to take part, then they should do so when bilateral relations are at their most positive. The content of the pressure is also important. Pressure will be less likely to be effective on issues closely tied to the nation's interest or integrity, such as the rights of minorities in separatist regions like Kashmir and Catalonia. When pressure does address these issues, it may receive more popular support when it explicitly focuses on the issue as a violation of individual rights rather than a suppression of a minority group's right to self-determination.

Pressure that explicitly targets government leaders will also be less likely to evoke a defensive reaction. While this kind of pressure may be censored in more authoritarian states, the link between the leadership elites and the nation as a whole might be broken in other ways, for example, if the public views their leaders as betraying the nation in an international dispute, or as failing to satisfactorily provide for their needs. In a similar way, pressure on states with strong partisan political divides will be far less likely to backfire than pressure on one-party states where the ruling party has cultivated a close link to the nation.

And finally, factual reporting of new human rights abuses will be less likely to backfire than demands for governments to change their existing long-standing policies. Look back to the role of Voice of America in the late 1980s in passing on unfiltered news about human rights abuses. There is even evidence that this kind of naming of specific incidents, if high profile and prominent enough, like the news of shootings around Tiananmen Square in 1989 or Tibet in 2008, may eventually push the regime's media to address the abuses, further raising awareness of the issue among the population.

As an example, take international criticism of Chinese authorities' reaction to the COVID-19 epidemic. My experiment in the United Kingdom shows that at the early stages, foreign criticism of the Conservatives' policies made people more aware of their government's failures. And the evidence from this book suggests that international pressure might have had a similar impact in China at the epidemic's emergence in January and February 2020. At this time, news about authorities' delayed response to the outbreak was still coming through and domestic criticism was growing. External disapproval would have shone a light onto the initial cover-up and played into public disaffection and, if it had come from multilateral groups like the World Health Organization, may even have appeared like a genuine international effort to help contain the virus. By the time we reached May, however, there was little new to say about the events of December and January, and domestic public opinion had calcified in support of the government's successful later containment of the virus. At this time, the Trump administration's openly disingenuous efforts to repeatedly attack China's response were much more likely to backfire.

The point is that while autocrats may well censor the most effective pressure, with the right timing, targeting, topic, and source, the international human rights community can minimize the likelihood that its actions will be used as propaganda tools. There is a swell of populist and nationalist authoritarians rising across the globe, and while criticism, threats, and entreaties irritate, embarrass, and cajole these leaders on the international stage, without careful consideration they may strengthen and embolden them at home.

APPENDIX 1

Database and Regression Tables for Chapter 5

Here is a short summary of the data used in this chapter and some of the main statistical results. For full information on how the data was constructed and full statistical tables, please see jamiegruffyddjones.com.

To create a sample database of this information I used media, nongovernmental organization (NGO), governmental, and international organizational sources. I began with the *Lexis Nexus* database and recorded all instances of foreign criticism and other pressure on human rights in China mentioned in English-language news stories since 1979. To supplement this I used official sources: UN draft resolutions or official reports on human rights in China (http://www.un.org/en/sc); European Parliament resolutions on human rights in China (http://www.europarl.europa.eu/); US congressional bills, acts and resolutions, and sanctions on human rights in China; Congressional Executive Committee on China annual reports (https://www.congress.gov and http://www.cecc.gov/); and reports from the two major NGOs working on human rights in China, Human Rights Watch and Amnesty International (https://www.hrw.org/ and https://www.amnesty.org/en/). I also examined all resolutions and official statements from regional groupings. Almost all the resolutions and statements from these groupings are purely directed at their region, however, so very few address human rights in China. Finally, I included all instances of meetings between country leaders and the Dalai Lama (https://www.dalailama.com).

Table A1.1 Descriptive Statistics about Number of Cases of Pressure on Human Rights in China and Proportion of Cases Reported in *People's Daily*, 1979–2011

	Total Cases of Pressure, 1979–2011	Total Cases Reported in *People's Daily*, 1979–2011	Proportion of Cases Reported
All pressure	1,337	228	0.1735
From the United States	461	149	0.323
From other Western sources	311	49	0.158
From non-Western sources	59	2	0.034
Total from the United Nations	96	19	0.198
From international NGOs	434	14	0.032
Pressure on issues of territorial integrity	436	101	0.229
Specific pressure	251	10	0.040
General pressure	742	178	0.239
Policy pressure	171	45	0.263
Also reported in the *New York Times*	229	80	0.351

Table A1.2 Predicted Probability of Reporting International Pressure in the *People's Daily* (人民日报) by Source of Pressure

	With All United Nations	With UN Split
United States	0.289	0.297
	(0.0264)	(0.0269)
Other West	0.137	0.136
	(0.0212)	(0.0211)
Non-West	0.0262	0.0263
	(0.0186)	(0.0187)
International NGO	0.0570	0.0549
	(0.0159)	(0.0154)
United Nations (all)	0.209	
	(0.0473	
United Nations (draft resolutions)		0.901
		(0.112)
United Nations (not draft resolutions)		0.0519
		(0.0297)
Observations	1,166	1,166

Standard errors in parentheses.

Table A1.3 Predicted Probability of Reporting International Pressure in the *People's Daily* by Type of Pressure

	All Reports
General	0.157
	(0.0162)
Policy	0.256
	(0.0367)
Specific	0.0652
	(0.0208)
Observations	1,337

Standard errors in parentheses.

Table A1.4 Predicted Probability of Reporting International Pressure in the *People's Daily* by Topic of Territorial Integrity

	All Reports
Nonterritorial	0.118
	(0.0188)
Territorial	0.197
	(0.0518)
Observations	1,337

Standard errors in parentheses.

Table A1.5 Predicted Probability of Reporting International Pressure in the *People's Daily* by Whether Pressure Has Previously Appeared in the *New York Times*

	All Reports
Not reported in *New York Times*	0.125
	(0.006)
Reported in *New York Times*	0.238
	(0.0381)
Observations	1,337

Standard errors in parentheses.

Table A1.6 Timing of All Reported US Pressure in the *People's Daily*

	US Pressure Only: Chinese Visit to United States in Last 28 Days	US Pressure Only: US Visit to China in Last 28 Days	US Pressure Only: US Visit to China in Last 7 Days
International incidents with the United States last 28 days	0.0959*** (0.0321)	0.0887*** (0.0324)	0.0887*** (0.0324)
Chinese official visit to United States last 28 days	−0.016*** (0.0045)		
US official visit to China last 28 days		0.0006 (0.0079)	
US official visit to China last 7 days			−0.0201*** (0.0061)
US pressure last 28 days	0.0141*** (0.00216)	0.0136*** (0.00214)	0.0136*** (0.00214)
New York Times stories last 28 days	−0.0064* (0.0039)	−0.00603 (0.00391)	−0.00605 (0.00388)
Unrest last 28 days	1.38e-05** (6.79e-06)	−1.36e-05** (6.89e-06)	−1.36e-05** (6.89e-06)
Repression last 28 days	1.90e-05* (8.46e-06)	1.98e-05* (8.41e-06)	1.97e-05* (8.41e-06)
Lianghui and next 28 days	0.0666*** (0.0180)	0.0331*** (0.00835)	0.0332*** (0.00847)
Date	1.05e-06** (4.43e-07)	−9.53e-07** (4.48e-07)	−1.00e-06** (4.47e-07)
Constant	−0.0396*** (0.00796)	−0.0397*** (0.00809)	−0.0399*** (0.00808)
N	12,025	12,025	12,025

Standard errors in parentheses.

*** $p < 0.01$, ** $p < 0.05$, * $p < 0.1$.

APPENDIX 2
Regression Table for Chapter 8

Table A2.1 Impact of Dalai Lama (DL) Meeting and its Interaction with People's Stated Level of National Pride on Perceptions of China's Level of Democracy

	DL Meeting Only		Interaction of Meeting and National Pride	
	Ordered Logit	Ordinary Least Squares	Ordered Logit	Ordinary Least Squares
	Province Controls	Province Fixed Effects	Province Controls	Province Fixed Effects
Dalai Lama meeting	0.359***	0.569***	−1.295**	−0.977
	(0.105)	(0.140)	(0.580)	(0.663)
National pride			0.279***	0.312***
			(0.100)	(0.114)
DL * pride			0.461***	0.429**
			(0.161)	(0.182)
Urban	0.275**	0.508***	0.251**	0.440***
	(0.110)	(0.143)	(0.111)	(0.141)
Birth year	−0.0170***	−0.0244***	−0.0170***	−0.0233***
	(0.00364)	(0.00437)	(0.00365)	(0.00433)
Education level	−0.0852***	−0.0722**	−0.0981***	−0.0912***
	(0.0290)	(0.0349)	(0.0292)	(0.0347)
Female	−0.00264	0.183	−0.00242	0.174
	(0.106)	(0.129)	(0.106)	(0.128)
Buddhist	0.201	−0.0494	0.283	0.0365
	(0.183)	(0.218)	(0.182)	(0.217)
Tibetan minority province	0.186		0.155	
	(0.169)		(0.169)	
Provincial Purchasing Power Parity (PPP)	−5.34e-05***		−6.12e-05***	
	(1.81e-05)		(1.82e-05)	
Constant cut1	−37.69***		−36.93***	
	(7.061)		(7.111)	
Constant cut2	−36.97***		−36.21***	
	(7.059)		(7.109)	
Constant cut3	−36.30***		−35.51***	
	(7.058)		(7.107)	

Table A2.1 *Continued*

	DL Meeting Only		Interaction of Meeting and National Pride	
	Ordered Logit	Ordinary Least Squares	Ordered Logit	Ordinary Least Squares
	Province Controls	Province Fixed Effects	Province Controls	Province Fixed Effects
Constant cut4	−35.90*** (7.057)		−35.11*** (7.106)	
Constant cut5	−34.84*** (7.054)		−34.01*** (7.104)	
Constant cut6	−34.17*** (7.052)		−33.32*** (7.102)	
Constant cut7	−33.46*** (7.050)		−32.58*** (7.099)	
Constant cut8	−32.45*** (7.046)		−31.54*** (7.095)	
Constant cut9	−31.91*** (7.044)		−31.00*** (7.094)	
Constant		53.91*** (8.471)		50.86*** (8.432)
N	1,221	1,221	1,213	1,213
R-squared		0.070		0.096
Number of provinces		21		21

***$p < 0.01$, **$p < 0.05$, *$p < 0.1$.

Results are given for ordered logit models, with provinces as controls, and for ordinary least squares models, using provincial fixed effects.

APPENDIX 3

Details of Survey Experiment in the United Kingdom, 2020, for Chapter 9

The survey was taken by 418 British respondents through Amazon's Mechanical Turk platform, from April 22 to 25, 2020. Respondents were asked a number of demographic questions, including their exposure to the virus and their past voting habits, before being randomly provided with one of the two prompts listed below. (Half of Prompt 2's respondents randomly received "politicians" and half randomly received "experts." This made no difference to the results.) They were then asked questions about their opinions of the British government's response to the virus, its performance in general, and their future voting intentions.

PROMPT 1

UK Response to Coronavirus

Coronavirus-19 (COVID-19) was first identified in Wuhan, China, in December 2019 and has now reached at least 210 countries. Almost two months after the World Health Organization declared COVID-19 a "public health emergency," the British government announced a countrywide lockdown to contain the virus, including restriction on freedom of movement and the closure of pubs, restaurants, and retailers.

PROMPT 2

Foreign (Politicians/Experts) Criticize UK Response to Coronavirus

In recent days, a series of foreign (politicians/health experts) have come out to heavily criticize the British response to the COVID-19 disease outbreak.

Coronavirus-19 (COVID-19) was first identified in Wuhan, China, in December 2019 and has now reached at least 210 countries. Almost two months after the World Health Organization declared COVID-19 a "public health emergency," the British government announced a countrywide lockdown to contain the virus, including restriction on freedom of movement and the closure of pubs, restaurants, and retailers.

Notes

Chapter 1

1. Reprinted in Solzhenitsyn, Aleksandr (2018) *Détente, Democracy and Dictatorship*, 37. Routledge.
2. Zissis, C. (2007) Backgrounder: Olympic pressure on China. *New York Times*, 4 May.
3. See Dean, R. N. (1980) Contacts with the West: The dissidents' view of Western support for the human rights movement in the Soviet Union. *Universal Human Rights*, 2, 47; Peterson, C. (2012) *Globalizing Human Rights: Private Citizens, the Soviet Union, and the West*. Vol. 1. Routledge. According to Soviet dissident Yuri Galanskov: "The Western press, and especially the Western radio stations broadcasting in Russian publicize the arbitrariness and acts of crude coercion by Soviet official personnel, and thus force the state bodies and officials to take action. In this way the Western press and radio are fulfilling the tasks of what is at present lacking in Russia, an organized opposition, and thereby stimulating out national development." Quoted in Dean, R. N. (1980), 54.
4. Turn to chapter 4 for a discussion of these events in full.
5. Recent political science studies have found that under certain conditions public shaming, international law, economic sanctions, and military intervention can all reduce human rights violations. For a couple of examples on the impact of **shaming**, see Hendrix, C. S., & Wong, W. H. (2013) When is the pen truly mighty? Regime type and the efficacy of naming and shaming in curbing human rights abuses. *British Journal of Political Science*, 43(3), 651–672; Murdie, A. M., & Davis, D. R. (2012) Shaming and blaming: Using events data to assess the impact of human rights INGOs. *International Studies Quarterly*, 56(1), 1–16. On **law**, see, for example: Simmons, B. A. (2009) *Mobilizing for Human Rights: International Law in Domestic Politics*. Cambridge University Press; Lupu, Y. (2015) Legislative veto players and the effects of international human rights agreements. *American Journal of Political Science*, 59(3), 578–594. On **sanctions**: Peksen, D. (2009) Better or worse? The effect of economic sanctions on human rights. *Journal of Peace Research*, 46(1), 59–77; Krain, M. (2014) The effects of diplomatic sanctions and engagement on the severity of ongoing genocides or politicides. *Journal of Genocide Research*, 16(1), 25–53. And on **military interventions**: Murdie, A., & Davis, D. R. (2010) Problematic potential: The human rights consequences of peacekeeping interventions in civil wars. *Human Rights Quarterly*, 32(1), 50–73; Bell, S. R., Murdie, A., Blocksome, P., & Brown, K. (2013) "Force multipliers": Conditional effectiveness of military and INGO human security interventions. *Journal of Human Rights*, 12(4), 397–422.

6. Foot, R. (2000) *Rights beyond Borders: The Global Community and the Struggle over Human Rights in China*. Oxford University Press.
7. Kent, A. (2011) *China, the United Nations, and Human Rights: The Limits of Compliance*. University of Pennsylvania Press; Wan, M. (2001) *Human Rights in Chinese Foreign Relations: Defining and Defending National Interests*. University of Pennsylvania Press; Kinzelbach, K. (2013) Resisting the Power of Human Rights: The People's Republic of China. In: Risse, T., & Sikkink, K. (eds.) *The Persistent Power of Human Rights: From Commitment to Compliance*. Cambridge University Press, 164–181. We are primarily talking about civil and political rights here. China's performance in economic and social rights (the right to work, education, housing, health, and food) has improved dramatically since the 1980s (see Alston, P. [2016] How seriously does China take economic and social rights? *Unpublished Manuscript*). But the international human rights community has rarely targeted China over these rights.
8. Economist Intelligence Unit's Democracy Index 2020. See https://www.eiu.com/topic/democracy-index.
9. Freedom House's Freedom in the World Index. See https://freedomhouse.org/countries/freedom-world/scores.
10. Reporters Without Borders' World Press Freedom Index 2020. See https://rsf.org/en/world-press-freedom-index.
11. See, for example: Norris, P., & Inglehart, R. (2018) *Cultural Backlash: The Rise of Authoritarian Populism*. Cambridge University Press; Carothers, T. (2006) The backlash against democracy promotion. *Foreign Affairs*, 85(2), 55–68; Risse, T., & Babayan, N. (2015) Democracy promotion and the challenges of illiberal regional powers: introduction to the special issue. *Democratization*, 22(3), 381–399.
12. Kinzelbach, K. (2013); Keck, M., & Sikkink, K. (1998) *Activists beyond Borders: Advocacy Networks in International Politics*. Cornell University Press.
13. Richardson, S. (2016) How to deal with China's human rights abuses. *Human Rights Watch*, 1 September.
14. Nathan, A. J. (1994) Human rights in Chinese foreign policy. *China Quarterly*, 139, 622–643; Kent, A. (2011) *China, the United Nations, and Human Rights: The Limits of Compliance*. University of Pennsylvania Press.
15. Nathan, A. J. (1994), 643.
16. World Values Survey (2018). See www.worldvaluessurvey.org.
17. On the CIRI empowerment index see http://www.humanrightsdata.com/.
18. Washington Post (2015) China's domestic violence law is a victory for feminists. But they say it doesn't go far enough. *Washington Post*, 29 December.
19. Diplomat (2014) Is China rethinking the death penalty? *The Diplomat*, 26 November
20. Kinzelbach, K. (2014) *The EU's Human Rights Dialogue with China: Quiet Diplomacy and Its Limits*. Routledge, 179.
21. Christian Science Monitor (2012) In China, public outcry softens sentence for Wu Ying. *Christian Science Monitor*, 22 May.
22. Ibid.
23. Wang, J., & Lu, Y. (2012) Social issues and judicial justice: Using the Li Chang Kui case to understand the impact of public opinion on the death penalty. *Legal System*

and Economy, 2. (As with other Chinese sources, title translated from Chinese by the author.)
24. Christian Science Monitor (2011) China's debate on the death penalty becomes increasingly open. *Christian Science Monitor*, 28 September.
25. Roth, K. (2015) For human rights, majority opinion isn't always important. *Open Democracy*.
26. Koo, J. W. (2015) Public opinion on human rights is the true gauge of progress. *Open Democracy*.
27. Hassid, J., & Brass, J. N. (2014) Scandals, media and good governance in China and Kenya. *Journal of Asian and African Studies*.
28. Davis, D. R., Murdie, A., & Steinmetz, C. G. (2012) "Makers and shapers": Human rights INGOs and public opinion. *Human Rights Quarterly*, 34(1), 199–224; Ausderan, J. (2014) How naming and shaming affects human rights perceptions in the shamed country. *Journal of Peace Research*, 51(1), 81–95; Marinov, N. (n.d.) International Actors as Critics of Domestic Freedoms. *Working Paper*; Hendrix, C. S., & Wong, W. H. (2013).
29. Simmons, B. A. (2009); McEntire, K. J., Leiby, M., & Krain, M. (2015) Human rights organizations as agents of change: An experimental examination of framing and micromobilization. *American Political Science Review*, 109(3), 407–426; Gulnaz A., Chilton, A. S., & Usman, Z. (n.d.) The Effect of Endorsement from International Organizations on Support for Women's Rights: Evidence from an Experiment in Pakistan. *Working Paper*; Wallace, G. P. R. (2013) International law and public attitudes toward torture: An experimental study. *International Organization*, 67, 105–140; Chilton, A. S. (2014) The influence of international human rights agreements on public opinion: An experimental study. *Chicago Journal of International Law*, 15, 110–137.
30. Davis, D. R., Murdie, A., & Steinmetz, C. G. (2012); Ausderan, J. (2014); Marinov, N. (2016).
31. Kuran, T. (1991) Now out of never: The element of surprise in the East European revolution of 1989. *World Politics*, 44(1), 7–48.
32. Geddes, B., & Zaller, J. (1989) Sources of popular support for authoritarian regimes. *American Journal of Political Science*, 33(2), 319–347, 319.
33. Orttung, R., & Walker, C. (2014) Authoritarian regimes retool their media-control strategy. *Washington Post*, 10 January.
34. https://www.freedomhouse.org/sites/default/files/Worst%20of%20the%20Worst%202012%20final%20report.pdf.
35. International Business Times (2015) Xi Jinping UK state visit: Who are the protesters targeting China's leader and what do they want? *International Business Times*, 20 October.
36. New York Times (2015) Xi Jinping's Britain visit ends amid criticism of arrest of dissidents in London. *New York Times*, 23 October.
37. China Digital Times (2014) Minitrue: China ranks 175th in Press Freedom Index. *China Digital Times*, 12 February.
38. China Digital Times (2014) Minitrue: Scrub Obama's call for open internet. *China Digital Times*, 14 November.
39. In the World Values Survey Fourth Wave, from 2000 to 2004.

40. Author's database.
41. Guardian (2016) Ilham Tohti, Uighur imprisoned for life by China, wins major human rights prize. *The Guardian*, 11 October.
42. New York Times (2016) Ilham Tohti, Uighur scholar in Chinese prison, is given human rights award. *New York Times*, 11 October.
43. Congressional-Executive Committee on China (2011) One year after the Nobel Peace Prize award to Liu Xiaobo: Conditions for political prisoners and prospects for political reform. *Congressional-Executive Committee on China*, 6 December.
44. Guardian (2014) China condemned for charging Uighur academic Ilham Tohti with separatism. *The Guardian*, 26 February.
45. Xinhua (2016) Foreign Ministry: China strongly opposes the award given to Ilham Tohti by human rights groups. *Xinhua*, 12 October.
46. Global Times (2016) Western human rights prize given to one who "sits in jail." *Global Times*, 12 October.
47. As a small selection: Anderlini, J. (2020) Xi Jinping faces China's Chernobyl moment. *Financial Times*, 10 February; Adonis, A. (2020) Why coronavirus is China's Chernobyl. *New European*, 16 April; Topaloff, L. K. (2020) Is COVID-19 China's "Chernobyl moment"? *The Diplomat*, 4 March.
48. Gorbachev, M. (2006) Turning point at Chernobyl. *Project Syndicate*, 14 April.
49. Eribo, F., & Gaddy, G. D. (1992). Pravda's coverage of the Chernobyl nuclear accident at the threshold of glasnost. *Howard Journal of Communications*, 3(3–4), 242–252.
50. People's Daily (2020) Australian media: If in the end the CCP has taught us a lesson, what can we do? *People's Daily*, 13 March.
51. Moravcsik, A. (1995) Explaining international human rights regimes: Liberal theory and Western Europe. *European Journal of International Relations*, 1(2), 157–189.
52. Ibid.
53. Ibid., 175.
54. Some of these meetings or funding might be held in private or deliberately kept secret. While this may well be an indirect attempt to improve human rights by improving the capabilities of activist groups, if this kind of covert assistance is not made public, then it would not be a direct attempt to change the behavior of the target government.
55. Katrin Kinzelbach has an excellent analysis of private human rights diplomacy in her 2014 book: *The EU's Human Rights Dialogue with China: Quiet Diplomacy and Its Limits*. Routledge.
56. See Risse, T., Ropp, S. C., & Sikkink, K. (1999); Keck, M. E., & Sikkink, K. (1998).
57. See http://www.universal-rights.org/human-rights/human-rights-resolutions-portal/ and https://freedomhouse.org/report/freedom-press/freedom-press-2016.
58. Hendrix, C. S., & Wong, W. H. (2013).
59. See, for example, Mao Zedong's speech in 1950: Mao, Z. (1950) *Women Have Gone to the Labour Front. The Socialist Upsurge in China's Countryside*.
60. Luo, C., Ding, W. H., & Zhao, W. (2014) Factual framework and emotional discourse: News frame and discourse analysis in editorial of "Global Times" editorial and Hu Xijin's Microblog. *International Journalism*, 36(8), 38–55.

61. Financial Times (2016) Battling for influence—Hu Xijin, editor-in-chief, Global Times. *Financial Times*, 14 November.
62. Zhang, T. F., & Chen, L. J. (2014) On the nationalist tendency of the "Global Times"— Taking the Diaoyu Islands report as an example. *News University*, (3), 66–74.
63. For example: China Digital Times (2014) Minitrue: Global Times on "terrorist hometown." *China Digital Times*, 29 May.
64. New York Times (2016) Tabloid editor and ex-diplomat square off over China's foreign policy. *New York Times*, 8 April.
65. Fish, E. (2017) China's angriest newspaper doesn't speak for China. *Foreign Policy*, 28 April.
66. Although not always: Carlson, A., & Oaks, A. (2012) Is China's Global Times misunderstood? *The Diplomat*, 14 September.
67. Tai, Q. (2014).
68. Qiang, X. (2011) The battle for the Chinese Internet. *Journal of Democracy*, 22(2), 47–61.
69. For example, Radio Free Asia (2015) China's five feminists call for UN pressure on Beijing. *Radio Free Asia*, 6 July.
70. Primiano, C. B. (2015) The impact of international perception on China's approach to human rights. *East Asia*, 32(4), 401–419.
71. For example, The Inquirer (1997) Release of dissident Wei Jingsheng. *The Inquirer*, 17 November.

Chapter 2

1. Kunda, Z. (1990) The case for motivated reasoning. *Psychological Bulletin*, 108(3), 480; Taber, C. S., & Lodge, M. (2006) Motivated skepticism in the evaluation of political beliefs. *American Journal of Political Science*, 50(3), 755–769.
2. Lord, C. G., Ross, L., & Lepper, M. R. (1979) Biased assimilation and attitude polarization: The effects of prior theories on subsequently considered evidence. *Journal of Personality and Social Psychology*, 37(11), 2098; Kruglanski, A. W., & Webster, D. M. (1996) Motivated closing of the mind: "Seizing" and "freezing." *Psychological Review*, 103(2), 263; Kunda, Z. (1990).
3. Taber, C. S., & Lodge, M. (2006).
4. Tajfel, H. (ed.) (1978) *Differentiation between Social Groups: Studies in the Social Psychology of Intergroup Relations*. Academic Press.
5. Zheng, Y., & Zheng, Y. (1999) *Discovering Chinese Nationalism in China: Modernization, Identity, and International Relations*. Cambridge University Press; Pye, L. W. (1993) How China's nationalism was Shanghaied. *Australian Journal of Chinese Affairs*, (29), 107–133; Tang, W., & Darr, B. (2012) Chinese nationalism and its political and social origins. *Journal of Contemporary China*, 21(77), 811–826; Rozman, G. (2011) Chinese national identity and its implications for international relations in East Asia. *Asia-Pacific Review*, 18(1), 84–97; Tang, W., & He, G. (2010)

Separate but Loyal: Ethnicity and Nationalism in China. East-West Center; Townsend, J. (1992) Chinese nationalism. *Australian Journal of Chinese Affairs*, (27), 97–130. For a contrary perspective, see Li, L. (2015). China's rising nationalism and its forefront: Politically apathetic youth. *China Report*, 51(4), 311–326.

6. Tang, W., & Darr, B. (2012); Tang, W., & He, G. (2010).
7. Excluding people who said "don't know" or refused to answer the question. http://www.worldvaluessurvey.org.
8. Zhao, S. S. (2004); He, B. (2018) *Nationalism, National Identity and Democratization in China*. Routledge.
9. Through protests on the street: Rosen, S., & Fewsmith, J. (2001) The domestic context of chinese foreign policy: Does "public opinion" matter? In Lampton, D. M. (ed.) *The Making of Chinese Foreign and Security Policy in the Era of Reform 1978–2000*. Stanford University Press, 151–190; Weiss, J.C. (2014); Reilly, J. (2012) *Strong Society, Smart State: The Rise of Public Opinion in China's Japan Policy*. Columbia University Press; and online: Zhang, Y., Liu, J., & Wen, J. R. (2018) Nationalism on Weibo: Towards a multifaceted understanding of Chinese nationalism. *China Quarterly*, 235, 758–783.
10. Tajfel, H., & Turner, J. C. (1979) An integrative theory of intergroup conflict. *Social Psychology of Intergroup Relations*, 33(47), 74; Tajfel, H., & Turner, J. C. (1986) The social identity theory of intergroup behavior. In Worchel, S. & Austin, W. (eds.), *Psychology of Intergroup Relations*. Chicago: Nelson-Hall, 7–24; Rubin, M., & Hewstone, M. (1998) Social identity theory's self-esteem hypothesis: A review and some suggestions for clarification. *Personality and Social Psychology Review*, 2(1), 40–62.
11. Steele, C. M. (1988) The psychology of self-affirmation: Sustaining the integrity of the self. *Advances in Experimental Social Psychology*, 21, 261–302; Sherman, D. K., & Kim, H. S. (2005) Is there an" I" in "team"? The role of the self in group-serving judgments. *Journal of Personality and Social Psychology*, 88(1), 108.
12. I have drawn out the intuition behind social identity theory in broad strokes. The theory itself has taken on many nuances and critiques since its inception. For a summary see McKeown, S., Haji, R., & Ferguson, N. (2016) *Understanding Peace and Conflict through Social Identity Theory. Contemporary Global Perspectives*. Springer, chapters 1–2. The basic insight for our purposes, however, is the key role that our ingroup's prestige or status plays for our own self-esteem.
13. Martiny, S. E., & Rubin, M. (2016) Towards a clearer understanding of social identity theory's self-esteem hypothesis. In McKeown, S., Haji, R., & Ferguson, N. (eds.) *Understanding Peace and Conflict Through Social Identity Theory*, 19–32. Springer; Martiny, S. E., Kessler, T., & Vignoles, V. L. (2012) Shall I leave or shall we fight? Effects of threatened group-based self-esteem on identity management strategies. *Group Processes and Intergroup Relations*, 15, 39–55; Baumeister, R. F., Smart, L., & Boden, J. M. (1996) Relation of threatened egotism to violence and aggression: The dark side of high self-esteem. *Psychological Review*, 103, 5–33.

14. Steele, C. M. (1988); Branscombe, N. R., Spears, R., Ellemers, N., & Doosje, B. (2002) Intragroup and intergroup evaluation effects on group behavior. *Personality and Social Psychology Bulletin*, 28(6), 744–753.
15. See, for example: Chapman, T. L., & Reiter, D. (2004) The United Nations Security Council and the rally 'round the flag effect. *Journal of Conflict Resolution*, 48(6), 886–909; Baker, W. D., & Oneal, J. R. (2001) Patriotism or opinion leadership? The nature and origins of the "rally 'round the flag" effect. *Journal of Conflict Resolution*, 45(5), 661–687; Hetherington, M. J., & Nelson, M. (2003) Anatomy of a rally effect: George W. Bush and the war on terrorism. *PS: Political Science & Politics*, 36(1), 37–42.
16. Brody, R. A. (1991) *Assessing the President*. Stanford University Press; Mueller, J. E. (1970) Presidential popularity from Truman to Johnson. *American Political Science Review*, 64, 18–33.
17. Sherman, D. K., & Cohen, G. L. (2002) Accepting threatening information: Self-affirmation and the reduction of defensive biases. *Current Directions in Psychological Science*, 11(4), 119–123.
18. Green, D. P., Palmquist, B., & Schickler, E. (2004) *Partisan Hearts and Minds: Political Parties and the Social Identities of Voters*. Yale University Press; Steele, C. M. (1988); Sherman, D. K., & Cohen, G. L. (2002); Nyhan, B., & Reifler, J. (n.d.) The roles of information deficits and identity threat in the prevalence of misperceptions. *Unpublished Manuscript*; de Hoog, N. (2013) Processing of social identity threats. *Social Psychology*, 44, 361–372.
19. Hornsey, M. J. (2005) Why being right is not enough: Predicting defensiveness in the face of group criticism. *European Review of Social Psychology*, 16(1), 301–334, 303.
20. Hornsey, M. J., & Imani, A. (2004) Criticizing groups from the inside and the outside: An identity perspective on the intergroup sensitivity effect. *Personality and Social Psychology Bulletin*, 30(3), 365–383.
21. Hornsey, M. J., Trembath, M., & Gunthorpe, S. (2004) "You can criticize because you care": Identity attachment, constructiveness, and the intergroup sensitivity effect. *European Journal of Social Psychology*, 34(5), 499–518.
22. See, for example: Miller, P. R., & Conover, P. J. (2015) Red and blue states of mind: Partisan hostility and voting in the United States. *Political Research Quarterly*, 68(2), 225–239.
23. Lambert, A. J., Scherer, L. D., Schott, J. P., Olson, K. R., Andrews, R. K., O'Brien, T. C., & Zisser, A. R. (2010). Rally effects, threat, and attitude change: An integrative approach to understanding the role of emotion. *Journal of Personality and Social Psychology*, 98(6), 886; Lambert, A. J., Schott, J. P., & Scherer, L. (2011).
24. Bullock, J. G., Gerber, A. S., Hill, S. J., & Huber, G. A. (2015) Partisan bias in factual beliefs about politics. *Quarterly Journal of Political Science*, 10, 519–578. Engaging in "social competition"—from social media wars to business feuds—can be an effective way of bolstering self-esteem for groups who feel that their status is being tested or threatened (Reid, S. A., Giles, H., & Abrams, J. R. [2004] A social identity model of media usage and effects. *Zeitschrift für Medienpsychologie*, 16[1], 17–25).

25. Lau, R. R., Sears, D. O., & Jessor, T. (1990) Fact or artifact revisited: Survey instrument effects and pocketbook politics. *Political Behavior*, 12(3), 217–242; Weeks, B. E. (2015) Emotions, partisanship, and misperceptions: How anger and anxiety moderate the effect of partisan bias on susceptibility to political misinformation. *Journal of Communication*, 65(4), 699–719.
26. See http://www.culturalcognition.net/blog/2016/12/2/is-cultural-cognition-an-instance-of-bounded-rationality-a-t.html for a summary of this multipaper study.
27. De Hoog, N. (2013); Taber, M., & Lodge, C. S. (2006); Redlawsk, D. P. (2002) Hot cognition or cool consideration? Testing the effects of motivated reasoning on political decision making. *Journal of Politics*, 64(4), 1021–1044.
28. Lodge, M., & Taber, C. (2000) Three steps toward a theory of motivated political reasoning. In Chong, D. & Kuklinski, J. H. (eds.) *Elements of Reason: Cognition, Choice, and the Bounds of Rationality*. Cambridge University Press, 183–213; Taber, M., & Lodge, C. (2006); Redlawsk, D. P. (2002); Trevors, G. J., Muis, K. R., Pekrun, R., Sinatra, G. M., & Winne, P. H. (2016) Identity and epistemic emotions during knowledge revision: A potential account for the backfire effect. *Discourse Processes*, 53(5–6), 339–370; Nauroth, P., Gollwitzer, M., Bender, J., & Rothmund, T. (2015) Social identity threat motivates science-discrediting online comments. *PLoS One*, 10(2), e0117476; Nyhan, B., & Reifler, J. (2010) When corrections fail: The persistence of political misperceptions. *Political Behavior*, 32(2), 303–330; Schaffner, B. F., & Roche, C. (2016) Misinformation and motivated reasoning: Responses to economic news in a politicized environment. *Public Opinion Quarterly*, 81(1), 86–110.
29. Schaffner, B. F., & Roche, C. (2016).
30. Schaffner, B. F., & Luks, S. (2018) Misinformation or expressive responding? What an inauguration crowd can tell us about the source of political misinformation in surveys. *Public Opinion Quarterly*, 82(1), 135–147; Bullock, J. G., Gerber, A. S., Hill, S. J., & Huber, G. A. (2015); Berinsky, A. J. (2018) Telling the truth about believing the lies? Evidence for the limited prevalence of expressive survey responding. *Journal of Politics*, 80(1), 211–224.
31. Greenwald, A. G., Poehlman, T. A., Uhlmann, E. L., & Banaji, M. R. (2009) Understanding and using the Implicit Association Test: III. Meta-analysis of predictive validity. *Journal of Personality and Social Psychology*, 97, 17–41.
32. Gerber, A. S., & Huber, G. A. (2009) Partisanship and economic behavior: Do partisan differences in economic forecasts predict real economic behavior? *American Political Science Review*, 103(3), 407–426.
33. Nauroth, P., Gollwitzer, M., Bender, J., & Rothmund, T. (2015).
34. Trevors, G. J., Muis, K. R., Pekrun, R., Sinatra, G. M., & Winne, P. H. (2016).
35. Davenport, C. (2015) *How Social Movements Die: Repression and Demobilization of the Republic of New Africa*. Cambridge University Press; Lichbach, M. I. (1998) *The Rebel's Dilemma*. University of Michigan Press; Moore, W. H. (1998) Repression and dissent: Substitution, context, and timing. *American Journal of Political Science*, 42(3), 851–873.
36. Dickson, E. (n.d.) On the (In)effectiveness of Collective Punishment: An Experimental Investigation. *Working Paper*; Opp, K-D., & Roehl, W. (1990) Repression,

micromobilization, and political protest. *Social Forces*, 69(2), 521–547; Francisco, R. A. (1995) The relationship between coercion and protest: An empirical evaluation in three coercive states. *Journal of Conflict Resolution*, 39(2), 263–282; Mason, T. D., & Krane, D. (1989) The political economy of death squads: Toward a theory of the impact of state-sanctioned terror. *International Studies Quarterly*, 33(2), 175–198; Hess, D., & Martin, B. (2006) Repression, backfire, and the theory of transformative events. *Mobilization*, 11(2), 249–267.
37. Fang, K., & Repnikova, M. (2018). Demystifying "Little Pink": The creation and evolution of a gendered label for nationalistic activists in China. *New Media & Society*, 20(6), 2162–2185; Liu, H. (2019) *From Cyber-Nationalism to Fandom Nationalism*. Routledge.
38. The "naming" side of "naming and shaming."
39. Gränzer, S. (1999) Changing discourse: Transnational advocacy networks in Tunisia and Morocco. In Risse, T., Ropp, S. C., & Sikkink, K. (eds.) *The Power of Human Rights: International Norms and Domestic Change*. Cambridge University Press, 109–133.
40. See, for example, Hong Kong pro-democracy protestors' flying of the American flag in late 2019 in celebration of the President Trump's signing of the Hong Kong Human Rights and Democracy Act, which would potentially impose sanctions in the event of any crackdown. Also see Murdie, A., & Peksen, D. (2014) The impact of human rights INGO shaming on humanitarian interventions. *Journal of Politics*, 76(1), 215–228.
41. Grauvogel, J., Licht, A. A., & Von Soest, C. (2017) Sanctions and signals: How international sanction threats trigger domestic protest in targeted regimes. *International Studies Quarterly*, 61(1), 86–97. Murdie and Bhasin find more mixed results, that foreign criticism only encourages protest if there is a strong international NGO presence in the country (Murdie, A., & Bhasin, T. [2011] Aiding and abetting: Human rights INGOs and domestic protest. *Journal of Conflict Resolution*, 55[2], 163–191).
42. Della Porta, D. D. M. (2006) *Social Movements: An Introduction*. 2nd ed. Blackwell Publishing; Stephan, M. J., & Chenoweth, E. (2008). Why civil resistance works: The strategic logic of nonviolent conflict. *International Security*, 33(1), 7–44.
43. Grauvogel, J., Licht, A. A., & von Soest, C. (2017).
44. International Campaign for Tibet (2007) Crackdown on celebrations in Tibet as Dalai Lama receives Gold Medal award in week of Party Congress. *International Campaign for Tibet*, 23 January; Outlook India (2008) China arrests over 300 monks for staging protests in Tibet. *Outlook India*, 11 March.
45. There are other plausible motivations, such as defending other social groups not mentioned here. I focus on the most prominent.
46. This might range from personally being a member of a discriminated-against group to working for an organization that benefits from stricter national security practices.
47. Nyhan, B., & Reifler, J. (2019) The roles of information deficits and identity threat in the prevalence of misperceptions. *Journal of Elections, Public Opinion and Parties*, 29(2), 222–244; Nyhan, B. (2021).
48. Nyhan, B., & Reifler, J. (2010).

49. Nyhan, B., Reifler, J., & Ubel, P. A. (2013) The hazards of correcting myths about health care reform. *Medical Care*, 51(2), 127–132.
50. Schaffner, B. F., & Roche, C. (2016).
51. Wood, T., & Porter E. (2019). The elusive backfire effect: Mass attitudes' steadfast factual adherence. *Political Behavior*, 41(1), 135–163.
52. Pan, J., & Xu, Y. (2018) China's ideological spectrum. *Journal of Politics*, 80(1), 254–273.
53. Hornsey, M. J., Robson, E., Smith, J., Esposo, S., & Sutton, R. M. (2008) Sugaring the pill: Assessing rhetorical strategies designed to minimize defensive reactions to group criticism. *Human Communication Research*, 34(1), 70–98.
54. These kinds of groups, like the UN Human Rights Council Special Procedures, also provide a sense of authoritative, independent expertise. Regardless of the "hostility" of the source toward their nation, there is extensive evidence that people are much more likely to be persuaded by comments that come from a more trustworthy and expert source (see, e.g., Sternthal, B., Dholakia, R., & Leavitt, C. [1978] The persuasive effect of source credibility: Tests of cognitive response. *Journal of Consumer Research*, 4[4], 252–260; Pornpitakpan, C. [2004] The persuasiveness of source credibility: A critical review of five decades' evidence. *Journal of Applied Social Psychology*, 34[2], 243–281).
55. This argument brings up another implication. Pressure that is more coercive, like warnings of military intervention or harsh economic sanctions, should be more likely to appear as hostile than mild appeals for restraint, and therefore should be more likely to provoke a backfire. I did not have the space in this book to test this proposition, but this is a plausible extension for any future work on this topic.
56. Christensen, T. J., Garver, J. W., Hu, W., Huang, Y., Wan, M., Yu, B., Zhang, M. J., & Zhao, S. (1999) *In the Eyes of the Dragon: China Views the World*. Rowman & Littlefield. This rhetoric has increased in recent years. See, for example: Kuo, L. (2019) "We'll fight to the end": China's media ramps up rhetoric in US trade war. *The Guardian*, 23 May.
57. Quoted in Weiss, J. C. (2019) How hawkish is the Chinese public? Another look at "rising nationalism" and Chinese foreign policy. *Journal of Contemporary China*, 28(119), 679–695.
58. Tan, Q. (2011) The change of public opinion on US-China relations. *Asian Perspective*, 35(2), 211–237.
59. See https://www.pewresearch.org/global/2012/10/16/chapter-2-china-and-the-world/.
60. Medeiros, E. S. (2019) The changing fundamentals of US-China relations. *Washington Quarterly*, 42(3), 93–119.
61. The relationship between China and Pakistan, according to the then-president of Pakistan: Sharif, M. S. (2015) Xi's heartwarming visit demonstrates iron brotherhood of China and Pakistan. *Global Times*, 1 June.
62. McGranahan, C. (2010) *Arrested Histories: Tibet, the CIA, and Memories of a Forgotten War*. Duke University Press.
63. This might help explain the contradictory results from two recent studies on the impact of international law. In one experiment, Americans told that torture violated international legal agreements became more likely to oppose its use (Wallace, G. P.

R. [2013]), but in another, Turkish citizens told that their country's refugee policy was illegal under international law became even more supportive of the policy (Cope, K. L., & Crabtree, C. [2019] A nationalist backlash to international refugee law: evidence from a survey experiment in Turkey. *Virginia Public Law and Legal Theory Research Paper*, 2018-33). The issue of refugees and borders is much more closely tied to the nation and its territory than that of torture, and pressure on this issue is, therefore, more likely to backfire.

64. Tai finds that news on separatist movements is highly likely to be censored (Tai, Q. Q. [2014] China's media censorship: A dynamic and diversified regime. *Journal of East Asian Studies*, 14[2], 185–210). "Tibet" itself is also a commonly censored term, https://tibet.net/tibet-among-chinas-top-censored-search-keywords/.
65. Petty, R. E., & Cacioppo, J. T. (1984) The effects of involvement on responses to argument quantity and quality: Central and peripheral routes to persuasion. *Journal of Personality and Social Psychology*, 46(1), 69.
66. Luchok, J. A., & McCroskey, J. C. (1978) The effect of quality of evidence on attitude change and source credibility. *Southern Journal of Communication*, 43(4), 271–282
67. Hendrix, C. S., & Wong, W. H. (2013).
68. Lhasa resident quoted in *Human Rights Watch*: https://www.hrw.org/report/2010/07/21/i-saw-it-my-own-eyes/abuses-chinese-security-forces-tibet-2008-2010.
69. New York Times (2008) Bush to urge China to improve human rights. *New York Times*, 6 August.
70. Hendrix, C. S., & Wong, W. H. (2013) make this distinction.
71. Zhang, L. Q., & Dominick, J. R. (1998) Penetrating the great wall: The ideological impact of voice of America newscasts on young Chinese intellectuals of the 1980s. *Journal of Radio Studies*, 5(1), 82–101, 94.
72. Tai, Q. Q. (2016) Western media exposure and Chinese immigrants' political perceptions. *Political Communication*, 33(1), 78–97.
73. While a "specific" critique is not necessarily the same as a "novel" critique, the mechanism is the same, and in practice previously unheard criticism almost always references specific violations rather than general critiques. In chapter 5 I only examine the impact of specific violations.
74. Another consequence of this argument, again not something I test in this book, is that the size of the violation should matter. The larger the perceived injustice, the more visible and shocking the violation, and the more close to home it is for people, then the harder it is to ignore. It is harder to make people view criticism of torture and mass murder in their own community as an issue of international competition than, say, criticism of police surveillance of an unrelated ethnic group across the other side of the country.
75. Lord, C. G., Ross, L., & Lepper, M. R. (1979); Kunda, Z. (1990).
76. de Hoog, N. (2013); Steele, C. M. (1988).
77. Tajfel, H., & Turner, J. C. (1979).
78. Wimmer, A. (2017).
79. As Reicher and colleagues say, referring to twentieth-century dictatorships: "if followers identify with a group which is embodied through the leader, then an attack

on the leader becomes not only an attack on the group but also an attack on oneself." Reicher, S., Haslam, S. A., Platow, M., & Steffens, N. (2016) Tyranny and leadership. In McKeown, S., Haji, R., & Ferguson, N. (eds.) *Understanding Peace and Conflict through Social Identity Theory. Contemporary Global Perspectives*, 71–87, 81. Springer.
80. Zhao, S. (1998) A state-led nationalism: The patriotic education campaign in post-Tiananmen China. *Communist and Post-Communist Studies*, 31(3), 287–302.
81. Zhao, S. (1998); CPC Central Committee (1994) *Outline on the Implementation of Education in Patriotism*. Government Printing Office; People's Daily (1991) General Secretary Jiang Zemin's letter to Li Tieying and He Dongchang stresses the implementation of education on Chinese modern and contemporary history. *People's Daily*, 1 June
82. Bian, Y., Shu, X., & Logan, J. R. (2001) Communist Party membership and regime dynamics in China. *Social Forces*, 79(3), 805–841; Dickson, B. J. (2014) Who wants to be a communist? Career incentives and mobilized loyalty in China. *China Quarterly*, 217, 42–68
83. 2019 Statistical Bulletin of the Chinese Communist Party. See http://www.12371.cn/2020/06/30/ARTI1593514894217396.shtml.
84. Zhao, S. (2016) Xi Jinping's Maoist revival. *Journal of Democracy*, 27(3), 83–97; Fan, J., Zhang, T., & Zhu, Y. (2016) Behind the personality cult of Xi Jinping. *Foreign Policy*, 8 March; Shirk, S. L. (2018) China in Xi's "new era": The return to personalistic rule. *Journal of Democracy*, 29(2), 22–36.
85. Zhang, T., & Zhu, Y. (2016).
86. People's Daily (2018) Seize this historical opportunity. *People's Daily*, 14 January.
87. People's Daily (2013) Xi Jinping's election as president gives sails to the Chinese dream. *People's Daily*, 14 March.
88. King, G., Pan, J., & Roberts, M. E. (2013).
89. Timmons, H. (2015) How the New York Times is eluding censors in China. *Quartz*, 6 April.
90. Jones-Rooy, A. (n.d.) Legitimacy and Credibility: The Media as a Political Tool in China and Other Autocracies. *Working Paper*; Chen, J., & Xu, Y. (2017) Why do authoritarian regimes allow citizens to voice opinions publicly? *Journal of Politics*, 79(3), 792–803; Roberts, M. E., & Stewart, B. (n.d.) Localization and Coordination: How Propaganda and Censorship Converge in Chinese Newspapers. *Working Paper*.
91. Brady, A. M. (2009) *Marketing Dictatorship: Propaganda and Thought Work in Contemporary China*. Rowman & Littlefield Publishers.

Chapter 3

1. https://www.hrw.org/world-report/2012/country-chapters/china-and-tibet.
2. For example: People's Daily (2012) How does building houses for people violate human rights? *People's Daily*, 27 January (translated from Chinese by the author, as are all the following cited *People's Daily* reports).

3. Ibid.
4. People's Daily (2012) Refute Human Rights Watch's one-sided views on China's judicial reform. *People's Daily*, 28 January.
5. Roberts, M. (2018) *Censored: Distraction and Diversion inside China's Great Firewall*. Princeton University Press.
6. Zhao, Y. (1998). *Media, Market, and Democracy in China: Between the Party Line and the Bottom Line*. University of Illinois Press; Repnikova, M. (2017). *Media Politics in China: Improvising Power under Authoritarianism*. Cambridge University Press. Roberts, M. (2018).
7. Zhao, Y. (1998).
8. Edelstein, A. S., & Liu, A. P. L. (1963) Anti-Americanism in Red China's People's Daily: A functional analysis. *Journalism Quarterly*, 40(2), 187–195; Lee, C. C. (1981) The United States as seen through the People's Daily. *Journal of Communication*, 31(4), 92–101.
9. People's Daily (1959) With an evil Cold War strategy, the US uses the Tibetan insurgency to invade China. *People's Daily*, 13 April.
10. People's Daily (1959) Distorting the truth in Tibet, British newspapers reveal their imperialist ambitions and viciously attack China. *People's Daily*, 8 April.
11. List of resolutions accessed from tibet.net/wp-content/uploads/2013/10/International-rsolutions-on-Tibet.pdf.
12. People's Daily (1961) Anti-Chinese wave under US control. *People's Daily*, 23 December.
13. People's Daily (1959) Vehemently protest American hijacking of the United Nations to interfere in China's internal affairs. *People's Daily*, 24 October.
14. People's Daily (1965) Another shameful record from the UN. *People's Daily*, 21 October.
15. People's Daily (1959) Opposing American intensification of the Cold War. *People's Daily*, 24 October.
16. People's Daily (1961) Condemn America's forcing the UN General Assembly to block the restoration of China's legal rights. *People's Daily*, 25 December.
17. People's Daily (1965) Another shameful record from the UN. *People's Daily*, 21 October.
18. People's Daily (1965) Deputy Prime Minister Chen Yi held a press conference. *People's Daily*, 17 October.
19. People's Daily (1965) The United States and India once again turn the "Tibet question" into an anti-Chinese farce at the UN General Assembly. *People's Daily*, 21 December.
20. The United Kingdom's Foreign and Commonwealth archive for the period reveals concerns about attacks on the British embassy and uprisings in Hong Kong but next to no mention of any bloodshed on the mainland.
21. Foot, R. (2000), 87.
22. Cohen, R. (1987) People's Republic of China: The human rights exception. *Human Rights Quarterly*, 9(4), 447–549.
23. Chen, D. (2005) Explaining China's changing discourse on human rights, 1978–2004. *Asian Perspective*, 29(3), 155–182.

24. Foot, R. (2000).
25. Foot, R. (2000), 97.
26. Taken from http://dalailama.com/messages/tibet/five-point-peace-plan.
27. Vause, W. G. (1989) Tibet to Tiananmen: Chinese human rights and United States foreign policy. *Vanderbilt Law Review,* 42, 1575.
28. An act that sets the rules for the State Department's foreign relations.
29. Taken from http://www.dalailama.com/messages/tibet/strasbourg-proposal-1988.
30. People's Daily (1987) Tibetan people eat their own grapes. *People's Daily,* 15 September.
31. People's Daily (1987) Separatists work with the Dalai Lama to manufacture trouble. *People's Daily,* 3 October; People's Daily (1987) Lhasa riots. *People's Daily,* 4 October.
32. People's Daily (1988) Chinese embassy in Switzerland refutes Dalai Lama's speech. *People's Daily,* 23 June.
33. People's Daily (1987) US Senate passes so-called "Tibet problem" amendment. *People's Daily,* 8 October.
34. People's Daily (1987) China's American embassy condemns Congress for interfering in China. *People's Daily,* 11 November.
35. New York Times (1987) Beijing is backed by administration on unrest in Tibet. *New York Times,* 7 October.
36. Li, J. (2012) *China's America: The Chinese View the United States, 1900–2000.* SUNY Press.
37. Li, T. (1988) *Comparative Study of Reciprocal Coverage of the People's Republic of China in the Washington Post and the United States in the People's Daily in 1986: A Case Study of Foreign News within the Context of the Debate of the New World Information Order* (Doctoral dissertation, Oklahoma State University).
38. Harding, H. (2000) *A Fragile Relationship: The United States and China since 1972.* Brookings Institution Press.
39. See, for example, Ding, X. L. (2006) *The Decline of Communism in China: Legitimacy Crisis, 1977–1989.* Cambridge University Press.
40. Weiss, J. C. (2014).
41. Stockmann, D. (2013) *Media Commercialization and Authoritarian Rule in China.* Cambridge University Press.
42. New York Times (1989) Crackdown in Beijing. Excerpts from Bush's news conference. *New York Times,* 6 June.
43. New Straits Times (1989) World leaders outraged by army action. *New Straits Times,* 6 June.
44. New York Times (1989) Turmoil in China: Kremlin dismayed, says aide. *New York Times,* 9 June.
45. This is all summarized in detail by Foot, R. (2000).
46. Following a similar logic to that of Hendrix, C. S., & Wong, W. H. (2013), discussed in Chapter 2.
47. People's Daily (1989) President Bush condemns the situation in China. *People's Daily,* 8 June.

48. People's Daily (1989) Fang Lizhi "evacuation" to the American embassy. *People's Daily*, 8 June.
49. People's Daily (1989) Fang Lizhi and his wife "seek protection." *People's Daily*, 13 June.
50. People's Daily (1989) The American embassy's so-called "protection" of Fang Lizhi. *People's Daily*. 9 June.
51. For example People's Daily (1989) Voice of America makes up story of Northwest National Cotton Factory workers out of nothing. *People's Daily*, 17 June; People's Daily (1989) Voice of America continues to make things up. *People's Daily*, 19 June; People's Daily (1989) Voice of America lies about Zhang Weiping's arrest. *People's Daily*, 20 June.
52. He, Z., & Zhu, J. (1994) The "Voice of America" and China: Zeroing in on Tiananmen Square. *Journalism and Communication Monographs*, no. 143.
53. Newsweek (2015) Covering the Tiananmen Square massacre, then and now. *Newsweek*, 4 June; New York Times (1989) Voice of America has won the ear of China. *New York Times*, 9 May.
54. He, Z., & Zhu, J. (1994).
55. Schmutz, G. M. (1989) *Sociologie de la Chine et sociologie chinoise*. Librairie Droz.
56. Milwaukee Journal (1987) Voice of America broadcasts give Chinese facts—and fits. *Milwaukee Journal*, 27 March.
57. Schmutz, M. (1989).
58. Zhang, L., & Dominick, J. R. (1998).
59. Ibid., 92.
60. People's Daily (1989) The Ministry of Foreign Affairs raises serious complaints at Fang Lizhi's so-called "protection" at the US embassy. *People's Daily*, 10 June.
61. People's Daily (1989) Voice of America's indecent actions. *People's Daily*, 12 June.
62. People's Daily (1989) Voice of America continues to make things up. *People's Daily*, 19 June.
63. People's Daily (1989) Accusing the US government and Voice of America. *People's Daily*, 18 June.
64. People's Daily (1989) Accusing the US government and Voice of America. *People's Daily*, 18 June.
65. Zhang, L., & Dominick, J. R. (1998), 91.
66. Berg, J. S. (2008) *Broadcasting on the Short Waves, 1945 to Today*. McFarland, 47.
67. http://www.publications.parliament.uk/pa/cm199900/cmselect/cmfaff/574/0061310.htm.
68. Zhang, H., Dickey, D., & Jackson, D. S. (2011) *Radio Silence in China: VOA Abandons the Airwaves*. Heritage Foundation Lecture.
69. UN Sub-Commission on Prevention of Discrimination and Protection of Minorities: Resolution 1989/5.
70. The Republic of China on Taiwan had held the "China" seat in the UN Security Council until 1971.
71. Foot, R. (2000): 121.
72. Ibid.

73. UN Sub-Commission on Prevention of Discrimination and Protection of Minorities: Resolution 1991/L.19.
74. http://www.ohchr.org/EN/AboutUs/Pages/WhatWeDo.aspx.
75. Lebovic, J. H., & Voeten, E. (2006) The politics of shame: The condemnation of country human rights practices in the UNCHR. *International Studies Quarterly*, 50(4), 861–888; Vadlamannati, K. C., Janz, N., & Berntsen, Ø. I. (2018) Human rights shaming and FDI: Effects of the UN Human Rights Commission and Council. *World Development*, 104, 222–237; Wright, J., & Escribà-Folch, A. (2009). Are dictators immune to human rights shaming? Institut Barcelona d'Estudis Internacionals (IBEI). *Working Paper*.
76. Zhao, S. (2005) China's pragmatic nationalism: Is it manageable? *Washington Quarterly*, 29(1), 131–144.
77. Stockmann, D. (2013), 56; Esarey, A. (2005) Cornering the market: State strategies for controlling China's commercial media. *Asian Perspective*, 37–83; Roberts, M. E. (2018).
78. Quoted in Brady, A. M. (2017) Guiding hand: The role of the CCP Central Propaganda Department in the current era. In Brodsgaard, K. E. (ed.) *Critical Readings on the Communist Party of China*, 752–772, p. 771. Brill.
79. For example: Los Angeles Times (2004) U.N. rights panel criticizes Cuba, N. Korea. *Los Angeles Times*, 16 April.
80. This story mentioned nothing about a resolution, so I do not include it in Figure 3. People's Daily (1991) Our UN conference representative points out that Tibet is an unalienable part of China's territory. *People's Daily*, 16 August.
81. People's Daily (1989) The UN human rights subcommittee passed a China-related resolution. *People's Daily*, 3 September.
82. People's Daily (1989) Failure of an anti-China plot. *People's Daily*, 26 November.
83. People's Daily (1996) West's use of human rights to interfere in China's internal affairs fails again. *People's Daily*, 24 April.
84. Ibid.
85. People's Daily (1993) So-called "China's human rights situation" draft resolution, supported by minority of Western countries, dies in its foetal stages. *People's Daily*, 12 March.
86. People's Daily (1992) Our representative in the Human Rights Council exposes the lies of the "Tibet human rights question." *People's Daily*, 27 February.
87. People's Daily (2001) Condemn the United States for interfering in China's Internal Affairs. *People's Daily*, 19 April.
88. Foot, R. (2000), 165.
89. People's Daily (1997) Our ambassador elaborates on human rights to refute unfounded accusations. *People's Daily*, 17 November.
90. Foot, R. (2000).
91. People's Daily (2001) From international human rights law and America's "human rights diplomacy." *People's Daily*, 10 May.
92. http://www.state.gov/documents/organization/252967.pdf.

93. For example, Washington Times (2016) "Global governance crisis" causes rise in human rights abuses, State Department finds. *Washington Times*, 13 April; USA Today (2016) Syria listed as worst country on human rights, State Department report says. *USA Today*, 13 April.
94. People's Daily (1990) Foreign Ministry spokesman discusses the US State Department human rights report *People's Daily*, 22 February; People's Daily (1992) China's Human Rights Research Council comments on the US human rights report and China's re-education through labour. *People's Daily*, 3 February.
95. Chinese Embassy in the United States (2003) Human rights records in the United States. *Chinese Embassy in the United States*, 23 October.
96. People's Daily (2014) The US's anti-China "human rights war" has already exhausted its playbook. *People's Daily*, 1 March.
97. People's Daily (2011) The human rights teacher can rest. *People's Daily*, 12 April.
98. Global Times (2015) The US is too arrogant in the Sino-US human rights dispute. *Global Times*, 27 June.
99. People's Daily (2015) China releases report in fight back against American human rights allegations. *People's Daily*, 27 June.

Chapter 4

1. China Digital Times (2008) Lhasa witness, March 2008. *China Digital Times*, 16 May.
2. Human Rights Watch (2010) China: Witnesses lift veil on abuses by security forces in Tibet. *Human Rights Watch*, 21 July.
3. New York Times (2008) Violence in Tibet. *New York Times*, 15 March.
4. Telegraph (2008) Tibet protest crackdown claims up to 100 lives. *The Telegraph*, 15 March.
5. Telegraph (2008) Could Tibet be another Tiananmen? *The Telegraph*, 15 March.
6. New York Times (2008) China: CNN apologizes over Tibet comments. *New York Times*, 16 May.
7. UN News Centre (2008) Tibet: Ban Ki-moon urges restraint by authorities amid reported violence, deaths. *UN News Centre*, 17 March.
8. The White House (2008) Remarks by President Bush and Prime Minister Kevin Rudd of Australia in a joint press conference. *White House*, 28 March.
9. Reuters (2008) Taiwan criticizes China over Tibet. *Reuters*, 15 March.
10. Hindustan Times (2008) Pranab Mukherjee, Indian foreign minister. *Hindustan Times*, 22 April.
11. Voice of America Tibetan (2008) Nobel Laureates urge China to open talks with Dalai Lama. *Voice of America Tibetan*, 21 March.
12. Guardian (2008) Olympic athletes sign letter urging China to respect Tibet freedoms. *The Guardian*, 7 August.
13. European Commission (2008) Declaration by the presidency on behalf of the EU on the situation in Tibet. *European Commission*, 19 March.

14. New York Times (2008) Europe and US press China over Tibet. *New York Times*, 27 March.
15. European Parliament (2008) European Parliament resolution of 10 April 2008 on Tibet. *European Parliament*, 10 April.
16. CNN (2008) Protesting Tibetan exiles arrested in Nepal. *CNN*, 29 March.
17. China Digital Times (2008) Video: Tibet students protest on campuses in Lanzhou and Beijing. *China Digital Times*, 18 March.
18. See Hong, F., & Zhouxiang, L. (2012) The politicisation of the Beijing Olympics. *International Journal of the History of Sport*, 29(1), 1–29.
19. Hong, F., & Zhouxiang, L. (2012).
20. NPR (2008) Calls for Olympics boycott follow Tibet crackdown. *NPR*, 15 March.
21. BBC (2008) Polish PM's no to Olympic opening. *BBC*, 27 March.
22. Guardian (2008) Merkel says she will not attend opening of Beijing Olympics. *The Guardian*, 29 March.
23. BBC (2008) Sarkozy threat to Olympic opening. *BBC*, 25 March.
24. http://www.danwei.org/net_nanny_follies/youtube_blocked_in_china_1.php.
25. Wall Street Journal (2008) News of protests is hard to find in China—in media or on-line. *Wall Street Journal*, 18 March.
26. Christian Science Monitor (2008) China blocks YouTube, reporters over Tibet news. *Christian Science Monitor*, 18 March.
27. People's Daily (2008) A few people in Lhasa fight, shoot and burn. *People's Daily*, 15 March; Xinhua (2008) Tibet's representative answers reporters' questions. *Xinhua*, 15 March.
28. Guardian (2008) State TV switches to non-stop footage of Chinese under attack. *The Guardian*, 18 March.
29. HRW (2008) China's forbidden zones. *Human Rights Watch*, 22 June.
30. Barnett, R. (2009) The Tibet protests of spring, 2008. *China Perspectives*, (3), 6.
31. China Digital Times (2008) Netizens find space to comment on Lhasa riots. *China Digital Times*, 16 March.
32. Global Times (2008) Western media makes false reports about Tibet to trick the global audience. *Global Times*, 22 March.
33. For example: People's Daily (2008) China's embassies and consulates strongly condemn the violence of Tibetan separatists. *People's Daily*, 22 March; People's Daily (2008) Foreign Ministry spokesman answers journalist questions on French President Sarkozy and the Olympic Games. *People's Daily*, 27 March; People's Daily (2008) China expresses strong dissatisfaction with the EU foreign affairs ministers' informal meeting. *People's Daily*, 31 March.
34. South China Morning Post (2008) Censor loosens strings in publicity war. *South China Morning Post*, 9 April.
35. People's Daily (2008) Ignorance or prejudice. *People's Daily*, 28 March; People's Daily (2008) Black and white cannot be reversed. *People's Daily*, 27 March.
36. China Daily (2008) German news television regrets error in covering Tibet riots. *China Daily*, 14 March.

37. People's Daily (2008) China's Association for Journalists issues strong condemnation of Western media's distortions of the Lhasa incident. *People's Daily*, 27 March.
38. People's Daily (2008) Foreign Ministry spokesman answers journalist questions on the French Embassy and the Tibet question. *People's Daily*, 27 March.
39. Global Times (2008) Western media makes false reports about Tibet to trick the global audience. *Global Times*, 22 March.
40. People's Daily (2008) News workers and experts. *People's Daily*, 29 March.
41. People's Daily (2008) Violence through words. *People's Daily*, 17 April.
42. People's Daily (2008) Is attacking disabled people what Tibetan separatists call human rights? *People's Daily*, 12 April.
43. For example: People's Daily (2008) France may ask the EU whether to jointly boycott the Olympic Games opening ceremony. *People's Daily*, 24 April; People's Daily (2008) The French government advocates boycotting Chinese goods. *People's Daily*, 15 April.
44. People's Daily (2008) Word games cannot mask the true spirit of "Tibetan independence." *People's Daily*, 1 April.
45. Denis-Remis, C., Lebraty, J. F., & Philippe, H. (2013) The 2008 anti-French demonstrations in China: Learning from a social media crisis. *Journal of Contingencies and Crisis Management*, 21(1), 45–55.
46. See http://www.water-cube.com/en/other/profile/2014/110928.html.
47. China Daily (2008) CNN: What's wrong with you? *China Daily*, 2 April.
48. Weiss, J. C. (2014), 241.
49. Washington Post (2008) Beijing's crackdown gets strong domestic support. *Washington Post*, 17 March.
50. Weiss, J. C. (2014).
51. Nyiri, P., Zhang, J., & Varrall, M. (2010) China's cosmopolitan nationalists: "Heroes" and "traitors" of the 2008 Olympics. *China Journal*, (63), 25–55.
52. Telegraph (2008) Beijing Olympics 2008: Amnesty International torture ads dropped. *The Telegraph*, 16 July.
53. Kyodo (2008) Rights group says man goes missing after applying for protest in Beijing. *Kyodo*, 13 August.
54. New York Times (2008) Bush to urge China to improve human rights. *New York Times*, 6 August.
55. Telegraph (2008) Beijing Olympics 2008: Amnesty International torture ads dropped. *The Telegraph*, 6 August.
56. LA Times (2002) China censors Bush speech in print. *Los Angeles Times*, 23 February.
57. Harris, J. F., & Pomfret, J. (1998) Summit Debate Buoys U.S. Hopes. *Washington Post*, 28 June.
58. Reuters (2015) China's Xi to be feted on British trip despite criticism. *Reuters*, 19 October.
59. New York Times (2015) Xi Jinping's Britain visit ends amid criticism of arrest of dissidents. *New York Times*, 23 October.
60. Guardian (2012) India cracks down on Tibetan protests during Chinese leader's visit. *The Guardian*, 18 March.

61. Independent (1994) Li Peng finds friendly faces in Bucharest. *The Independent*, 11 July.
62. The Age (1994) Li Peng loses his cool as Germans raise rights issue. *The Age*, 9 July.
63. The Independent (1994) Chinese PM breaks off visit to Germany. *The Independent*, 9 July.
64. People's Daily (1990) On the meeting between President Weizsäcker and the Dalai Lama. *People's Daily*, 10 July.
65. For example: Xinhua (2008) The French leader's mistaken act to meet with the Dalai Lama grossly interferes with China's internal affairs. *Xinhua*, 8 December.
66. Global Times (2008) French President Sarkozy ignores China's warnings and meets the Dalai Lama. *Global Times*, 7 December.
67. The Observer (2008) Chinese web users give Sarkozy a roasting. *The Observer*, 12 May.
68. China Daily (2015) Dalai Lama meeting, a political gimmick? *China Daily*, 2 February.
69. People's Daily (2015) Calling the Dalai Lama a "good friend," what does Obama mean? *People's Daily*, 7 February.
70. Global Times (2015) Foreign media reports Obama and Dalai Lama meeting. *Global Times*, 2 February.
71. The exception being People's Daily (1995) Foreign Ministry spokesman holds press conference expressing dissatisfaction with EU interference. *People's Daily*, 20 December.
72. Amnesty International (2008) China: Call for release of Hu Jia as he receives European Parliament Sakharov Prize. *Amnesty International*, 24 October.
73. Guardian (2010) Liu Xiaobo Nobel win prompts Chinese fury. *Guardian*, 8 October.
74. Norway hosts the prize.
75. Guardian (2010) Eighteen more countries refuse to attend Nobel peace prize ceremony. *Guardian*, 7 December.
76. CNN (2010) China blanks Nobel Peace prize searches. *CNN*, 8 October.
77. China Digital Times (2010) Twitter reactions to Liu Xiaobo's Nobel Peace Prize. *China Digital Times*, 8 October.
78. Ibid.
79. Reporters without Borders (2010) Arrests, censorship and propaganda in reaction to Liu Xiaobo's Nobel. *Reporters without Borders*, 8 October.
80. Ibid.
81. CNN (2010) China blanks Nobel Peace prize searches. *CNN*, 8 October.
82. China Digital Times (2010) New directives from the Ministry of Truth, October 8, 2010. *China Digital Times*, 8 October.
83. People's Daily (2010) Peace Prize for misleading policies. *People's Daily*, 17 October.
84. Roberts, M. E. (2018).
85. People's Daily (2010) Against the wishes of the Nobel Peace Prize. *People's Daily*, 5 November.
86. BBC (2010) China jails prominent Uighur academic Ilham Tohti for life. *BBC*, 23 September.
87. Examples of some of the stories through 2014: People's Daily (2014) Central Nationalities University academic Ilham Tohti is arrested. The US puts pressure on

China. *People's Daily*, 18 January; People's Daily (2014) The US calls on China to release Ilham Tohti. *People's Daily*, 31 July; People's Daily (2014) The Chinese side's response to American calls to release Ilham Tohti: Interference in China's internal affairs. *People's Daily*, 1 August; People's Daily (2014) A case record of Ilham Tohti's trial for separatism. *People's Daily*, 24 September; People's Daily (2014) Ilham Tohti sentenced in second trial for separatism. *People's Daily*, 21 November.
88. People's Daily (2014) Central Nationalities University academic Ilham Tohti is arrested. The US puts pressure on China. *People's Daily*, 18 January.
89. Guardian (2014) China condemned for charging Uighur academic Ilham Tohti with separatism. *Guardian*, 26 February.
90. People's Daily (2014) Central Nationalities University academic Ilham Tohti is arrested. The US puts pressure on China. *People's Daily*, 18 January.
91. Xinhua (2014) A country should not use double standards to interfere in other countries' internal affairs. *Xinhua*, 2 August.
92. China Digital Times (2014) Minitrue: Ilham Tohti's life sentence. *China Digital Times*, 24 September.
93. http://blog.feichangdao.com/2014/01/xu-zhiyong-sentenced-to-4-years.html.
94. Ibid.
95. People's Daily (2014) Xu Zhiyong sentenced to four years in prison for gathering people to disturb public order. *People's Daily*, 26 January.
96. Global Times (2014) Xu Zhiyong sentenced to four years, the law's criteria are clear. *Global Times*, 27 January.
97. People's Daily (2014) The West's "plot" to support Chinese dissidents. *People's Daily*, 28 January.
98. China Digital Times (2014) Sensitive words: Xu Zhiyong, offshore money, more. *China Digital Times*, 14 February.
99. As an unscientific estimate, around 32 out of 162 total posts were critical in some way of the verdict or of the CCP. Global Times (2014) Xu Zhiyong sentenced to four years, the law's criteria are clear. *Global Times*, 27 January.
100. In this case, only three of sixty-nine posts could be deemed as being critical. Global Times (2014) The West's "plot" to support Chinese dissidents. *Global Times*, 28 January.
101. Fu, H. (2018) The July 9th (709) crackdown on human rights lawyers: Legal advocacy in an authoritarian state. *Journal of Contemporary China*, 27(112), 1–15.
102. http://blog.feichangdao.com/2015/07/sina-weibo-hides-censorship-of-lawyers.html.
103. https://www.weibo.com/2328516855/CqFqi8xtC.
104. Xinhua (2015) The Ministry of Public Security unveils the "rights defenders'" dark plans. *Xinhua*, 12 July.
105. Xinhua (2015) The American response to the detention of troublesome lawyers should be scoffed at. *Xinhua*, 14 July.
106. People's Daily (2014) The West's protection of Chinese separatists is useless. *People's Daily*, 25 September.
107. BBC (2015) Pu Zhiqiang: China rights lawyer gets suspended jail sentence. *BBC Online*, 22 December; People's Daily (2015) Pu Zhiqiang's three-year suspended sentence shows the dignity of Chinese law. *People's Daily*, 22 December.

108. Xinhua (2015) Pu Zhiqiang is sentenced to three years on probation. *Xinhua*, 22 December.
109. Global Times (2015) How can the West judge the Pu Zhiqiang case? *Global Times*, 9 December.
110. People's Daily (1994) Hong Kong people comment. *People's Daily*, 2 March.
111. People's Daily (1994) An NPC spokesman condemns the British interference in China's internal affairs. *People's Daily*, 23 April.
112. Guardian (2014) China censors images of Hong Kong protests in TV broadcasts to mainland. *The Guardian*, 29 September.
113. China Digital Times (2014) Sensitive words: Hong Kong protests. *China Digital Times*, 29 September.
114. China Daily (2014) "Occupy Central" has become a political farce. *China Daily*, 17 October.
115. Global Times (2014) America watches Hong Kong's "universal elections." *Global Times*, http://opinion.huanqiu.com/special/Hong_Kong/.
116. BBC (2014) Hong Kong protests: Leader says "external forces" involved. *BBC*, 19 October.
117. SCMP (2015) Hong Kong's Occupy protest "was an attempt at colour revolution": PLA general. *SCMP*, 3 March.
118. China Digital Times (2014) Minitrue: Reprint news of US connections to HK activism. *China Digital Times*, 26 June.
119. Financial Times (2014) UK treads softly over Hong Kong protests. *Financial Times*, 29 September.
120. Al Jazeera (2014) Obama denies US role in Hong Kong protests. *Al Jazeera*, 12 November.
121. Asian Correspondent (2014) Merkel raises Hong Kong human rights ahead of China summit. *Asian Correspondent*, 4 October.
122. Interview with the author, July 2015.
123. China Digital Times (2014) HK activists, ex-pats say "foreign forces" not behind protests. *China Digital Times*, 31 October.
124. For example, with US congressional reports: International Business Times (2014) China condemns US for distorting facts about Hong Kong protests, asks it to stop interfering. *International Business Times,* 10 October; Global Times (2015) The US reports that China's human rights are deteriorating. *Global Times*, 10 October.
125. Guardian (2014) MPs' trip to China cancelled after row over Hong Kong protests debate. *The Guardian*, 24 November.
126. Global Times (2014) Hong Kong electoral reform: The UK should be a self-respecting audience. *Global Times*, 4 September.
127. Global Times (2014) The British parliament relies on "verbal cannons" to interfere with China's internal affairs. *Global Times*, 5 December.
128. See, for example, comments under two instances of British criticism of democracy in Hong Kong: https://www.weibo.com/2656274875/BluJLsIWe?refer_flag=1001030106_&type=comment#_rnd1524145250759 or https://www.weibo.com/

1618051664/BffyOimgy?refer_flag=1001030106_&type=comment#_rnd152414
5945196.
129. China Digital Times (2014) State media and public opinion on the HK protests. *China Digital Times*, 6 October; Washington Post (2014) In Beijing, support for dialogue in Hong Kong but not democracy. *Washington Post*, 6 October.
130. Sciutto, J., Borger, G., & Diamond, J. (2019) Trump promised Xi US silence on Hong Kong democracy protests as trade talks stalled. *CNN*, 4 October.
131. Cheng, K. (2019) UK report calls for "proportionate" police response to Hong Kong protests and end to violence. *HKFP*, 1 November.
132. Mai, J., Churchill, O., & Zhou, L. (2019) China accuses US and Britain of hypocrisy over violence in Hong Kong. *SCMP*, 12 November.
133. Reuters (2019) Thousands in Hong Kong celebrate at "Thanksgiving" rally after US legislation backs supporters. *Reuters*, 29 November.
134. People's Daily (2019) Seeing the double-faced American politicians. *People's Daily*, 26 November.
135. People's Daily (2019) The international community will reject evil deeds that incite riots (Zhong Sheng). *People's Daily*, 26 November.
136. Xinhua (2019) Xinhua News Agency commentator: The US should look in the mirror and abandon its double standards on human rights. *Xinhua*, 30 November.
137. Sukumaran, T. (2019) Carrie Lam should resign over Hong Kong protests: Malaysian leader Mahathir Mohamad. *SCMP*, 4 October.
138. Based on whether the news is featured in a news source revealed in a search on the Baidu search engine, using a logistic regression and controlling for the type of prisoner, their ethnicity, religion, sex, age, province, and the date they were arrested.
139. See the next chapter for a full analysis of this data and its sources.
140. Hu Jintao (2008) Speech to the People's Daily as part of inspection work. *People's Daily*, 23 June.
141. Ibid.
142. See Fan, Y. P., & Liu, J. (2011) Unified propaganda, centralized channeling, and unified guidance—The historical evolution of the CCP's media thought in the new era. *Journal of Lanzhou University*, 39(4), 6–13 or Zheng, B. W. (2021) On the core and essence of the CCP's media thought in the past 100 years. *News Lovers*, 9.
143. Gang, Q., & Bandurski, D. (2011) China's emerging public sphere: The impact of media commercialization, professionalism, and the Internet in an era of transition. In Shirk, S. L. (ed.) *Changing Media, Changing China*, 38–76. Oxford University Press.
144. Ibid.
145. People's Daily (2009) Guiding online public opinion: Four keywords. *People's Daily*, 3 June.
146. People's Daily (2008) Dare to speak, speak early, speak well: Put in practice public opinion guidance for 2008 in the People's Daily. *People's Daily*, 24 December.
147. Roberts, M. E. (2018).

Chapter 5

1. Vox (2016) Hong Kong's disappearing bookseller controversy, explained. *Vox*, 19 January; Los Angeles Times (2016) Hong Kong publisher suspends plans for book critical of Chinese president. *Los Angeles Times*, 28 January.
2. As reported in the South China Morning Post (2016) New claim Lee Bo sent a video and a letter to his wife saying his visit to mainland was "personal decision." *SCMP*, 10 January. Also see http://www.scmp.com/topics/hong-kong-bookseller-disappearances for a summary of the events.
3. United Kingdom Foreign and Commonwealth Office (2016) *Six Monthly Report to Parliament on Hong Kong: July–December 2015*. FCO.
4. Guardian (2016) Britain accuses China of serious breach of treaty over "removed" Hong Kong booksellers. *The Guardian*, 12 February.
5. In the *People's Daily*, *Global Times*, and *South-East Online* among many others.
6. Beijing Youth Daily (2016) UK issues a report on the so-called Hong Kong problem. *Beijing Youth Daily*, 13 February.
7. Global Times (2016) The Global Times discusses British report on Hong Kong: Don't make a fuss. *Global Times*, 14 February.
8. Guardian (2013) David Cameron protests to Chinese president after UK journalist barred. *The Guardian*, 3 December.
9. Reuters (2014) U.N. rights watchdog calls for open elections in Hong Kong. *Reuters*, 23 October.
10. Parts of this chapter, including replication material, are included in Gruffydd-Jones, J. J. (2019) Citizens and condemnation: Strategic uses of international human rights pressure in authoritarian states. *Comparative Political Studies*, 52(4), 579–612.
11. Shambaugh, D. (2007) China's propaganda system: Institutions, processes and efficacy. *China Journal*, (57), 25–58.
12. Repnikova, M. (2017), 83.
13. Ibid.
14. Lei, Y. W. (2018) *The Contentious Public Sphere: Law, Media, and Authoritarian Rule in China*. Princeton University Press.
15. Lei, Y. W. (2018); Roberts, M. E. (2018).
16. Repnikova, M. (2017).
17. http://cmp.hku.hk/2016/03/03/39672/.
18. Lei, Y. W. (2018), 17.
19. Stockmann, D. (2013).
20. Using the 人民日报 (*People's Daily*) search engine.
21. I estimate versions of the following equation:

$$\text{Report of international pressure} = \alpha + \beta_1 \text{Source} + \beta_2 \text{Territorial} + \beta_3 \text{Type} + \beta_4 \text{New York Times} + \varepsilon$$

Testing instead for the number of reports, using a negative binomial model for count data, brings almost identical findings.

One concern about this design is that the types of pressure are likely to be correlated with the sources of pressure. For example, criticism from international NGOs is much more likely to be about specific abuses or jailed dissidents, whereas criticism from the US president is much more likely to be quite general. Finding that "general" pressure is reported more often may just reflect the fact that this kind of pressure is more likely to have come from the United States. To deal with this, I conduct tests using fixed effects by type when testing for the impact of the source and using fixed effects by source when testing for the impact of the type of pressure. In other words, when looking at the impact of the source of pressure, I only compare "policy" pieces to other "policy" pieces, "general" pieces to other "general" pieces, and "specific" pieces to other "specific" pieces. When looking at the impact of the type of pressure, I only compare pressure that comes from the United States to other pressure that comes from the United States, and so on. These changes bring almost identical findings. In robustness checks I also included a number of different controls, such as the date and time of year of the pressure. None of these made any difference to the results.

22. For those interested, full details of these robustness checks are available online on jamiegruffyddjones.com.
23. China Digital Times (2017) China controls information about Liu Xiaobo. *China Digital Times*, 12 July.
24. China Digital Times (2017) Despite censorship, netizens remember Liu Xiaobo. *China Digital Times*, 14 July; Global Times (2017) People waiting for China's collapse will suffocate. *Global Times*, 17 July.
25. I also include as a separate category appeals for jailed dissidents (this might include appeals for their release or criticism of their treatment in prison). I include this as a separate group because while the appeals involve specific pieces of information about a new rights abuse, the arrests could also be seen as part of existing policy decisions to crack down on crime or dissidence.
26. China Digital Times (2014) Minitrue: Scrub Obama's call for open Internet. *China Digital Times*, 14 November.
27. International Federation of Journalists (2010) Voices of courage: Press freedom in China 2010. *IFJ*, https://ifex.org/images/china/2011/02/01/voices_of_courage.pdf.
28. While we can only guess at the reasons for this, one plausible explanation is that, unlike crackdowns on political prisoners, censorship affects every Chinese person with an internet connection, and experience of censorship may adversely affect regime support (Roberts, M. E. [2018]).
29. As will be discussed in the next chapter.
30. As just one example, see People's Daily (2010) The "Google incident" is a case of prejudice. *People's Daily*, 26 January.
31. For example: Amnesty International (1992) Chiran 02/92: People's Republic of China: Drugs and the death penalty in 1991. *Amnesty International*, 1 February, reported in People's Daily (1992) Foreign Ministry spokesman speaks. *People's Daily*, 21 February; Amnesty International (1994) China: The death penalty: Unprecedented rise in death sentences and executions since September 1993. *Amnesty International*,

1 January, reported in People's Daily (1994) Our representative in Geneva refutes Amnesty International's attack on China. *People's Daily*, 24 February.
32. For example: Washington Post (2004) China rebuts U.S. criticism on rights. *Washington Post*, 31 March.
33. For example: People's Daily (1989) Voice of America makes up story of Northwest National Cotton Factory workers out of nothing. *People's Daily*, 17 June; People's Daily (1989) Voice of America continues to make things up. *People's Daily*, 19 June; People's Daily (1989) Voice of America lies about Zhang Weiping's arrest. *People's Daily*, 20 June; People's Daily (1989) Playing games with the truth, Voice of America again makes up new lies. *People's Daily*, 23 June.
34. This excludes Taiwan, since while it is an issue of territorial integrity for many Chinese, criticism of human rights in Taiwan would be directed at the Taiwanese government rather than the CCP.
35. http://tibet.net/2018/01/tibet-among-chinas-top-censored-search-keywords/.
36. Repnikova, M. (2017), 81.
37. This is highly statistically significant. These results still hold when we exclude pressure that focuses only on the traditionally "less sensitive" matter of Hong Kong.
38. Pressure that comes "from" a particular source includes comments or actions originating from any media or commercial organization, religious group or individual in that country or region, and official parliamentary, legislative, and executive comments.
39. I include the European Union, plus countries from Western Europe, Canada, Australia, and New Zealand. I do not include the former Soviet bloc as these are less likely to be seen as traditional allies of the United States.
40. I include all non-Western countries, including US allies in East Asia and those with whom China has territorial disputes, such as the Philippines and Japan. Pressure is less likely to arise from these sources in the first place and, because of the use of English-language sources, may be underrepresented in the database. However, if anything, if my hypothesis about Western and non-Western sources is correct, only including more prominent non-English-language pressure that has reached English-language media should bias my results in the opposite direction from the prediction—their relative prominence should make them *more* likely to be reported in the *People's Daily*.
41. For example: People's Daily (1989) Fang Lizhi "evacuation" to the American embassy *People's Daily*, 8 June; and People's Daily (1989) President Bush condemns the situation in China. *People's Daily*, 8 June.
42. People's Daily (1989) The UK unilaterally delays the Sino-UK conference. *People's Daily*, 18 June.
43. People's Daily (1989) On Pelosi's "double standards." *People's Daily*, 13 April.
44. People's Daily (2008) The NPC spokesman comments on the US congressional anti-China Tibet resolution. *People's Daily*, 13 April.
45. People's Daily (2008) Push through the falsehoods and uncover the truth. *People's Daily*, 27 March.
46. Polskie Radio (2008) Poland threatens to boycott Beijing Olympics. *Polskie Radio*, 15 March.

47. Guardian (2008) Merkel says she will not attend opening of Beijing Olympics. *The Guardian*, 19 March.
48. For example: Agence France-Presse (2009) France concerned over Xinjiang riots. *Agence France-Presse*, 7 July.
49. BBC (2009) Turkey calls international community to show more concern for China's Uighurs. *BBC*, 9 July.
50. BBC (2009) Iran daily deplores government "indifference" to "killings" in Xinjiang. *BBC*, 13 July.
51. BBC (2009) Azeri opposition parties criticize China over "atrocities against Uighurs." *BBC*, 13 July.
52. Reuters (2009) China dismisses accusation of Xinjiang genocide. *Reuters*, 14 July.
53. http://www.oic-oci.org/topicdetail.asp?tid=256.
54. People's Daily (2009) The public falsehoods of Western media have received strong protests. *People's Daily*, 14 July; Beijing Daily (2009) A published article demonstrates the double standards of Western media. *Beijing Daily*, 13 July.
55. Al Jazeera (2020) African nationals "mistreated, evicted" in China over coronavirus. *Al Jazeera*, 12 April.
56. CBS (2020) McDonald's apologizes after restaurant in China bans black people. *CBS*, 17 April.
57. Cahlan, S., & Lee, J. (2020) Video evidence of anti-black discrimination in China over coronavirus fears. *Washington Post*, 18 June.
58. Daily Nation (2020) Kenyans in China: Rescue us from hell. *Daily Nation*, 11 April.
59. https://twitter.com/femigbaja/status/1248698266889457664.
60. France24 (2020) African ambassadors write letter of complaint to China over "discrimination." *France24*, 13 April.
61. https://www.sahrc.org.za/index.php/sahrc-media/news-2/item/2329-media-statement-sahrc-calls-for-non-discrimination-in-the-global-struggle-against-covid-19.
62. Davison, H. (2020) Chinese official: Claims of racial targeting are "reasonable concerns." *The Guardian*, 13 April; Global Times (2020) Who is behind the fake news of "discrimination" against Africans in China? *Global Times*, 16 April.
63. http://www.cidca.gov.cn/2020-04/14/c_1210558192.htm.
64. People's Daily (2020) Ministry of Foreign Affairs responds to questions around Guangdong's anti-epidemic measures for African citizens in China. *People's Daily*, 13 April; People's Daily (2020) Treat deported foreigners in accordance with the law. *People's Daily*, 13 April.
65. For example: https://baijiahao.baidu.com/s?id=1664003219991652705&wfr=spider&for=pc.
66. Global Times (2020) The Namibian ambassador criticises the "China discriminates against black people" video spreading through Africa. *Global Times*, 15 April
67. People's Daily (2020) The American side is arrogant and provocative. *People's Daily*, 14 April.
68. See Olander, E. (2020) A Western (read US) role in what's happening in Guangzhou emerges as a key Chinese message point. *China Africa Blog*, 14 April.
69. Using a time series model, I estimate versions of the following equation:

$$\text{Report of international pressure}_t = \alpha + \beta_1 \text{US Incident}_{t-1,t-29} + \beta_2 \text{War Anniversary}_{t-1,t-29}$$
$$+ \beta_3 \text{International Pressure}_{t-1,t-29} + \beta_4 \text{Controls}_{t-1,t-29}$$
$$+ \text{lag} + f(\text{Time}) + \varepsilon_t$$

70. Taken from Weiss, J. C. (2014) *Powerful Patriots: Nationalist Protest in China's Foreign Relations*. Oxford University Press. None of these incidents should be linked to foreign human rights pressure. I do not include anti-CNN protests in 2008 as these were directly linked to existing criticism.
71. Nitsch, V. (2007) State visits and international trade. *World Economy*, 30(12), 1797–1816.
72. Lebovic, J. H., & Saunders, E. N. (2016) The diplomatic core: The determinants of high-level us diplomatic visits, 1946–2010. *International Studies Quarterly*, 60(1), 107–123.
73. Drawn from the Global Database of Events, Language and Tone (GDELT). GDELT is built from automated content analysis of news articles, with upwards of 250 million global events based on open-source data from a wide range of news sources, including online sources (Schrodt, P. [2013] GDELT: Global Data on Events, Location, and Tone. Presentation for the Conflict Research Society, Essex University, 17 September).
74. Each of the time series results are robust to alternative analytical tests, controls, and time periods.
75. H. Res. 178: https://www.govtrack.us/congress/bills/106/sres103/text/is.
76. For example: People's Daily (1999) The ugly face of the human rights guardian. *People's Daily*, 16 May.
77. People's Daily (1999) The NPC spokesman comments on the US congressional anti-China resolution. *People's Daily*, 31 May.
78. Using a time series model with the same controls, $p = 0.066$.
79. One plausible explanation is that leaders have more choice over the countries they visit than the ones they receive, and that they primarily travel to those countries when they have something to "sell" or "sign," as suggested by Lebovic, J. H., & Saunders, E. N. (2016).
80. New York Times (1989) U.S. suspends high-level links to China as crackdown goes on. *New York Times*, 21 June.
81. Agence France Presse (1995) China cancels trips, warns of more response over Lee visit. *Agence France Presse*, 25 May. These retaliatory cancellations are regular occurrences even beyond the fraught US-China relationship. In 2017 Pakistan Foreign Minister Khawaja Mohammed Asif canceled his visit to the United States and visited China instead, following President Trump's criticism of Pakistan, while in 2012 top Chinese official Wu Bangguo canceled his visit to the United Kingdom in protest of Prime Minister David Cameron's meeting with the Dalai Lama.
82. The correlation between meetings and reports is a strong 0.39 (until 2012, after which the sheer importance of the relationship meant that meetings have occurred every year, regardless of the strength of bilateral relations).
83. See Kinzelbach, K. (2014).

84. There is no less American pressure at these times, and non-US pressure is reported at the same rate as at other times.
85. Again taken from Weiss, J. C. (2014).
86. King, G., Pan, J., & Roberts, M. E. (2013).
87. Lorentzen, P. (2013) Regularizing rioting: Permitting public protest in an authoritarian regime. *Quarterly Journal of Political Science*, 8(2), 127–158; Lorentzen, P. (2014) China's strategic censorship. *American Journal of Political Science*, 58(2), 402–414.
88. Plantan, E., & Cairns, C. (2017) Why Autocrats Sometimes Relax Censorship: Signalling Government Responsiveness on Chinese Social Media. *Working Paper*.
89. Miller, A. (2015) The trouble with factions. *China Leadership Monitor*, 46, 1–12.
90. Stockmann, D. (2013).
91. Shirk, S. L. (2007) Changing media, changing foreign policy in China. *Japanese Journal of Political Science*, 8(1), 43–70, 55.
92. Jones-Rooy, A. (2012); Roberts, M.E., & Stewart, B.M. (2017).
93. CNN (2003) China censors CNN SARS report. *CNN*, 15 May.
94. Wall Street Journal (2003) Quarantine China. *WSJ*, 31 March.
95. BBC (2003) China under fire for virus spread. *BBC*, 6 April.
96. CNN (2003) China censors CNN SARS report. *CNN*, 15 May.
97. People's Daily (2003) WHO commends China and ASEAN for strengthening cooperation to deal with SARS. *People's Daily*, 30 April.
98. Guardian (2008) Chinese figures show fivefold rise in babies sick from contaminated milk. *The Guardian*, 2 December.
99. ABC (2008) FDA detains many foods from China for melamine test. *ABC*, 14 November.
100. Reuters (2008) China needs more coherent food-safety system: U.N. *Reuters*, 22 October.
101. Reuters (2008) China milk scandal deplorable, says WHO. *Reuters*, 25 September.
102. ABC (2008) FDA detains many foods from China for melamine test. *ABC*, 14 November.
103. Reuters (2008) China milk scandal deplorable, says WHO. *Reuters*, 25 September.
104. Xinhua (2008) WHO assists China in dealing with "problem milk powder" incidents. *Xinhua*, 21 September.
105. Global Times (2008) WHO wants China to explain why it delayed the release of tainted milk powder. *Global Times*, 19 September.
106. Ruan, L., Knockel, J., & Crete-Nishihata, M. (2020) Censored contagion: How information on the coronavirus is managed on Chinese social media. *Citizen Lab*, 3 March, https://citizenlab.ca/2020/03/censored-contagion-how-information-on-the-coronavirus-is-managed-on-chinese-social-media/.
107. Qiang, G. (2020) As an epidemic raged, what kept Party media busy? *China Media Project*, 30 January.
108. Qiang, G. (2020) What ails the People's Daily? *China Media Project*, 24 February.

109. Ruan, L., Knockel, J., & Crete-Nishihata, M. (2020); Reuters (2020) China's online censors tighten grip after brief coronavirus respite. *Reuters*, 11 February.
110. Zheng, C. C. (2020) Covid-19 in China: From "Chernobyl moment" to impetus for nationalism. *Made in China Journal*, 4 May, https://madeinchinajournal.com/2020/05/04/covid-19-in-china-from-chernobyl-moment-to-impetus-for-nationalism/.
111. Global Times (2020) Chinese vigilant on deifying writer Fang Fang amid publication of Wuhan diary in English. *Global Times*, 8 April.
112. China Digital Times (2020) Translation: Backlash to Wuhan Diary "reveals a serious problem society must correct." *China Digital Times*, 21 April.
113. Dunst, C. (2020) Beijing's propaganda is finding few takers. *Foreign Affairs*, 20 April; Foreign Policy (2020) China's neighbors face a belligerent post-pandemic Beijing. *Foreign Policy*, 29 April.
114. See, for example, from late April: People's Daily (2020) What the United States is concealing behind the "concealment theory." *People's Daily*, 29 April; People's Daily (2020) The US Republican Party's "China attack" memo was exposed by Hua Chunying's repost. *People's Daily*, 26 April.
115. See Baidu search news results here (https://www.baidu.com/s?ie=utf-8&cl=2&medium=0&rtt=1&bsst=1&rsv_dl=news_t_sk&tn=news&word=甩锅+美国+新冠病毒) for the extent of the coverage of this topic. One example from March: People's Daily (2020) American politicians "pass the buck" to China, hurting only themselves. *People's Daily*, 21 March.
116. People's Daily (2020) US media: Pompeo is America's China-attack-dog. *People's Daily*, 12 May.
117. People's Daily (2020) Zhong Sheng: Lies will eventually be exposed. *People's Daily*, 11 June.
118. CCTV (2020) Pompeo, spreading "political viruses," is becoming the public enemy of mankind. *CCTV News*, 28 April; see Dong, D. (2020) Pompeo: "Public enemy." *China Media Project*, 7 May, for a summary of some of these outbursts.
119. Global Times (2020) Chinese vigilant on deifying writer Fang Fang amid publication of Wuhan diary in English. *Global Times*, 8 April.
120. Zheng, C. C. (2020); Kim, J. (2020). The Chinese people step up to enforce China's nationalist propaganda. *The Diplomat*, 5 May; Wang, V., & Qin, A. (2020) As coronavirus fades in China, nationalism and xenophobia flare. *New York Times*, 16 April.
121. China Digital Times (2020) Netizens demand free speech after death of disciplined Wuhan doctor. *China Digital Times*, 6 February; China Digital Times (2020) Minitrue: Control temperature on death of Coronavirus whistleblower. *China Digital Times*, 6 February; Deutsche Welle (2020) Coronavirus: Li Wenliang's death "a moment of awakening" for China. *DW*, 14 February.
122. Zheng, C. C. (2020).
123. Xie, E. (2020) Coronavirus journal Wuhan Diary continues to upset Chinese nationalists. *SCMP*, 3 May.
124. Voice of America (2020) China, Vietnam top virus response survey, but for different reasons. *VoA*, 21 May; Wu, C. (2020) How Chinese citizens view their government's Coronavirus response. *The Conversation*, 4 June.

125. Sharma, Y. (2020) Government targets academic critics of COVID-19 response. *University World News*, 12 May.
126. Quoted in Stockmann, D. (2013), 56.
127. A search for the report with the *Lexus Nexis* database reveals only two mentions in non-Chinese newspapers, both occurring after the report was featured in Chinese media.
128. Human Rights Watch (2015) World Report 2015: China, https://www.hrw.org/world-report/2015/country-chapters/china-and-tibet.
129. People's Daily (2015) Inclusive development: The emphasis of Tibet's human rights progress. *People's Daily*, 3 February.
130. Xinhua (2015) Signed article: The just path of justice reform and human rights protection. *Xinhua*, 2 February.
131. People's Daily (2015) Human Rights Watch: The broken reviewer. *People's Daily*, 2 February.
132. Gauthier, U. (2015) Après les attentats, la solidarité de la Chine n'est pas sans arrière-pensées. *L'Obs*, 18 November.
133. Global Times (2015) Why China can't stand the French reporter Guo Yu. *Global Times*, 26 December.
134. For example: People's Daily (2015) Goodbye Guo Yu, China will not see you off. *People's Daily*, 27 December.
135. For example: Guardian (2015) French journalist accuses China of intimidating foreign press. *The Guardian*, 26 December; and Reuters (2015) French journalist forced to leave China after article on troubled Xinjiang. *Reuters*, 31 December.
136. Global Times (2015) Guo Yu nakedly fights for terrorism. *Global Times*, 28 December.

Chapter 6

1. Hong Fincher, L. (2016) China's Feminist Five. *Dissent*, Fall 2016.
2. http://blog.feichangdao.com/2015/04/sina-weibo-censors-searches-about-five.html.
3. Irish Times (2015) China rejects Hillary Clinton's criticism over treatment of feminist activists. *Irish Times*, 9 April.
4. Reuters (2015) Global campaign preceded surprise move to free Chinese activists. *Reuters*, 7 May.
5. Zhao, S. L. (2015) The inspirational backstory of China's feminist five. *Foreign Policy*, 17 April.
6. Parts of this chapter are also included in Gruffydd-Jones, J. J. (2019).
7. Song, R. X., & Song, R. Z. (1624) Nu Lunyu [The Analects for Women], as quoted in Chen D. Y. (1937) *Zhongguo Funu Shenghuoshi [Women's Life in China]*, 115. Shangwu.

8. Bossen, L., Xurui, W., Brown, M. J., & Gates, H. (2011) Feet and fabrication: Footbinding and early twentieth-century rural women's labor in Shaanxi. *Modern China*, 37(4), 347–383.
9. Mackie, G. (1996) Ending footbinding and infibulation: A convention account. *American Sociological Review*, 61(6), 999–1017.
10. Levy, H. S. (1966) *Chinese Footbinding: The History of a Curious Erotic Custom*. W. Rawls.
11. Ko, D. (2005) *Cinderella's Sisters: A Revisionist History of Footbinding*. University of California Press.
12. *Chinese Recorder and Missionary Journal* (1896) December. Shanghai, 617, quoted in Whitefield, B. (2008) The Tian Zu Hui (Natural Foot Society): Christian women in China and the fight against footbinding. *Southeast Review*, 203, 207.
13. Drucker, A. R. (1981). The influence of Western women on the anti-footbinding movement 1840–1911. *Historical Reflections/Réflexions Historiques*, 8(3), 179–199.
14. Whitefield, B. (2008).
15. Appiah, K. A. (2010) The art of social change. *New York Times*, 22 October.
16. Drucker, A. R. (1981).
17. Zhao, S. S. (2005) China's pragmatic nationalism: Is it manageable? *Washington Quarterly*, 29(1), 131–144.
18. Shiying, W. (1984) Yihetuan yundong shi baokan wenzhang suoyin. [A listing of newspaper and periodical articles on the history of the Boxer movement]. In *Yihetuan yundong shi lunwen xuan [Selected essays on the history of the Boxer movement]*. Zhonghua Shuju.
19. Zhang, K. Y., & Tian, T. (2010) Xin shiji zhi chu de Xinhai geming shi yanjiu [Research on the Xinhai revolution at the start of the new century]. *Zhejiang shehui kexue*, 9, 89–98.
20. Greenhalgh, S. (1977) Bound feet, hobbled lives: Women in old China. *Frontiers: A Journal of Women Studies*, 2(1), 7–21.
21. Lee, W. Y. (1995) Women's education in traditional and modern China. *Women's History Review*, 4(3), 345–336.
22. Keck, M. E., & Sikkink, K. (1998).
23. Drucker, A. R. (1981).
24. Keck, M. E., & Sikkink, K. (1998).
25. Keck and Sikkink (1998) compare this to the campaign against female circumcision in Kenya, where powerful organized opposition among the Kikuyu successfully framed the Western campaign as a colonial attack on traditional customs.
26. Kang Youwei, cited in Appiah, K. A. (2011) *The Honor Code: How Moral Revolutions Happen*, 60. WW Norton & Company.
27. Mao, Z. (1950).
28. Zhou, J. (2013) Keys to women's liberation in Communist China: An historical overview. *Journal of International Women's Studies*, 5(1), 67–77.
29. Fincher, L. H. (2014) *Leftover Women: The Resurgence of Gender Inequality in China*. Bloomsbury.

30. Howell, J. (1997) Post-Beijing reflections: Creating ripples, but not waves in China. *Women's Studies International Forum*, 20(2), 235–252.
31. Fry, L. (2011) Chinese women and economic human rights. *Human Rights and Human Welfare*. Accessed at: https://web.archive.org/web/20180423024007id_/https://www.du.edu/korbel/hrhw/researchdigest/china/WomenChina.pdf.
32. Chia, R. C., Allred, L. J., & Jerzak, P. A. (1997) Attitudes toward women in Taiwan and China. *Psychology of Women Quarterly*, 21(1), 137–150.
33. https://data.worldbank.org/indicator/SL.TLF.CACT.FE.ZS?locations=CN.
34. Lee, J., Campbell, C., & Tan, G. (1992) Infanticide and family planning in late imperial China: The price and population history of rural Liaoning, 1774–1873. In Rawski, T. G., & Li, L. M. (eds.) *Chinese History in Economic Perspective*. Berkeley: University of California Press, 145–176.
35. Wang, Z. (1997) Maoism, feminism, and the UN conference on women: Women's studies research in contemporary China. *Journal of Women's History*, 8(4), 126–152, 127.
36. For example: BBC Online (1999) China hits back at women's rights criticism. *BBC Online*, 4 February.
37. In addition to the dramatic growth of the #MeToo movement (see Zeng, J. [2019] You say #MeToo, I say #MiTu: China's online campaigns against sexual abuse. In *#MeToo and the Politics of Social Change*, 71–83. Palgrave Macmillan, for a discussion of this movement).
38. Fincher, L. H. (2014).
39. China News (2011) China's domestic violence data is sparse, *China News*, 21 October.
40. China Daily Forum (2012) Bloody brides in abuse protest. *China Daily Forum*, 15 February.
41. See China Law Translate (2015) Thicker than water: An overview of China's new Domestic Violence Law. *China Law Translate*, 31 December.
42. Fincher, L. H. (2014).
43. NPR (2013) American woman gives domestic abuse a face, and voice, in China. *NPR*, 7 February.
44. Fincher, L. H. (2014).
45. Lü, P. (2018) Two years on: Is China's Domestic Violence Law working? *Amnesty International*, 7 March.
46. Howell, J. (1997), quoted in New York Times (1995) Hillary Clinton in China, details abuse of women. *New York Times*, 6 September.
47. Weekend Australian (1995) Strongarm tactics. *Weekend Australian*, 9 September
48. New York Times (1995) Meeting of women says surveillance by China must end. *New York Times*, 9 September.
49. Reuters (2015) Global campaign preceded surprise move to free Chinese activists. *Reuters*, 7 May.
50. Radio Free Asia (2015) Chinese activists slam ruling party's record on women's rights. *Radio Free Asia*, 28 September.
51. New York Times (2015) Despite release, feminists' case shows China's hostility toward civic action. *New York Times*, 14 April.

52. Global Times Online (2015) Social commentary: Protecting feminism is not a reason to protest on the streets. *Global Times*, 9 April.
53. Roberts, M. (2018).
54. Diplomat (2016) Why China dreads a Hillary Clinton presidency. *The Diplomat*, 10 February.
55. People's Daily Online (2015) Hillary learns how to be a big mouth and makes herself very "low." *People's Daily Online—Global Times*, 28 September.
56. BBC Online (2015) China angered by Hillary Clinton tweet on women's rights. *BBC Online*, 28 September.
57. Taken from Lowy Interpreter (2015) The backlash to Clinton's gender criticism explained. *Lowy Interpreter*, 8 October.
58. China Change (2016) Guo Jianmei, Zhongze, and the empowerment of women in China. *China Change*, 14 February.
59. For those interested in the full survey texts and outcomes, please go to jamiegruffyddjones.com.
60. See China Internet Watch (2015) *China Internet Statistics*, https://app.box.com/s/pk6vwre4unf0i4n071stncqt4q9hglnr.
61. Yang, G. (2009) *The Power of the Internet in China: Citizen Activism Online*. Columbia University Press.
62. The randomization procedure was successful with no statistically significant differences between the groups.
63. Reuters (2016) E.U. "extremely troubled" by "deterioration" of China's human rights. *Reuters*, 9 December.
64. Global Times (2016) European and American ambassadors prejudice human rights. *Global Times*, 2 February.
65. Alongside Japan—although human rights criticism rarely comes from Tokyo.
66. People's Daily (2015) Why is China-Africa cooperation thriving? *People's Daily English Language Edition*, 7 December.
67. Schatz, R. T., & Lavine, H. (2007) Waving the flag: National symbolism, social identity, and political engagement. *Political Psychology*, 28(3), 329–355.
68. Hassin, R. R., Ferguson, M. J., Shidlovski, D., & Gross, T. (2007) Subliminal exposure to national flags affects political thought and behavior. *Proceedings of the National Academy of Sciences*, 104(50), 19757–19761.
69. If we assume the scale is a continuous one.
70. Guardian (2016) Women's rights crackdown exposes deepening crisis in Chinese society. *The Guardian*, 5 February; Global Times (2016) Women's legal aid center in Beijing closed. *Global Times*, 2 February.
71. Washington Post (2016) On eve of Iowa, Hillary Clinton chides China on women's rights. Here's why. *Washington Post*, 1 February.
72. Global Times (2016) Western media hypes the Zhongze closure incident. *Global Times*, 16 February.
73. Lei, Y. W. (2018); Washington Post (2013) In China, Communist Party takes unprecedented step: It is listening. *Washington Post*, 2 August.
74. Caixin (2018) After outcry, Weibo does U-turn on gay content ban. *Caixin*, 16 April.

NOTES 217

75. Bullock, J. G., Gerber, A. S., Hill, S. J., & Huber, G. A. (2015).
76. I randomly vary the number of "likes" on the post to check whether survey respondents are genuinely treating the fake post as they would a real one. Theories of how people conform in social situations expect that greater likes, comments, and shares should make people more willing to also like the post (Asch, S. E. [1955] Opinions and social pressure. *Scientific American*, 193[5], 31–35), and this is indeed what happens, with 2,042 as opposed to 45 existing likes increasing new likes by 5.2%.
77. Appiah, K. A. (2010).
78. http://www3.weforum.org/docs/WEF_GGGR_2017.pdf. It fell to 106th place by 2020.
79. Kelley, J. D., & Simmons, B. A. (2015) Politics by number: Indicators as social pressure in international relations. *American Journal of Political Science*, 59(1), 55–70, 55.
80. China Digital Times (2014) Minitrue: China ranks 175th in Press Freedom Index. *China Digital Times*, 12 February.
81. The randomization procedure was again successful.
82. Both statistically nonsignificant increases.
83. On a technical note, this also helps address a concern with the first study, that before reading the second piece of criticism targeting government leaders, survey respondents had already answered a number of questions about their attitudes. This makes it difficult to prove whether the subsequent change in people's responses came from the second prompt or from having already answered those extra questions and thought some more about women's rights. We can, however, still make an accurate comparison against those who received no prompt, because they had answered all the same questions.
84. An increase of around 6.2 percentage points, but only significant at $p = 0.14$.
85. Weiss, J. C. (2013) Authoritarian signaling, mass audiences, and nationalist protest in China. *International Organization*, 67(1), 1–35; Weatherley, R. (2014) *Making China Strong: The Role of Nationalism in Chinese Thinking on Democracy and Human Rights*. Palgrave Macmillan.
86. One interesting question is why also providing people with something that highlights their national identity (whether exposing them to a small Chinese flag or emphasizing comparisons to other nations) should have no effect on their response to criticism of the country as a whole. Certainly, the hostility theory predicts that it would just intensify people's defensiveness. One plausible reason we didn't see this is because this kind of criticism already made people very aware of their country and how it was comparing to others. An extra flag or explicit comparison made little difference.
87. When targeting the nation, donations increase by a statistically significant 13.4 percentage points, but when leaders are targeted, donations increase only by a nonsignificant 3.8 percentage points.
88. Some see this very common diplomatic response as an especially weak reaction to foreign provocations, so people may be expressing their dissatisfaction with this language.
89. A picture of a fist made of a Chinese flag slamming into a fist of an American flag, over an image of the world.

90. For a summary of the "rally 'round the flag" effect in response to existential threats see Lambert, A. J., Schott, J. P., & Scherer, L. (2011) Threat, politics, and attitudes: Toward a greater understanding of rally-'round-the-flag effects. *Current Directions in Psychological Science*, 20(6), 343–348.
91. The percentage who either disagree or strongly disagree with the statement that women's rights are "not good enough" drops from 50.5% to 36.4% after reading about American comments.
92. Stockmann, D. (2013), 94.
93. See, for example, the overtly heavy censorship of the Panama Papers leak of Xi Jinping's family wealth or of media attacks on Xi's personalist leadership: China Digital Times (2016) Minitrue: Panama Papers and foreign media attacks. *China Digital Times*, 4 April; China Digital Times (2016) Minitrue: "Delete all content related to Panama Papers." *China Digital Times*, 6 April; China Digital Times (2016) Minitrue: Delete "'Daddy Xi' ignites leader worship." *China Digital Times*, 6 April.
94. Thomson, A., & Sylvester, R. (2020) We have a moral duty to stand up for Hong Kong against bullying China. *The Times*, 23 May.
95. Faulconbridge, G. (2020) China's "nervous" Xi Jinping risks new cold war, last British governor of Hong Kong says. *The Independent*, 30 May.
96. For example: Xinhua (2020) Myths, farces, weakness: Comments on Patten and Pompeo's remarks on Hong Kong. *Xinhua*, 27 May.
97. Zaller, J. (1992) *The Nature and Origins of Mass Opinion*. Cambridge University Press.

Chapter 7

1. Names in this chapter are all pseudonymous to preserve interviewees' anonymity.
2. Later to be revealed as hypothetical.
3. Interviews lasted between fifteen and forty-five minutes and were all conducted in Mandarin.
4. Mainka, S. A., & Mills, J. A. (1995) Wildlife and traditional Chinese medicine: Supply and demand for wildlife species. *Journal of Zoo and Wildlife Medicine*, 26(2), 193–200.
5. https://wildaid.org/resources/prince-william-david-beckham-and-yao-ming-saving-wildlife-for-future-generations/
6. Foreign Policy (2017) Don't get too excited about China's ivory ban. *Foreign Policy*, 10 January.
7. Blok, A. (2008). Contesting global norms: Politics of identity in Japanese pro-whaling countermobilization. *Global Environmental Politics*, 8(2), 39–66.
8. Schroeder, M. (2008) The construction of China's climate politics: Transnational NGOs and the spiral model of international relations. *Cambridge Review of International Affairs*, 21(4), 505–525.
9. The Atlantic (2012) China has no good answer to the U.S. embassy pollution-monitoring. *The Atlantic*, 13 June.

10. http://www.pewresearch.org/fact-tank/2015/12/10/as-smog-hangs-over-beijing-chinese-cite-air-pollution-as-major-concern/.
11. Through virtual private networks (VPNs) or foreign travel.
12. Zaller, J. (1992).
13. Overseas students and staff were only exposed to criticism from the United States, so no comparison is possible.
14. One common way of accounting for whether people are thinking through their responses or reacting automatically is to examine how long it takes them to respond to a question, known as "response latency." Citizens who counterargue critical information should spend more time doing so than those who respond automatically. And in the previous chapter I find that those who read about American pressure on their country as a whole did indeed take 2.47 seconds longer in deciding whether to like the *Weibo* post ($p < 0.1$) but 1.27 seconds fewer when they were told that the pressure targeted their leaders only, suggesting that when American pressure targeted China as a country, people thought more deeply through their answer. On response latency, see Petersen, M. B., Skov, M., Serritzlew, S., & Ramsay, T. (2013) Motivated reasoning and political parties: Evidence for increased processing in the face of party cues. *Political Behavior*, 35, 831–854. Also see Schaffner, B. F., & Roche, C. (2016).
15. For summary of coverage, see Guardian (2010) Twitter gaffe: US embassy announces "crazy bad" Beijing air pollution. *Guardian*, 19 November.
16. Global Times (2012) The US Embassy should respond positively to the Environmental Agency's appeal. *Global Times*, 6 June.
17. https://www.weibo.com/1974576991/ymAQauh68?refer_flag=1001030106_&type=comment#_rnd1525871315315.
18. https://chinadigitaltimes.net/2012/06/netizen-voices-clearing-the-air/.
19. For a discussion of framing effects in the United States, see, for example: Chong, D., & Druckman, J. N. (2007) Framing public opinion in competitive democracies. *American Political Science Review*, 101(04), 637–655.

Chapter 8

1. Parts of this chapter are featured in Gruffydd-Jones, J. J. (2018) Meeting the Dalai Lama and perceptions of democracy in China: A quasi-natural experiment. *Democratization*, 25(4), 652–672.
2. White House Press Office (2014) Readout of the president's meeting with his Holiness the XIV Dalai Lama. *White House Press Office*, 21 February.
3. Global Times (2011) China opposes Obama's meeting with the Dalai Lama. *Global Times*, 16 July.
4. White House Press Secretary (2008) Statement of US support for democratic dissidents. *White House Press Secretary*, 1 May.
5. LA Times (1988) Reagan meets 96 Soviet dissidents. *Los Angeles Times*, 31 May.
6. Sharansky, N. (2008) The dissident choice. *Los Angeles Times*, 24 November.

7. Fuchs, A., & Klann, N. H. (2013) Paying a visit: The Dalai Lama effect on international trade. *Journal of International Economics*. 91(1), 164–177.
8. Washington Post (2009) Obama's meeting with the Dalai Lama is delayed. *Washington Post*, 5 October.
9. Ibid.
10. Telegraph (2009) Barack Obama cancels meeting with Dalai Lama "to keep China happy." *The Telegraph*, 5 October.
11. UNPO (2010) Tibet: Swiss refusal to meet Dalai Lama draws criticism. *UNPO*, 17 March, http://www.unpo.org/article/10873.
12. For a discussion of costly signals in international relations, see Fearon, J. (1997) Signaling foreign policy interests: Tying hands versus sinking costs. *Journal of Conflict Resolution*, 41(1), 68–90.
13. Ibid.
14. ChinaFile (2015) What's the case for heads of state meeting the Dalai Lama? *ChinaFile*, 5 February.
15. White House (2011) The president's meeting with his Holiness the XIV Dalai Lama. *White House Press Office*, 17 July.
16. Guardian (2011) Barack Obama meets the Dalai Lama at the White House. *The Guardian*, 16 July.
17. In Pakistan for example: Express Tribune (2011) Obama meets with Dalai Lama despite Chinese opposition. *Express Tribune*, 17 July.
18. The Journal (2011) Obama-Lama summit goes ahead but China ain't pleased. *The Journal*, 17 July.
19. Reuters (2011) China calls on US to cancel Dalai Lama meeting. *Reuters*, 15 July.
20. Global Times (2011) China opposes Obama's meeting with the Dalai Lama. *Global Times*, 16 July.
21. People's Daily (2011) Trying to cover up interference. *People's Daily*, 17 July.
22. People's Daily (2011) Deep care: A great leap forward. *People's Daily*, 17 July.
23. Roberts, M. E. (2018). We have evidence for this from the 2014 Obama-Dalai Lama meeting, when the department issued a call to use "only Xinhua and national media copy" (China Digital Times [2014] Minitrue: Obama's meeting with the Dalai Lama. *China Digital Times*, 21 February).
24. Global Times (2011) Obama meets Dalai Lama. *Global Times*, 17 July.
25. Global Times (2011) As long as Tibet is stable, Dalai is just a pawn. *Global Times*, 18 July.
26. Global Times (2011) Obama meets the Dalai, China expresses indignation. *Global Times*, 18 July.
27. Global Times (2011) Obama meets the Dalai, reiterates his opposition to Tibetan independence. *Global Times*, 17 July.
28. The y-axis is a comparative indicator of search volume, so a score of sixty-one for 达赖 (Dalai) on July 18 equates to about 1.7 times the number of searches as the thirty-six for 胡锦涛 (Hu Jintao).
29. Due to transportation reasons—much of these provinces is highly remote.

30. I also look at different time frames in my robustness checks, namely ten and fifteen days. These make little difference. Why choose July 17 as a cutoff point rather than July 16, the day the forthcoming meeting was announced? This is simply because of the level of media attention on both dates. While the announcement on July 16 saw a small article in the *Global Times*, the meeting itself took place just half an hour before July 17 began, and received a large amount of press coverage, taking up most of the first three pages in the *People's Daily*. And this was a conservative choice, because even if some respondents had heard the news on the July 16, choosing July 17 as a cutoff should underreport rather than overreport any findings. In any case, the choice of date has little effect on the results.
31. Dickson, B. (2016) *The Dictator's Dilemma: The Chinese Communist Party's Strategy for Survival*. Oxford University Press.
32. Ibid.
33. Lu, J., & Shi, T. (2015) The battle of ideas and discourses before democratic transition: Different democratic conceptions in authoritarian China. *International Political Science Review*, 36(1), 20–41.
34. Entropy balancing matches covariates across pre- and post- meeting groups. Hainmueller, J. (2012) Entropy balancing for causal effects: A multivariate reweighting method to produce balanced samples in observational studies. *Political Analysis*, 20(1), 25–46.
35. Using the following model:

    Belief China is Democratic = $\alpha + \beta_1$Meeting + β_2NationalPride + β_3Pride* Meeting
    $+ \beta_4$Individual level controls + β_4Provincial Fixed Effects/
    β_4Provincial level contols + ε_t

36. This is highly statistically significant. Turn to Appendix 2 for statistical tables. Full analysis of the statistical design and results are available at jamiegruffyddjones.com.
37. These results all still hold when we look at the ten and fifteen days either side of the meeting, and if we use July 16 as a cutoff date instead of July 17.
38. There was a 10-percentage-point jump for each of these measures after the meeting.
39. Mueller, J. E. (1973) *War, Presidents, and Public Opinion*. Wiley; Dinesen, P. T., & Jæger, M. M. (2013) The effect of terror on institutional trust: New evidence from the 3/11 Madrid terrorist attack. *Political Psychology*, 34(6), 917–926.
40. Davis, D. W., & Silver, B. D. (2004) Civil liberties vs. security: Public opinion in the context of the terrorist attacks on America. *American Journal of Political Science*, 48(1), 28–46.
41. Jiang, J., & Yang, D. L. (2016).
42. King, G., et al. (2013).
43. People's Daily (2011) Deep care: A great leap forward. *People's Daily*, 17 July.
44. Bullock, J. G., et al. (2015).
45. People's Daily (2011) Actively promote the military academy education. *People's Daily*, 9 July.
46. People's Daily (2011) First half-year GDP grew by 9.6%. *People's Daily*, 9 July.
47. Xinhua (2011) Xinjiang's Hotan police station attacked by a mob. *Xinhua*, 19 July.

48. And if we include both the meeting and the attacks in the same regression equation, only the meeting continues to have a positive impact on perceptions, while the attacks have a negative effect.
49. Davis, D. W., & Silver, B. D. (2004); Merolla, J. L., & Zechmeister, E. J. (2009) *Democracy at Risk: How Terrorist Threats Affect the Public*. University of Chicago Press.
50. Summed up in Global Times (2014) Supporting Chinese dissidents: The Western conspiracy. *Global Times*, 28 January.
51. AP (2008) Tibet ordered to ramp up propaganda education against Dalai Lama. *Associated Press*, 3 April.

Chapter 9

1. See, for example: Keck, M. E., & Sikkink, K. (1998); Kinzelbach, K. (2013).
2. For example: China Digital Times (2014) Minitrue: Hush story on Xi's praise for patriotic bloggers. *China Digital Times*, 16 October; China Media Project (2018) English news brief on presidential term change angers leaders. *China Media Project*, 1 March.
3. China Digital Times (2016) Minitrue: Delete op-ed on Tsai Ing-Wen. *China Digital Times*, 16 May.
4. China Digital Times (2016) Minitrue: Delete Global Times editorial on bookseller. *China Digital Times*, 17 June.
5. Global Times (2015) Hostile forces target younger generation. *Global Times*, 25 May.
6. China Digital Times (2015) All websites must urgently delete the Global Times commentary, "Overseas Forces Attempt to Incite Post-80s, 90s Generation." *China Digital Times*, 26 May.
7. Guardian (2015) Chinese students in the west call for transparency over Tiananmen Square. *The Guardian*, 26 May.
8. Brutger, R., & Strezhnev, A. (2022) International Disputes, Media Coverage, and Backlash against International Law. *Journal of Conflict Resolution*, Online First; Chapman, T., & Chaudoin, S. (2020) Public reactions to international legal institutions: The ICC in a developing country. *Journal of Politics*, 82(4), 1305–1320.
9. Gustavsson, G. (2020) The risk of Sweden's coronavirus strategy? Blind patriotism. *Washington Post*, 3 May.
10. Jetschke, A. (1999) Linking the unlinkable: International norms and nationalism in Indonesia and the Philippines. In Risse-Kappen, T., Ropp, S. C., & Sikkink, K. (eds.) *The Power of Human Rights: International Norms and Domestic Change*. Cambridge University Press, 134–171.
11. Manila Times (2016) Academic: "Duterte held up a long-hidden looking glass to the US." *Manila Times*, 12 September.
12. Scheindlin, D. (2016) Human rights and public opinion in Israel: Anger vs. pragmatism. *Open Global Rights*, 26 October; Hermann, T. (2015) Wanted in Israel: Democratic leadership. *Open Global Rights*, 7 October.

13. Grossman, G., Manekin, D., & Margalit, Y. (2018) How sanctions affect public opinion in target countries: Experimental evidence from Israel. *Comparative Political Studies*, 51(14), 1823–1857.
14. Lupu, Y., & Wallace, G. P. (2019) Violence, nonviolence, and the effects of international human rights law. *American Journal of Political Science*, 63(2), 411–426.
15. Reicher, S., Haslam, S. A., Platow, M., & Steffens, N. (2016).
16. Readers may have noted that this conclusion is almost the exact opposite to that of Hendrix and Wong 2013, who argue that shaming is likely to be most effective in heavily restricted media environments. The difference may come down to the fact that these authors examine press and NGO reports, reports that rely heavily on news of specific abuses, and do not include the arguably more high-profile diplomatic criticisms, which are often far more generic. As chapters 5 and 6 show, these different kinds of shaming have very different impacts.
17. BBC (2014) How far do EU-US sanctions on Russia go? *BBC*, 15 September.
18. Russia Today (2016) "Senseless carnival": Lawmaker blasts PACE over latest anti-Russian resolution. *Russia Today*, 13 October.
19. For example: Russia Today (2016) Russia to respond to any new US sanctions with "painful" measures—deputy FM. *Russia Today*, 16 October.
20. Russia Today (2014) Senator warns of foreign provocation targeting upcoming Russian polls. *Russia Today*, 19 January.
21. Huffington Post (2016) Putin sanctioned his own people. But it helped him win. *Huffington Post*, 23 September.
22. Levitsky, S., & Way, L. (2002) The rise of competitive authoritarianism. *Journal of Democracy*, 13(2), 51–65.
23. As has been shown in other studies of transnational persuasion: Bush, S. S., & Jamal, A. A. (2015) Anti-Americanism, authoritarian politics, and attitudes about women's representation: Evidence from a survey experiment in Jordan. *International Studies Quarterly*, 59(1), 34–45; Dragojlovic, N. (2013, 2015).
24. Ausderan, J. (2014)
25. Lupu, Y., & Wallace, G. P. (2019).
26. Daily Monitor (2014) NRM was built on nationalism, says Museveni. *Daily Monitor*, 1 December.
27. Foreign Policy (2016) Is the U.S. military propping up Uganda's "elected" autocrat? *Foreign Policy*, 18 February.
28. Ibid.
29. http://www.pewglobal.org/2015/06/23/1-americas-global-image/.
30. https://freedomhouse.org/report/freedom-press/2016/uganda.
31. Shepherd, N. (2014) The politics of Uganda's anti-homosexuality legislation. *Chatham House*, 24 February.
32. http://www.pewglobal.org/2013/06/04/the-global-divide-on-homosexuality/.
33. Al Jazeera (2014) Europe backs sanctions over anti-gay laws. *Al Jazeera*, 13 March.
34. Shepherd, N. (2014).
35. Washington Post (2014) Ugandan leader signs harsh anti-gay bill despite warning from Obama administration. *Washington Post*, 14 February.

36. Allen, E. P. (2014).
37. Al Jazeera (2014) Ugandan president signs anti-gay law. *Al Jazeera,* 25 February
38. For example: New Vision (2014) Museveni responds to Obama over anti-gay bill. *New Vision,* 21 February; New Vision (2014) Uganda accuses World Bank of blackmail. *New Vision,* 3 March
39. Allen, E. P. (2014)
40. In 2015, 90% agreed very strongly with the statement "Homosexuality is inconsistent with Ugandan culture and religious norms and should therefore continue to be illegal in this country" (Afrobarometer 2015).
41. Washington Post (2014).
42. Before rising again to 76% positive in 2015 (http://www.pewglobal.org/2015/06/23/1-americas-global-image/).
43. Afrobarometer 2012 and 2015.
44. Daily Monitor (2014) Stop political arrests or lose US trade—Obama. *Daily Monitor,* 14 July.
45. Huffington Post (2014) Uganda President Yoweri Museveni wants to have anti-gay law re-issued. *Huffington Post,* 12 August.
46. Manila Times (2016) Academic: "Duterte held up a long-hidden looking glass to the US." *Manila Times,* 12 September.
47. CNN (2016) After cursing Obama, Duterte expresses regret. *CNN,* 6 September.
48. Ranger, T. (2004) Nationalist historiography, patriotic history and the history of the nation: The struggle over the past in Zimbabwe. *Journal of Southern African Studies,* 30(2), 215–234.
49. https://freedomhouse.org/report/freedom-press/2015/Zimbabwe.
50. Raftopoulos, B., & Savage, T. (2004) (eds.) *Zimbabwe: Injustice and Political Reconciliation.* African Minds.
51. Tendi, B. M. (2014) The origins and functions of demonisation discourses in Britain–Zimbabwe relations (2000–). *Journal of Southern African Studies,* 40(6), 1251–1269.
52. Ndlovu-Gatsheni, S. J. (2009) Making sense of Mugabeism in local and global politics: "So Blair, keep your England and let me keep my Zimbabwe." *Third World Quarterly,* 30(6), 1139–1158.
53. See, for example: Movement for Democratic Change Press Release (2002) Zimbabwe: MDC welcomes EU decision to extend targeted sanctions. *AllAfrica,* 23 July.
54. Grauvogel, J., Licht, A. A., & Von Soest, C. (2017).
55. Grauvogel, J. (2018) *The "Internal Opposition" Effect of International Sanctions: Insights from Burundi, Zimbabwe and a Qualitative Comparative Analysis of Sub-Saharan Africa* (Doctoral dissertation, University of Hamburg).
56. The Herald (2002), 9 April. Quoted from Phimister, I., & Raftopoulos, B. (2004) Mugabe, Mbeki & the politics of anti-imperialism. *Review of African Political Economy,* 31(101), 385–400.
57. The Chronicle (2016) Mr Obama, tear down these sanctions! *The Chronicle,* 7 October
58. International Business Times (2016) President Mugabe's regime blames Zimbabwe's economic woes on "international sanctions." *International Business Times,* 18 July.

59. Grauvogel, J. (2018).
60. The Chronicle (2016) Western countries' role in violent demos exposed. *The Chronicle*, 27 September.
61. The Chronicle (2016) Govt exposes US envoy hypocrisy. *The Chronicle*, 23 September.
62. Phimister, I., & Raftopoulos, B. (2004).
63. Bratton, M., Chikwana, A., & Sithole, T. (2005) Propaganda and public opinion in Zimbabwe. *Journal of Contemporary African Studies*, 23(1), 77–108.
64. Coltart, D. (2008) *A Decade of Suffering in Zimbabwe: Economic Collapse and Political Repression under Robert Mugabe*. CATO Institute.
65. Ibid.
66. United Nations Human Rights Council (2019) *Visit to the United Kingdom of Great Britain and Northern Ireland. Report of the Special Rapporteur on Extreme Poverty and Human Rights*, https://undocs.org/A/HRC/41/39/Add.1.
67. See the 2019 election manifesto, for example: https://labour.org.uk/manifesto-2019/.
68. For example: Gentleman, A., & Butler, P. (2014) Ministers savage UN report calling for abolition of UK's bedroom tax. *The Guardian*, 3 February; Spilling, R., & Robertson, A. (2019) Amber Rudd is to lodge a formal complaint over UN's "barely believable" poverty report accusing Britain of violating human rights obligations by creating "Dickensian" conditions for the poor. *Daily Mail*, 22 May.
69. For example: Booth, R., & Butler, P. (2018) UK austerity has inflicted "great misery" on citizens, UN says. *The Guardian*, 16 November; Chakrabortty, A. (2018) The epitaph for Tory austerity has been written, and it's damning. *The Guardian*, 16 November; Booth, R. (2018) "I'm scared to eat sometimes": UN envoy meets UK food bank users. *The Guardian*, 8 November; Booth, R., & Butler, P. (2018) "It's unfair": UN envoy meets children in Scotland to discuss poverty. *The Guardian*, 9 November; Booth, R. (2019) UN report compares Tory welfare policies to creation of workhouses. *The Guardian*, 22 May.
70. See https://labour.org.uk/wp-content/uploads/2019/11/Poverty-Britain_Ten-ways-the-Tories-have-entrenched-poverty-across-Britain.pdf.
71. For example, in *The Telegraph*: Ward, V. (2018) UK's welfare system is cruel and misogynistic, says UN expert after damning report on poverty. *The Telegraph*, 16 November; and with more aggrievance in the *Daily Mail*: Spilling, R., & Robertson, A. (2019) Amber Rudd is to lodge a formal complaint over UN's "barely believable" poverty report accusing Britain of violating human rights obligations by creating "Dickensian" conditions for the poor. *Daily Mail*, 22 May.
72. Doyle, J. (2012) How dare they! Britain condemned on human rights in UN report . . . by Iran, Russia and Cuba. *Daily Mail*, 9 June.
73. McNulty, D., Watson, N., & Philo, G. (2014) Human rights and prisoners' rights: The British press and the shaping of public debate. *Howard Journal of Criminal Justice*, 53(4), 360–376.
74. McGee, L., & Krever, M. (2020) Where did it go wrong for the UK on coronavirus? *CNN*, 1 May; Sawer, P. (2020) Britain criticised around the world for "complacent" and "calamitous" coronavirus response. *The Telegraph*, 6 May.
75. See appendix 3 for full text of the prompt.

76. And highly statistically significant.
77. The sample did pretty accurately account for the proportion of the whole UK population (including nonvoters) who voted Conservative in the last election (19.9% in the sample versus 19.6% in the population).
78. Even among those who said beforehand that they were "very proud" of their country, the criticism still cut their approval of the response by 8 percentage points.
79. Terman, R., & Gruffydd-Jones, J. (n.d.) Human Rights Shaming, Domestic Activism, and Nationalist Backlash. *Working Paper*.
80. Wong, S. H. W., & Wan, K. M. (2018) The housing boom and the rise of localism in Hong Kong: Evidence from the legislative council election in 2016. *China Perspectives*, 2018(2018/3), 31–40; Chan, E. (2000) Defining fellow compatriots as "others"—National identity in Hong Kong. *Government and Opposition*, 35(4), 499–519.
81. Fong, B. C. (2017) One country, two nationalisms: Center-periphery relations between Mainland China and Hong Kong, 1997–2016. *Modern China*, 43(5), 523–556.
82. Ibid.
83. Ibid.
84. Degolyer, M. E., & Scott, J. L. (1996) The myth of political apathy in Hong Kong. *Annals of the American Academy of Political and Social Science*, 547(1), 68–78.
85. Huffington Post (2014) Democracy protests divide Hong Kong. *Huffington Post*, 29 October.
86. China Digital Times (2014) C.Y. Leung takes tough stance ahead of talks. *China Digital Times*, 20 October; China Digital Times (2014) State media and public opinion on the HK protests. *China Digital Times*, 6 October.
87. Los Angeles Times (2014) In turbulent Hong Kong, conspiracy theories point West. *Los Angeles Times*, 9 October.
88. See chapter 4.
89. Yip, W. (2019) Beijing blames foreigners when Hong Kongers march. *Foreign Policy*, 19 June.
90. For a summary of these articles, see Ng, E. (2017) "Race traitors": Pro-Beijing papers accuse democracy figures of inviting US to interfere in Hong Kong. *HKFP*, 4 May.
91. According to *Reporters without Borders*, press freedom is declining but far higher than on the mainland: https://rsf.org/en/hong-kong.
92. Chan, J. M., & Lee, F. L. (2011) The primacy of local interests and press freedom in Hong Kong: A survey study of professional journalists. *Journalism*, 12(1), 89–105.
93. Lin, Z. (2016) Traditional media, social media, and alternative media in Hong Kong's Umbrella Movement. *Asian Politics & Policy*, 8(2), 365–372.
94. For an in-depth discussion of this, see Kuo, L., & Timmons, H. (2014) How China's anti-umbrella propaganda failed in Hong Kong. *Quartz*, 9 October.
95. Li, E. (2020) 280 Characters to change the world: Twitter in the Hong Kong protests. *Harvard International Review*, 1 April; Lee, F. L., Chen, H. T., & Chan, M. (2017) Social media use and university students' participation in a large-scale protest campaign: The case of Hong Kong's Umbrella Movement. *Telematics and Informatics*, 34(2), 457–469.

96. Chan, M. (2020) Partisan selective exposure and the perceived effectiveness of contentious political actions in Hong Kong. *Asian Journal of Communication*, 30(3–4), 1–18; Kobayashi, T. (2020) Depolarization through social media use: Evidence from dual identifiers in Hong Kong. *New Media & Society*, 22(8), 1339–1358.
97. In interviews with the author, 2015 and 2016.
98. McLaughlin, T. (2019) Hong Kong protesters appeal for international pressure on China at G-20. *Washington Post*, 26 June; Tam, F. (2019) Hong Kong protesters seek international support on rights. *Reuters*, 19 December.
99. Kobayashi, T. (2020); Lee, F. L. (2016) Impact of social media on opinion polarization in varying times. *Communication and the Public*, 1(1), 56–71.
100. Moravcsik, A. (1995). Explaining international human rights regimes: Liberal theory and Western Europe. *European Journal of International Relations*, 1(2), 157–189, 160. Also see Keck, M. E., & Sikkink, K. (1998); Simmons, B. (2009); Ropp, S. C., & Sikkink, K. (1999) The socialization of international human rights norms into domestic practices: Introduction. In Risse, T., Ropp, S. C., & Sikkink, K. (eds.) *The Power of Human Rights: International Norms and Domestic Change*, 1–39. Cambridge University Press.
101. Finnemore, M., & Sikkink, K. (1998) International norm dynamics and political change. *International Organization*, 52(4), 887–917.
102. Roth, K. (2015).
103. Economist (2016) Why do people in China give so little to charity? *The Economist*, 6 September.
104. Dimitrov, M., & Zhang, Z. (n.d.) Patterns of Protest Activity in China. *Working Paper*.
105. Reuters (2015).
106. In interviews with the author, 2015 and 2016.
107. Gruffydd-Jones, J. J. (2021) International attention and the treatment of political prisoners. *International Studies Quarterly*, 65(4), 999–1011.
108. Human Rights Watch (2017) The costs of international advocacy. China's interference in United Nations human rights mechanisms. *Human Rights Watch*, 5 September.
109. New York Times (2014) Norway's leaders snub Dalai Lama in deference to China. *New York Times*, 7 May.
110. Telegraph (2010) China warns Norway's Nobel Institute not to award peace prize to democracy activist Liu Xiaobo. *Daily Telegraph*, 28 September.
111. Risse, T., Ropp, S. C., & Sikkink, K. (1999).
112. Cardenas, S. (2004) Norm collision: Explaining the effects of international human rights pressure on state behavior. *International Studies Review*, 6(2), 213–232; Burgerman, S. (2001) *Moral Victories: How Activists Provoke Multilateral Action*. Cornell University Press.
113. Krasner, S. D. (1993) Sovereignty, regimes, and human rights. In Rittberger, V., & Mayer, P. (eds.) *Regime Theory and International Relations*. Oxford University Press.
114. For a different view, see Fincher, L. H. (2018) *Betraying Big Brother: The Feminist Awakening in China*. Verso Books.

115. China News Network (2020) Guangdong introduces steps for 9 industries: Implementing equal and non-discriminatory treatment for Chinese people and foreigners. *China News Network*, 3 May. Official Guangdong local government announcement here: http://amr.gd.gov.cn/zwgk/tzgg/content/post_2987464.html.
116. See http://ng.chineseembassy.org/eng/zngx/cne/t1775825.htm, for example.

Bibliography

Allen, E. P. (2014) Unintended consequences. *Foreign Policy,* 26 February.
Anjum, G., Chilton, A., & Usman, Z. (2021) United Nations endorsement and support for human rights: An experiment on women's rights in Pakistan. *Journal of Peace Research,* 58(3), 462–478.
Asch, S. E. (1955) Opinions and social pressure. *Scientific American,* 193(5), 31–35.
Ausderan, J. (2014) How naming and shaming affects human rights perceptions in the shamed country. *Journal of Peace Research,* 51(1), 81–95.
Baker, W. D., & Oneal, J. R. (2001) Patriotism or opinion leadership? The nature and origins of the "rally 'round the flag" effect. *Journal of Conflict Resolution,* 45(5), 661–687.
Barnett, R. (2009) The Tibet protests of spring, 2008. *China Perspectives,* 2009(3), 6–23.
Baumeister, R. F., Smart, L., & Boden, J. M. (1996) Relation of threatened egotism to violence and aggression: The dark side of high self-esteem. *Psychological Review,* 103, 5–33.
Bell, S. R., Murdie, A., Blocksome, P., & Brown, K. (2013) "Force multipliers": Conditional effectiveness of military and INGO human security interventions. *Journal of Human Rights,* 12(4), 397–422.
Berg, J. S. (2008) *Broadcasting on the Short Waves, 1945 to Today.* McFarland.
Berinsky, A. J. (2018) Telling the truth about believing the lies? Evidence for the limited prevalence of expressive survey responding. *Journal of Politics,* 80(1), 211–224.
Bian, Y., Shu, X., & Logan, J. R. (2001) Communist party membership and regime dynamics in China. *Social Forces,* 79(3), 805–841.
Blok, A. (2008) Contesting global norms: Politics of identity in Japanese pro-whaling countermobilization. *Global Environmental Politics,* 8(2), 39–66.
Bob, C. (ed.) (2011) *The International Struggle for New Human Rights.* University of Pennsylvania Press.
Bossen, L., Xurui, W., Brown, M. J., & Gates, H. (2011) Feet and fabrication: Footbinding and early twentieth-century rural women's labor in Shaanxi. *Modern China,* 37(4), 347–383.
Brady, A. M. (2009) *Marketing Dictatorship: Propaganda and Thought Work in Contemporary China.* Rowman & Littlefield Publishers.
Brady, A. M. (2017) Guiding hand: The role of the CCP Central Propaganda Department in the current era. In Brodsgaard, K. E. (ed.) *Critical Readings on the Communist Party of China,* 752–772. Brill.
Branscombe, N. R., Spears, R., Ellemers, N., & Doosje, B. (2002) Intragroup and intergroup evaluation effects on group behavior. *Personality and Social Psychology Bulletin,* 28(6), 744–753.
Bratton, M., Chikwana, A., & Sithole, T. (2005) Propaganda and public opinion in Zimbabwe. *Journal of Contemporary African Studies,* 23(1), 77–108.
Brody, R. A. (1991) *Assessing the President.* Stanford University Press.
Brutger, R., & Strezhnev, A. (n.d.) International Disputes, Media Coverage, and Backlash against International Law. *Working Paper.*

Bullock, J. G., Gerber, A. S., Hill, S. J., & Huber, G. A. (2015) Partisan bias in factual beliefs about politics. *Quarterly Journal of Political Science*, 10, 519–578.

Burgerman, S. (2001) *Moral Victories: How Activists Provoke Multilateral Action*. Cornell University Press.

Bush, S. S., & Jamal, A. A. (2015) Anti-Americanism, authoritarian politics, and attitudes about women's representation: Evidence from a survey experiment in Jordan. *International Studies Quarterly*, 59(1), 34–45.

Cardenas, S. (2004) Norm collision: Explaining the effects of international human rights pressure on state behavior. *International Studies Review*, 6(2), 213–232.

Carothers, T. (2006) The backlash against democracy promotion. *Foreign Affairs*, 85, 55.

Chan, E. (2000) Defining fellow compatriots as "others"—National identity in Hong Kong. *Government and Opposition*, 35(4), 499–519.

Chan, J. M., & Lee, F. L. (2011) The primacy of local interests and press freedom in Hong Kong: A survey study of professional journalists. *Journalism*, 12(1), 89–105.

Chan, M. (2020) Partisan selective exposure and the perceived effectiveness of contentious political actions in Hong Kong. *Asian Journal of Communication*, 30(3–4), 1–18.

Chapman, T. L., & Reiter, D. (2004) The United Nations Security Council and the rally 'round the flag effect. *Journal of Conflict Resolution*, 48(6), 886–909.

Chau, V. C. T. (1966) *The Anti-Footbinding Movement in China (1850–1912)*. Columbia University, Doctoral dissertation.

Chen, D. (2005) Explaining China's changing discourse on human rights, 1978–2004. *Asian Perspective*, 29(3), 155–182.

Chen D. Y. (1937) *Zhongguo Funu Shenghuoshi [Women's Life in China]*. Shangwu.

Chen, J. D., Pan, J., & Xu, Y. Q. (2015) Sources of authoritarian responsiveness: A field experiment in china. *American Journal of Political Science*, 60(2), 383–400.

Chen, J. D., & Xu, Y. Q. (2017) Why do authoritarian regimes allow citizens to voice opinions publicly? *Journal of Politics*, 79(3), 792–803.

Chia, R. C., Allred, L. J., & Jerzak, P. A. (1997) Attitudes toward women in Taiwan and China. *Psychology of Women Quarterly*, 21(1), 137–150.

Chilton, A. S. (2014) The influence of international human rights agreements on public opinion: An experimental study. *Chicago Journal of International Law*, 15, 110–137.

Chinese Communist Party Central Committee (1994) *Aiguo Zhuyi Jiaoyu Shishi Gangyao [Outline on the Implementation of Education in Patriotism]*. Government Printing Office.

Chong, D., & Druckman, J. N. (2007) Framing public opinion in competitive democracies. *American Political Science Review*, 101, 637–655.

Christensen, T. J., Garver, J. W., Hu, W., Huang, Y., Wan, M., Yu, B., Zhang, M. J., & Zhao, S. (1999) *In the Eyes of the Dragon: China Views the World*. Rowman & Littlefield.

Cohen, R. (1987) People's Republic of China: The human rights exception. *Human Rights Quarterly*, 9(4), 447–549.

Coltart, D. (2008) *A Decade of Suffering in Zimbabwe: Economic Collapse and Political Repression under Robert Mugabe*. CATO Institute.

Cope, K. L., & Crabtree, C. (2019) A nationalist backlash to international refugee law: Evidence from a survey experiment in Turkey. *Virginia Public Law and Legal Theory Research Paper*, 2018-33.

Crowther, N. (2015) "Small places, close to home": Successful communication on human rights. *Open Democracy*, 15 September.

Davenport, C. (2015) *How Social Movements Die: Repression and Demobilization of the Republic of New Africa*. Cambridge University Press.

Davis, D. R., Murdie, A., & Steinmetz, C. G. (2012) "Makers and shapers": Human rights INGOs and public opinion. *Human Rights Quarterly*, 34(1), 199–224.

Davis, D. W., & Silver, B. D. (2004) Civil liberties vs. security: Public opinion in the context of the terrorist attacks on America. *American Journal of Political Science*, 48(1), 28–46.

De Hoog, N. (2013) Processing of social identity threats. *Social Psychology*, 44, 361–372.

Degolyer, M. E., & Scott, J. L. (1996) The myth of political apathy in Hong Kong. *Annals of the American Academy of Political and Social Science*, 547(1), 68–78.

Della Porta, D. D. M. (2006) *Social Movements: An Introduction*. 2nd ed. Blackwell Publishing.

Denis-Remis, C., Lebraty, J. F., & Philippe, H. (2013) The 2008 anti-French demonstrations in China: Learning from a social media crisis. *Journal of Contingencies and Crisis Management*, 21(1), 45–55.

Dickson, B. J. (2014) Who wants to be a communist? Career incentives and mobilized loyalty in China. *China Quarterly*, 217, 42–68.

Dickson, B. J. (2016) *The Dictator's Dilemma: The Chinese Communist Party's Strategy for Survival*. Oxford University Press.

Dickson, E. (2007) On the (In)effectiveness of Collective Punishment: An Experimental Investigation. *Working Paper*.

Dimitrov, M., & Zhang, Z. (n.d.) Patterns of Protest Activity in China. *Working Paper*.

Dinesen, P. T., & Jæger, M. M. (2013) The effect of terror on institutional trust: New evidence from the 3/11 Madrid terrorist attack. *Political Psychology*, 34(6), 917–926.

Ding, X. L. (2006) *The Decline of Communism in China: Legitimacy Crisis, 1977–1989*. Cambridge University Press.

Dragojlovic, N. (2013) Leaders without borders: Familiarity as a moderator of transnational source cue effects. *Political Communication*, 30(2), 297–316.

Dragojlovic, N. (2015) Listening to outsiders: The impact of messenger nationality on transnational persuasion in the United States. *International Studies Quarterly*, 59(1), 73–85.

Drucker, A. R. (1981) The influence of Western women on the anti-footbinding movement 1840–1911. *Historical Reflections/Réflexions Historiques*, 8(3), 179–199.

Edelstein, A. S., & Liu, A. P. L. (1963) Anti-Americanism in Red China's People's Daily: A functional analysis. *Journalism Quarterly*, 40(2), 187–195.

Eribo, F., & Gaddy, G. D. (1992) Pravda's coverage of the Chernobyl nuclear accident at the threshold of glasnost. *Howard Journal of Communications*, 3(3–4), 242–252.

Esarey, A. (2005) Cornering the market: State strategies for controlling China's commercial media. *Asian Perspective*, 29(4), 37–83.

Fan, J., Zhang, T., & Zhu, Y. (2016) Behind the personality cult of Xi Jinping. *Foreign Policy*, 8 March.

Fan, Y. P., & Liu, J. (2011) Unified propaganda, centralized channeling, and unified guidance—The historical evolution of the CCP's media thought in the new era. *Journal of Lanzhou University*, 39(4), 6–13.

Fang, K., & Repnikova, M. (2018) Demystifying "Little Pink": The creation and evolution of a gendered label for nationalistic activists in China. *New Media & Society*, 20(6), 2162–2185.

Fincher, L. H. (2014) *Leftover Women: The Resurgence of Gender Inequality in China*. Bloomsbury.

Fincher, L. H. (2018) *Betraying Big Brother: The Feminist Awakening in China*. Verso Books.
Finnemore, M., & Sikkink, K. (1998) International norm dynamics and political change. *International Organization*, 52(4), 887–917.
Fong, B. C. (2017) One country, two nationalisms: Center-periphery relations between Mainland China and Hong Kong, 1997–2016. *Modern China*, 43(5), 523–556.
Foot, R. (2000) *Rights beyond Borders: The Global Community and the Struggle over Human Rights in China*. Oxford University Press.
Francisco, R. A. (1995) The relationship between coercion and protest: An empirical evaluation in three coercive states. *Journal of Conflict Resolution*, 39(2), 263–282.
Fry, L. (2011) Chinese women and economic human rights. *Human Rights and Human Welfare*, 41–56. Accessed at: https://web.archive.org/web/20180423024007id_/https://www.du.edu/korbel/hrhw/researchdigest/china/WomenChina.pdf
Frye, T. (2019) Economic sanctions and public opinion: Survey experiments from Russia. *Comparative Political Studies*, 52(7), 967–994.
Fu, H. (2018) The July 9th (709) crackdown on human rights lawyers: Legal advocacy in an authoritarian state. *Journal of Contemporary China*, 27(112), 1–15.
Fuchs, A., & Klann, N. H. (2013) Paying a visit: The Dalai Lama effect on international trade. *Journal of International Economics*, 91(1), 164–177.
Gang, Q., & Bandurski, D. (2011) China's emerging public sphere: The impact of media commercialization, professionalism, and the Internet in an era of transition. In Shirk, S. L. (ed.) *Changing Media, Changing China*, 38–76. Oxford University Press.
Geddes, B., & Zaller, J. (1989) Sources of popular support for authoritarian regimes. *American Journal of Political Science*, 33(2), 319–347.
Gerber, A. S., & Huber, G. A. (2009) Partisanship and economic behavior: Do partisan differences in economic forecasts predict real economic behavior? *American Political Science Review*, 103(3), 407–426.
Grauvogel, J. (2018) *The "Internal Opposition" Effect of International Sanctions: Insights from Burundi, Zimbabwe and a Qualitative Comparative Analysis of Sub-Saharan Africa*. Doctoral dissertation, University of Hamburg.
Grauvogel, J., Licht, A. A., & Von Soest, C. (2017) Sanctions and signals: How international sanction threats trigger domestic protest in targeted regimes. *International Studies Quarterly*, 61(1), 86–97.
Green, D. P., Palmquist, B., & Schickler, E. (2004) *Partisan Hearts and Minds: Political Parties and the Social Identities of Voters*. Yale University Press.
Greenhalgh, S. (1977) Bound feet, hobbled lives: Women in old China. *Frontiers: A Journal of Women Studies*, 2(1), 7–21.
Greenwald, A. G., Poehlman, T. A., Uhlmann, E. L., & Banaji, M. R. (2009) Understanding and using the Implicit Association Test: III. Meta-analysis of predictive validity. *Journal of Personality and Social Psychology*, 97, 17–41.
Grossman, G., Manekin, D., & Margalit, Y. (2018) How sanctions affect public opinion in target countries: Experimental evidence from Israel. *Comparative Political Studies*, 51(14), 1823–1857.
Gruffydd-Jones, J. J. (2018) Meeting the Dalai Lama and perceptions of democracy in China: A quasi-natural experiment. *Democratization*, 25(4), 652–672.
Gruffydd-Jones, J. J. (2019) Citizens and condemnation: Strategic uses of international human rights pressure in authoritarian states. *Comparative Political Studies*, 52(4), 579–612.

Gruffydd-Jones, J. J. (2021) The impacts of international attention on political prisoners in China. *International Studies Quarterly*, 65(4), 999–1011.

Hafner-Burton, E. M. (2008) Sticks and stones: Naming and shaming the human rights enforcement problem. *International Organization*, 62(4), 689–716.

Hainmueller, J. (2012) Entropy balancing for causal effects: A multivariate reweighting method to produce balanced samples in observational studies. *Political Analysis*, 20(1), 25–46.

Harding, H. (2000) *A Fragile Relationship: The United States and China since 1972*. Brookings Institution Press.

Hassid, J., & Brass, J. N. (2014) Scandals, media and good governance in China and Kenya. *Journal of Asian and African Studies*, 50(3), 325–342.

Hassin, R. R., Ferguson, M. J., Shidlovski, D., & Gross, T. (2007) Subliminal exposure to national flags affects political thought and behavior. *Proceedings of the National Academy of Sciences*, 104(50), 19757–19761.

He, Z., & Zhu, J. (1994) The "Voice of America" and China zeroing in on Tiananmen Square. *Journalism and Communication Monographs*, 143, 1–45.

Hendrix, C. S., & Wong, W. H. (2013) When is the pen truly mighty? Regime type and the efficacy of naming and shaming in curbing human rights abuses. *British Journal of Political Science*, 43(3), 651–672.

Hess, D., & Martin, B. (2006) Repression, backfire, and the theory of transformative events. *Mobilization*, 11(2), 249–267.

Hetherington, M. J., & Nelson, M. (2003) Anatomy of a rally effect: George W. Bush and the war on terrorism. *PS: Political Science & Politics*, 36(1), 37–42.

Hong, F., & Zhouxiang, L. (2012) The politicisation of the Beijing Olympics. *International Journal of the History of Sport*, 29(1), 1–29.

Hornsey, M. J. (2005) Why being right is not enough: Predicting defensiveness in the face of group criticism. *European Review of Social Psychology*, 16(1), 301–334.

Hornsey, M. J., & Imani, A. (2004) Criticizing groups from the inside and the outside: An identity perspective on the intergroup sensitivity effect. *Personality and Social Psychology Bulletin*, 30(3), 365–383.

Hornsey, M. J., Robson, E., Smith, J., Esposo, S., & Sutton, R. M. (2008) Sugaring the pill: Assessing rhetorical strategies designed to minimize defensive reactions to group criticism. *Human Communication Research*, 34(1), 70–98.

Hornsey, M. J., Trembath, M., & Gunthorpe, S. (2004) "You can criticize because you care": Identity attachment, constructiveness, and the intergroup sensitivity effect. *European Journal of Social Psychology*, 34(5), 499–518.

Howell, J. (1997) Post-Beijing reflections: Creating ripples, but not waves in China. *Women's Studies International Forum*, 20(2), 235–252.

Jiang, J., & Yang, D. L. (2016) Lying or believing? Measuring preference falsification from a political purge in China. *Comparative Political Studies*, 49(5), 600–634.

Jones-Rooy, A. (2012) Legitimacy and Credibility: The Media as a Political Tool in China and Other Autocracies. *Working Paper*.

Keck, M., & Sikkink, K. (1998) *Activists beyond Borders: Advocacy Networks in International Politics*. Cornell University Press.

Kelley, J. D., & Simmons, B. A. (2015) Politics by number: Indicators as social pressure in international relations. *American Journal of Political Science*, 59(1), 55–70.

Kent, A. (2011) *China, the United Nations, and Human Rights: The Limits of Compliance*. University of Pennsylvania Press.

King, G., Pan, J., & Roberts, M. E. (2013) How censorship in China allows government criticism but silences collective expression. *American Political Science Review*, 107(2), 326–343.

Kinzelbach, K. (2014) *The EU's Human Rights Dialogue with China: Quiet Diplomacy and Its Limits*. Routledge.

Ko, D. (2005) *Cinderella's Sisters: A Revisionist History of Footbinding*. University of California Press.

Kobayashi, T. (2020) Depolarization through social media use: Evidence from dual identifiers in Hong Kong. *New Media & Society*, 22(8), 1339–1358.

Koo, J. W. (2015) Public opinion on human rights is the true gauge of progress. *Open Democracy*, 3 July.

Krain, M. (2014) The effects of diplomatic sanctions and engagement on the severity of ongoing genocides or politicides. *Journal of Genocide Research*, 16(1), 25–53.

Krasner, S. D. (1993) Sovereignty, regimes, and human rights. In Rittberger, V., & Mayer, P. (eds.) *Regime Theory and International Relations*. Oxford University Press, 139–167.

Kruglanski, A. W., & Webster, D. M. (1996) Motivated closing of the mind: "Seizing" and "freezing." *Psychological Review*, 103(2), 263.

Kunda, Z. (1990) The case for motivated reasoning. *Psychological Bulletin*, 108(3), 480.

Kuran, T. (1991) Now out of never: The element of surprise in the East European revolution of 1989. *World Politics*, 44(1), 7–48.

Lambert, A. J., Scherer, L. D., Schott, J. P., Olson, K. R., Andrews, R. K., O'Brien, T. C., & Zisser, A. R. (2010) Rally effects, threat, and attitude change: An integrative approach to understanding the role of emotion. *Journal of Personality and Social Psychology*, 98(6), 886.

Lambert, A. J., Schott, J. P., & Scherer, L. (2011) Threat, politics, and attitudes: Toward a greater understanding of rally-'round-the-flag effects. *Current Directions in Psychological Science*, 20(6), 343–348.

Lebovic, J. H., & Saunders, E. N. (2016) The diplomatic core: The determinants of high-level us diplomatic visits, 1946–2010. *International Studies Quarterly*, 60(1), 107–123.

Lebovic, J. H., & Voeten, E. (2006) The politics of shame: The condemnation of country human rights practices in the UNCHR. *International Studies Quarterly*, 50(4), 861–888.

Lee, C. C. (1981) The United States as seen through the People's Daily. *Journal of Communication*, 31(4), 92–101.

Lee, F. L. (2016) Impact of social media on opinion polarization in varying times. *Communication and the Public*, 1(1), 56–71.

Lee, F. L., Chen, H. T., & Chan, M. (2017) Social media use and university students' participation in a large-scale protest campaign: The case of Hong Kong's Umbrella Movement. *Telematics and Informatics*, 34(2), 457–469.

Lee, J., Campbell, C., & Tan, G. (1992) Infanticide and family planning in late imperial China: The price and population history of rural Liaoning, 1774–1873. In Rawski, T. G., & Li. L. M. (eds.) *Chinese History in Economic Perspective*. Berkeley, 145–176.

Lee, W. Y. (1995) Women's education in traditional and modern China. *Women's History Review*, 4(3), 345–336.

Lei, Y. W. (2018) *The Contentious Public Sphere: Law, Media, and Authoritarian Rule in China*. Princeton University Press.

Levitsky, S., & Way, L. (2002) The rise of competitive authoritarianism. *Journal of Democracy*, 13(2), 51–65.

Levy, H. S. (1966) *Chinese Footbinding: The History of a Curious Erotic Custom*. W. Rawls.

Li, J. (2012) *China's America: The Chinese View the United States, 1900–2000.* SUNY Press.
Li, T. (1988) *Comparative Study of Reciprocal Coverage of the People's Republic of China in the Washington Post and the United States in the People's Daily in 1986: A Case Study of Foreign News within the Context of the Debate of the New World Information Order.* Doctoral dissertation, Oklahoma State University.
Lichbach, M. I. (1998) *The Rebel's Dilemma.* University of Michigan.
Lin, Z. (2016) Traditional media, social media, and alternative media in Hong Kong's Umbrella Movement. *Asian Politics & Policy,* 8(2), 365–372.
Liu, H. (2019) *From Cyber-Nationalism to Fandom Nationalism.* Routledge.
Lodge, M., & Taber, C. (2000) Three steps toward a theory of motivated political reasoning. In Chong, D., & Kuklinski, J. H. (eds.) *Elements of Reason: Cognition, Choice, and the Bounds of Rationality,* 183–213. Cambridge University Press.
Lord, C. G., Ross, L., & Lepper, M. R. (1979) Biased assimilation and attitude polarization: The effects of prior theories on subsequently considered evidence. *Journal of Personality and Social Psychology,* 37(11), 2098.
Lorentzen, P. (2013) Regularizing rioting: Permitting public protest in an authoritarian regime. *Quarterly Journal of Political Science,* 8(2), 127–158.
Lorentzen, P. (2014) China's strategic censorship. *American Journal of Political Science,* 58(2), 402–414.
Lu, J., & Shi, T. (2015) The battle of ideas and discourses before democratic transition: Different democratic conceptions in authoritarian China. *International Political Science Review,* 36(1), 20–41.
Luchok, J. A., & McCroskey, J. C. (1978) The effect of quality of evidence on attitude change and source credibility. *Southern Journal of Communication,* 43(4), 371–383.
Luo, C., Ding, W. H., & Zhao, W. (2014) Factual framework and emotional discourse: News frames and discourse analysis in "Global Times" editorials and Hu Xijin's Weibo. *International Journalism,* 36(8), 38–55.
Lupu, Y. (2015) Legislative veto players and the effects of international human rights agreements. *American Journal of Political Science,* 59(3), 578–594.
Lupu, Y., & Wallace, G. P. (2019) Violence, nonviolence, and the effects of international human rights law. *American Journal of Political Science,* 63(2), 411–426.
Mackie, G. (1996) Ending footbinding and infibulation: A convention account. *American Sociological Review,* 61(6), 999–1017.
Mainka, S. A., & Mills, J. A. (1995) Wildlife and traditional Chinese medicine: Supply and demand for wildlife species. *Journal of Zoo and Wildlife Medicine,* 26(2), 193–200.
Mao, Z. (1950) *People's Democratic Dictatorship.* Lawrence and Wishart.
Mao, Z. (1955) Women have gone to the labour front. In Mao, Z. (ed.) *Socialist Upsurge in China's Countryside,* Vol. 1, 357. Peking.
Marinov, N. (2016) International Actors as Critics of Domestic Freedoms. *Working Paper.*
Martiny, S. E., Kessler, T., & Vignoles, V. L. (2012) Shall I leave or shall we fight? Effects of threatened group-based self-esteem on identity management strategies. *Group Processes and Intergroup Relations,* 15, 39–55.
Martiny, S. E., & Rubin, M. (2016) Towards a clearer understanding of social identity theory's self-esteem hypothesis. In McKeown, S., Haji, R., & Ferguson, N. (eds.) *Understanding Peace and Conflict through Social Identity Theory,* 19–32. Springer.
Mason, T. D., & Krane, D. (1989) The political economy of death squads: Toward a theory of the impact of state-sanctioned terror. *International Studies Quarterly,* 33(2), 175–198.

McEntire, K. J., Leiby, M., & Krain, M. (2015) Human rights organizations as agents of change: An experimental examination of framing and micromobilization. *American Political Science Review*, 109(3), 407–426.

McGranahan, C. (2010) *Arrested Histories: Tibet, the CIA, and Memories of a Forgotten War.* Duke University Press.

McKeown, S., Haji, R., & Ferguson, N. (2016) *Understanding Peace and Conflict through Social Identity Theory. Contemporary Global Perspectives.* Springer.

McNulty, D., Watson, N., & Philo, G. (2014) Human rights and prisoners' rights: The British press and the shaping of public debate. *Howard Journal of Criminal Justice*, 53(4), 360–376.

Medeiros, E. S. (2019) The changing fundamentals of US-China relations. *Washington Quarterly*, 42(3), 93–119.

Merolla, J. L., & Zechmeister, E. J. (2009) *Democracy at Risk: How Terrorist Threats Affect the Public.* Chicago University Press.

Miller, A. (2015) The trouble with factions. *China Leadership Monitor*, 46, 1–12.

Miller, P. R., & Conover, P. J. (2015) Red and blue states of mind: Partisan hostility and voting in the United States. *Political Research Quarterly*, 68(2), 225–239.

Moore, W. H. (1998) Repression and dissent: Substitution, context, and timing. *American Journal of Political Science*, 42(3), 851–873.

Moravcsik, A. (1995) Explaining international human rights regimes: Liberal theory and Western Europe. *European Journal of International Relations*, 1(2), 157–189.

Mueller, J. E. (1970) Presidential popularity from Truman to Johnson. *American Political Science Review*, 64, 18–33.

Mueller, J. E. (1973) *War, Presidents, and Public Opinion.* Wiley.

Murdie, A., & Bhasin, T. (2011) Aiding and abetting: Human rights INGOs and domestic protest. *Journal of Conflict Resolution*, 55(2), 163–191.

Murdie, A., & Davis, D. R. (2010) Problematic potential: The human rights consequences of peacekeeping interventions in civil wars. *Human Rights Quarterly*, 32(1), 50–73.

Murdie, A., & Davis, D. R. (2012) Shaming and blaming: Using events data to assess the impact of human rights INGOs. *International Studies Quarterly*, 56(1), 1–16.

Murdie, A., & Peksen, D. (2014) The impact of human rights INGO shaming on humanitarian interventions. *Journal of Politics*, 76(1), 215–228.

Nathan, A. J. (1994) Human rights in Chinese foreign policy. *China Quarterly*, 139, 622–643.

Nauroth, P., Gollwitzer, M., Bender, J., & Rothmund, T. (2015) Social identity threat motivates science-discrediting online comments. *PLoS One,* 10(2), e011747.

Ndlovu-Gatsheni, S. J. (2009) Making sense of Mugabeism in local and global politics: "So Blair, keep your England and let me keep my Zimbabwe." *Third World Quarterly*, 30(6), 1139–1158.

Nitsch, V. (2007) State visits and international trade. *World Economy*, 30(12), 1797–1816.

Norris, P., & Inglehart, R. (2018) *Cultural Backlash: The Rise of Authoritarian Populism.* Cambridge University Press.

Nyhan, B. (2021) Why the backfire effect does not explain the durability of political misperceptions. *Proceedings of the National Academy of Sciences*, 118(15).

Nyhan, B., & Reifer, J. (2010) When corrections fail: The persistence of political misperceptions. *Political Behavior*, 32(2), 303–330.

Nyhan, B., & Reifler, J. (2019) The roles of information deficits and identity threat in the prevalence of misperceptions. *Journal of Elections, Public Opinion and Parties*, 29(2), 222–244.

Nyhan, B., Reifler, J., & Ubel, P. A. (2013) The hazards of correcting myths about health care reform. *Medical Care*, 51(2), 127–132.

Nyiri, P., Zhang, J., & Varrall, M. (2010) China's cosmopolitan nationalists: "Heroes" and "traitors" of the 2008 Olympics. *China Journal*, (63), 25–55.

Opp, K-D., & Roehl, W. (1990) Repression, micromobilization, and political protest. *Social Forces*, 69(2), 521–547.

Pan, J., & Xu, Y. Q. (2018) China's ideological spectrum. *Journal of Politics*, 80(1), 254–273.

Peksen, D. (2009) Better or worse? The effect of economic sanctions on human rights. *Journal of Peace Research*, 46(1), 59–77.

Pelika, S. L. (2007) *Picking Teams and Choosing Sides: Opinions as Symbols in the Policy Process*. Madison University Press.

Petersen, M. B., Skov, M., Serritzlew, S., & Ramsay, T. (2013) Motivated reasoning and political parties: Evidence for increased processing in the face of party cues. *Political Behavior*, 35, 831–854.

Petty, R. E., & Cacioppo, J. T. (1984) The effects of involvement on responses to argument quantity and quality: Central and peripheral routes to persuasion. *Journal of Personality and Social Psychology*, 46(1), 69.

Phimister, I., & Raftopoulos, B. (2004) Mugabe, Mbeki & the politics of anti-imperialism. *Review of African Political Economy*, 31(101), 385–400.

Plantan, E., & Cairns, C. (2017) Why Autocrats Sometimes Relax Censorship: Signalling Government Responsiveness on Chinese Social Media. *Working Paper*.

Pornpitakpan, C. (2004) The persuasiveness of source credibility: A critical review of five decades' evidence. *Journal of Applied Social Psychology*, 34(2), 243–281.

Primiano, C. B. (2015) The impact of international perception on China's approach to human rights. *East Asia*, 32(4), 401–419.

Raftopoulos, B., & Savage, T. (2004) *Zimbabwe: Injustice and Political Reconciliation*. African Minds.

Ranger, T. (2004) Nationalist historiography, patriotic history and the history of the nation: The struggle over the past in Zimbabwe. *Journal of Southern African Studies*, 30(2), 215–234.

Redlawsk, D. P. (2002) Hot cognition or cool consideration? Testing the effects of motivated reasoning on political decision making. *Journal of Politics*, 64(4), 1021–1044.

Reicher, S., Haslam, S. A., Platow, M., & Steffens, N. (2016) Tyranny and leadership. In McKeown, S., Haji, R., & Ferguson, N. (eds.) *Understanding Peace and Conflict through Social Identity Theory. Contemporary Global Perspectives*, 71–87. Springer.

Reid, S. A., Giles, H., & Abrams, J. R. (2004) A social identity model of media usage and effects. *Zeitschrift für Medienpsychologie*, 16(1), 17–25.

Repnikova, M. (2017) *Media Politics in China: Improvising Power under Authoritarianism*. Cambridge University Press.

Richardson, S. (2016) How to Deal with China's Human Rights Abuses. *Human Rights Watch*, 1 September.

Risse, T., & Babayan, N. (2015) Democracy promotion and the challenges of illiberal regional powers: Introduction to the special issue. *Democratization*, 22(3), 381–399.

Risse, T., Ropp, S. C., & Sikkink, K. (eds.) (1999) *The Power of Human Rights. International Norms and Domestic Change*. Cambridge University Press.

Risse, T., Ropp, S. C., & Sikkink, K. (eds.) (2013) *The Persistent Power of Human Rights: From Commitment to Compliance*. Cambridge University Press.

Roberts, M. (2018) *Censored: Distraction and Diversion Inside China's Great Firewall*. Princeton University Press.

Roberts, M. E., & Stewart, B. (2014) Localization and Coordination: How Propaganda and Censorship Converge in Chinese Newspapers. *Working Paper*, Harvard University.

Ropp, S. C., & Sikkink, K. (1999) The socialization of international human rights norms into domestic practices: Introduction. In Risse, T., Risse-Kappen, T., Ropp, S. C., & Sikkink, K. (eds.) *The Power of Human Rights: International Norms and Domestic Change*, 1–39. Cambridge University Press.

Rosen, S., & Fewsmith, J. (2001) The domestic context of Chinese foreign policy: Does "public opinion" matter? In Lampton, D. M. (ed.) *The Making of Chinese Foreign and Security Policy in the Era of Reform 1978–2000*, 155–163. Stanford University Press.

Roth, K. (2015) For human rights, majority opinion isn't always important. *Open Democracy*. 16 September.

Rubin, M., & Hewstone M. (1998) Social identity theory's self-esteem hypothesis: A review and some suggestions for clarification. *Personality and Social Psychology Review*, 2(1), 40–62.

Schaffner, B. F., & Luks, S. (2018) Misinformation or expressive responding? What an inauguration crowd can tell us about the source of political misinformation in surveys. *Public Opinion Quarterly*, 82(1), 135–147.

Schaffner, B. F., & Roche, C. (2016) Misinformation and motivated reasoning: Responses to economic news in a politicized environment. *Public Opinion Quarterly*, 81(1), 86–110.

Schatz, R. T., & Lavine, H. (2007) Waving the flag: National symbolism, social identity, and political engagement. *Political Psychology*, 28(3), 329–355.

Scheidlin, N. (2016) Why some human rights groups avoid public opinion research—and why they're wrong. *Open Democracy*, 11 January.

Schmutz, G. M. (1989) *Sociologie de la Chine et sociologie chinoise* (No. 84). Librairie Droz.

Schrodt, P. (2013) GDELT: Global Data on Events, Location, and Tone. Presentation for the Conflict Research Society, Essex University, 17 September.

Schroeder, M. (2008) The construction of China's climate politics: Transnational NGOs and the spiral model of international relations. *Cambridge Review of International Affairs*, 21(4), 505–525.

Shambaugh, D. (2007) China's propaganda system: Institutions, processes and efficacy. *The China Journal*, 57 (January), 25–58.

Sharansky, N. (2008) The dissident choice. *Los Angeles Times*, 24 November.

Shepherd, N. (2014) The politics of Uganda's anti-homosexuality legislation. *Chatham House*, 24 February.

Sherman, D. K., & Cohen, G. L. (2002) Accepting threatening information: Self-affirmation and the reduction of defensive biases. *Current Directions in Psychological Science*, 11(4), 119–123.

Sherman, D. K., & Kim, H. S. (2005) Is there an "I" in "team"? The role of the self in group-serving judgments. *Journal of Personality and Social Psychology*, 88(1), 108.

Shirk, S. L. (2007) Changing media, changing foreign policy in China. *Japanese Journal of Political Science*, 8(1), 43–70.

Shirk, S. L. (2011) *Changing Media, Changing China*. Oxford University Press.

Shirk, S. L. (2018) China in Xi's "new era": The return to personalistic rule. *Journal of Democracy*, 29(2), 22–36.

Shiying, W. (1984) Yihetuan yundong shi baokan wenzhang suoyin [Newspaper and periodical articles on the history of the Boxer movement]. In *Yihetuan yundong shi yanjiu* hui [Society for Research on the History of the Boxers] (ed.) Yihetuan yundong shi lunwen xuan [Selected essays on the history of the Boxer movement]. Zhonghua Shuju.

Sikkink, K. (1993) Human rights, principled issue-networks, and sovereignty in Latin America. *International Organization*, 47(3), 411–441.

Simmons, B. A. (2009) *Mobilizing for Human Rights: International Law in Domestic Politics*. Cambridge University Press.

Simmons, B. A. (2010) Treaty compliance and violation. *Annual Review of Political Science*, 13, 273–296.

Song, R. X., & Song, R. Z. (1624) *Nu Lunyu [The Analects for Women]*.

Steele, C. M. (1988) The psychology of self-affirmation: Sustaining the integrity of the self. *Advances in Experimental Social Psychology*, 21, 261–302.

Stephan, M. J., & Chenoweth, E. (2008) Why civil resistance works: The strategic logic of nonviolent conflict. *International Security*, 33(1), 7–44.

Sternthal, B., Dholakia, R., & Leavitt, C. (1978) The persuasive effect of source credibility: Tests of cognitive response. *Journal of Consumer Research*, 4(4), 252–260.

Stockmann, D. (2013) *Media Commercialization and Authoritarian Rule in China*. Cambridge University Press.

Taber, C. S., & Lodge, M. (2006) Motivated skepticism in the evaluation of political beliefs. *American Journal of Political Science*, 50(3), 755–769.

Tai, Q. Q. (2014) China's media censorship: A dynamic and diversified regime. *Journal of East Asian Studies*, 14(2), 185.

Tai, Q. Q. (2016) Western media exposure and chinese immigrants' political perceptions. *Political Communication*, 33(1), 78–97.

Tajfel, H. (ed.) (1978) *Differentiation between Social groups: Studies in the Social Psychology of Intergroup Relations*. Academic Press.

Tajfel, H., & Turner, J. C. (1979) An integrative theory of intergroup conflict. *Social Psychology of Intergroup Relations*, 33(47), 74.

Tajfel, H., & Turner, J. C. (1986) The social identity theory of intergroup behavior. In Worchel, S., & Austin, W. (eds.) *Psychology of Intergroup Relations*, 7–24. Chicago: Nelson-Hall.

Tan, Q. (2011) The change of public opinion on US-China relations. *Asian Perspective*, 35(2), 211–237.

Tendi, B. M. (2014) The origins and functions of demonisation discourses in Britain–Zimbabwe Relations (2000–). *Journal of Southern African Studies*, 40(6), 1251–1269.

Terman, R., & Gruffydd-Jones, J. (n.d.) Human Rights Shaming, Domestic Activism, and Nationalist Backlash. Working Paper.

Trevors, G. J., Muis, K. R., Pekrun, R., Sinatra, G. M., & Winne, P. H. (2016) Identity and epistemic emotions during knowledge revision: A potential account for the backfire effect. *Discourse Processes*, 53(5–6), 339–370.

Truex, R. (2016) *Making Autocracy Work*. Cambridge University Press.

Vadlamannati, K. C., Janz, N., & Berntsen, Ø. I. (2018) Human rights shaming and FDI: Effects of the UN Human Rights Commission and Council. *World Development*, 104, 222–237.

Vause, W. G. (1989) Tibet to Tienanmen: Chinese human rights and United States foreign policy. *Vanderbilt Law Review*, 42, 1575.

Wallace, G. P. R. (2013) International law and public attitudes toward torture: An experimental study. *International Organization*, 67, 105–140.

Wan, M. (2001) *Human Rights in Chinese Foreign Relations: Defining and Defending National Interests*. University of Pennsylvania Press.

Wang, J., & Lu, Y. (2012) Shehui Yulun Yu Sifa Zhengyi – Cong Li Changkui An Kan Shehui Yulun Dui Sixing Anjian de Yinxiang [Social issues and judicial justice: Using the Li Chang Kui case to understand the impact of public opinion on the death penalty]. *Legal System and Economy*, 2(2012), 154–155.

Wang, Z. (1997) Maoism, feminism, and the UN conference on women: Women's studies research in contemporary China. *Journal of Women's History*, 8(4), 126–152.

Wang, Z. (1999) *Women in the Chinese Enlightenment: Oral and Textual Histories*. University of California Press.

Weatherley, R. (2014) *Making China Strong: The Role of Nationalism in Chinese Thinking on Democracy and Human Rights*. Palgrave Macmillan.

Weeks, B. E. (2015) Emotions, partisanship, and misperceptions: How anger and anxiety moderate the effect of partisan bias on susceptibility to political misinformation. *Journal of Communication*, 65(4), 699–719.

Weiss, J. C. (2013) Authoritarian signaling, mass audiences, and nationalist protest in China. *International Organization*, 67(1), 1–35.

Weiss, J. C. (2014) *Powerful Patriots: Nationalist Protest in China's Foreign Relations*. Oxford University Press.

Weiss, J. C. (2019) How hawkish is the Chinese public? Another look at "rising nationalism" and Chinese foreign policy. *Journal of Contemporary China*, 28(119), 679–695.

Whitefield, B. (2008) The Tian Zu Hui (Natural Foot Society): Christian women in China and the fight against footbinding. *Southeast Review*, 203, 207.

Wimmer, A. (2017) Power and pride: National identity and ethnopolitical inequality around the world. *World Politics*, 69(4), 605–639.

Wong, S. H. W., & Wan, K. M. (2018) The housing boom and the rise of localism in Hong Kong: Evidence from the legislative council election in 2016. *China Perspectives*, 2018(3), 31–40.

Wood, T., & Porter, E. (2019) The elusive backfire effect: Mass attitudes' steadfast factual adherence. *Political Behavior*, 41(1), 135–163.

Wright, J., & Escribà-Folch, A. (2009) Are dictators immune to human rights shaming? Institut Barcelona d'Estudis Internacionals (IBEI). *Working Paper*.

Yang, G. (2009) *The Power of the Internet in China: Citizen Activism Online*. Columbia University Press.

Zaller, J. (1992) *The Nature and Origins of Mass Opinion*. Cambridge University Press.

Zeng, J. (2019) You say #MeToo, I say #MiTu: China's online campaigns against sexual abuse. In Fileborn, B., & Loney-Howes, R. (eds.) *#MeToo and the Politics of Social Change*, 71–83. Palgrave Macmillan.

Zhang, H., Dickey, D., & Jackson, D. S. (2011) Radio silence in China: VOA abandons the airwaves. *Heritage Foundation Lecture*, 1195.

Zhang, K. Y., & Tian, T. (2010) Xin shiji zhi chu de Xinhai geming shi yanjiu [Research on the Xinhai revolution at the start of the new century]. *Zhejiang shehui kexue*, 9, 89–98.

Zhang, L., & Dominick, J. R. (1998) Penetrating the great wall: The ideological impact of voice of America newscasts on young Chinese intellectuals of the 1980s. *Journal of Radio Studies*, 5(1), 82–101.

Zhang, T. F., & Chen, L. J. (2014) On the nationalist tendency of the "Global Times"—Taking the Diaoyu Islands report as an example. *News University*, (3), 66–74.

Zhao, S. (1998) A state-led nationalism: The patriotic education campaign in post-Tiananmen China. *Communist and Post-Communist Studies*, 31(3), 287–302.

Zhao, S. L. (2015) The inspirational backstory of China's feminist five. *Foreign Policy*, 17 April.

Zhao, S. S. (2005) China's pragmatic nationalism: Is it manageable? *Washington Quarterly*, 29(1), 131–144.

Zhao, S. S. (2016) Xi Jinping's Maoist revival. *Journal of Democracy*, 27(3), 83–97.

Zhao, Y. (1998) *Media, Market, and Democracy in China: Between the Party Line and the Bottom Line*. University of Illinois Press.

Zheng, B. W. (2021) On the core and essence of the CCP's media thought in the past 100 years. *News Lovers*, 9.

Zhou, J. (2013) Keys to women's liberation in Communist China: An historical overview. *Journal of International Women's Studies*, 5(1), 67–77.

Index

For the benefit of digital users, indexed terms that span two pages (e.g., 52–53) may, on occasion, appear on only one of those pages.

Tables and figures are indicated by *t* and *f* following the page number

activism:
    democracy, 61, 66, 67, 80, 164–65, 166
    direct impact of foreign pressure on, 23, 59, 66, 106, 168
    domestic violence, 5–6, 97, 102–5
    feminist five, 97, 102, 103–5
    footbinding, 98–99, 100–1
    gay rights in Uganda, 157
    Hong Kong, 65–67, 164–67
    impact of foreign pressure on public support for, 5, 106, 150–69
    impact on human rights, 6
    impact of public support on, 6, 111–12, 114, 167–68
    legal, 6, 64–65, 102–3
    nationalist, 22, 45, 57–58, 63–64, 100–1, 119–20
    pro-Tibet, 55, 57–59
    rights defense, 64–65
    Tibetan, 3, 23, 54, 55, 59–60
    women's rights, 5–6, 97, 102–5, 106
Activists beyond Borders, 100
African countries' response to Guangzhou racial discrimination, 82–83, 171
African Union
    Chinese response to criticism from, 107, 108–9, 108*f*, 122, 122*t*, 124–25
    citizens' views on, 127–28
    perceived hypocrisy from, 127
    relationship to China, 107–8, 128
air pollution. *See* pollution, air
alternative arguments:
    credibility, 36–38, 37*t*, 75–76
    factional, 87–88
    informational, 7–22, 35–36, 37
    news interest and prominence, 88–90, 91–94
American reaction to pressure, 163–64
Amnesty International, 22, 44, 51–52, 58, 78, 168
Analects of Women, 98

anti-China forces. *See* hostile (foreign) forces
anti-cnn.com, 57
APEC summit, 2014. *See also* pollution, air
Arab Spring, 92–93, 93*f*
Archibald Little, Mrs. 98–99
Asian Barometer survey, 133, 136–38, 141
austerity, criticism of, 161, 162
authoritarian regimes:
    ethics of researching, 12–13, 116–17, 120
    limit criticism of their rule, 7–9, 17, 35–36
    nationalist and partisan identities within, 24–25
    public opinion influence on human rights in, 5–6, 109–10, 167–68
    public support for, 140–42, 144, 157, 158*f*, 160, 161*f*
    relevance for researching, 12
    simplified model of response to international pressure, 25–26, 37*t*, 37
    United Nations condemnation of, 12
    See also censorship; Chinese Communist Party
awards:
    Congressional gold medal to Dalai Lama, 23, 59
    Martin Ennals prize to Ilham Tohti, 8–9
    Nobel peace prize to Liu Xiaobo, 8–9, 14, 61–62

Baidu, 55
Bandurski, David, 68–69
BBC, 36, 48, 56, 80–82, 89, 121
Beijing 2008 Olympic Games:
    boycott calls, 3, 55, 57
    Chinese public response to foreign criticism of, 3, 57–58
    foreign criticism of, 58
    protect the torch, 57–58
    torch relay, 3, 55, 57–58
bin Mohamad, Mahathir, 67

'black hands', 65–66, 165. *See also* Hong Kong
booksellers:
  criticism of, 71–72
  Lam Wing-Kee, 150–51
  Lee Bo, 71–72
Boxer Rebellion, 100
boycotts, 3, 55, 57, 82. *See also* sanctions
British food, 6
Bush, George H.W. 46–47
Bush, George W. 30, 54–55, 58, 134

Cafferty, Jack, 54, 56–57
Cameron, David, 72, 86–87
Carrefour boycott, 57, 60–61
Causeway Bay Books, 71–72. *See also* booksellers
CCP. *See* Chinese Communist Party
censorship:
  of calls for freedom of speech, 7–8, 58, 78
  of criticism of top leaders, 116
  of dissidents and activists, 62, 63, 64, 71–72, 97
  flooding, 61–62, 69–70, 136
  of health crises, 89–90
  of non-western foreign pressure, 72, 82–83, 104–5, 107–8, 171
  of pressure around diplomatic events in China, 58, 59, 84, 85–87, 86*f*
  of pressure around foreign visits, 58–59, 84, 85–87, 86*f*, 88–89
  of protests, 45, 46, 55–56, 65, 79, 97
  of sensitive topics, 30–31, 79
  of specific foreign pressure, 78, 79
  VPNs (Virtual Private Networks), 36, 68
Central Propaganda Department (CCPCD), 14. *See also* censorship; Neibu Tongxun; public opinion
channeling public opinion, 68–69. *See also* Chinese Communist Party
cheerleading, 20, 21, 22, 109–10, 142
Chernobyl, moment, 9
China Digital Times (CDT), 14, 61–62, 150–51
China's ideological spectrum, 24–25
ChinaMustExplain, 82
Chinese Communist Party:
  and Chinese medicine, 119–20
  and the Dalai Lama, 55, 57, 59, 60–61, 80–82
  employment of nationalism, 33, 49, 154
  party members versus leaders, 33
  pressure directed at party leaders, 33–34, 35*t*, 171–72
  propaganda system, 42, 49–50, 68–70, 73, 87–88, 150–51

and public opinion, 5–6, 109–10, 167–68
relationship to the state, 33–34
and women's rights, 101–5, 167–68, 170–71
See also authoritarian regimes
Chinese medicine:
  and the CCP, 119–20
  interviewees' knowledge of, 119–20, 121
  interviewees' opinion of foreign pressure over, 122, 122*t*, 123, 125, 126–27, 128, 129–30, 131, 152
  ivory, use of, 119
Cixi, Empress Dowager, 98–99
Clinton, Bill, 51, 58
Clinton, Hillary:
  criticism of censorship in China, 78
  criticism of feminist five arrests, 103, 104, 105–6
  criticism of women's rights in China in 1995 103
  target for Chinese state media, 104, 105–6
CNN, 54, 57, 80–82
colour revolutions, 65–66
commercial media expansion, 46, 49–50, 88, 91
comprehensive approach, 169
Congressional gold medal, 23, 59
Congressional-Executive Committee on China (CECC), 68, 105, 168. *See also* political prisoners
control over hostile narrative, 154–56, 156*t*
cooptation, 11
coronavirus. *See* COVID-19
counterarguments to criticism, 19–21, 25, 121, 123
COVID-19:
  China, criticism of response, 90–91
  United Kingdom, criticism of response, 162–63
  See also Guangzhou discrimination
credibility argument for international pressure, 36–38, 37*t*, 75–76
cross-national comparisons. *See* global rankings
cyber nationalists, 17. *See also* nationalist/nationalism

Daily Telegraph, 54
Dalai Lama:
  CCP rhetoric towards, 55, 57, 59, 60–61, 80–82
  Chinese interviewees' views of meetings with foreign leaders, 145
  Congressional gold medal award, impact of, 8–9, 59
  impact of meeting with Obama on Chinese public opinion, 139–44, 140*t*, 143*f*
  international policy towards meetings with, 145, 169–70

INDEX 245

meeting with Obama in 2011 133, 135–36, 137f
meetings with foreign leaders, 45, 59–61, 60f, 86–87, 134–35
protests against, 3, 57–58
similarity to other dissidents, 145
speech to European Union parliament, 44–45
'dare to speak, to speak early' 68–69, 90. See also delay in news coverage of crises
death penalty, 6, 78, 170
delay in state news coverage of crises, 45, 46, 55–56, 65, 79, 89–90, 97. See also 'dare to speak, to speak early'
democracy:
  activists for, 61, 66, 67, 80, 164–65, 166
  Chinese citizens' understanding of, 138–39, 141, 144
  impact of Dalai Lama meeting on perception of, 139–41, 140t, 142–44, 143f
  impact of Dalai Lama meeting on support for, 141, 144
  National Endowment for (NED), 65–66
  promotion, 134
  Zimbabwean citizens' satisfaction with, 160, 161f
  See also authoritarian regimes; democratic regimes
democratic regimes' response to pressure, 155, 163–64
Deng Xiaoping, 44, 45, 46
discrimination, racial:
  in Guangzhou, 82–83, 171
  in United States, 52, 127
dissidents:
  meetings with, 72, 145
  pressure over jailed, 11, 23, 44, 58, 61–64, 168
  See also activists; Dalai Lama; human rights lawyers; political prisoners
domestic violence:
  activism against, 5–6, 97, 102, 167–68, 170
  interviewees' views about, 123–25
  Kim Lee, 5–6, 102–3
  law against, 5–6, 102–3
  See also women's rights
Duterte, Rodrigo, 152–53, 158

Eliasson, Jan, 103
elite factions, 87–88
ethics:
  interviews, 120
  online surveys, 116–17
  research in china, 12–13
European Union (EU), 3, 44–45, 54–55

Fang Fang, 90–91
Fang Lizhi, 46–47, 80
fear, responding to surveys, 142. See also social pressure
feelings of the Chinese people, hurt, 59
feminist five:
  arrest, 97
  Hillary Clinton, 103, 104, 105–6
  importance to regime, 170–71
  international attention, 97, 103–6
  Li Tingting, 97
  release, 103–5, 168, 170–71
Fengrui law firm, 64
food safety. See Sanlu
Foot, Rosemary, 49, 51
football teams, 18
footbinding:
  Chinese activists, 99–101
  missionaries, 98–99, 100–1
  Natural Foot Society, 98–99
  origins and history, 98–99
  Qing government reaction to, 98–100
  See also women's rights
foreign media errors, 56
France:
  Carrefour boycott, 3, 57, 82
  Dalai Lama meeting, 62, 159
  Olympics boycott, 3, 55, 57
  Olympics torch protests, 55, 57
  Ursula Gauthier, 93–94
friendship deeper than the deepest sea, higher than the Himalayas, and sweeter than honey, 28, 192n.61

gamers, 21
Gauthier, Ursula, 93–94
Gbajabiamila, Femi, 82
genocide, accusations of, 82
global rankings
  civil and political freedoms, 4, 5–6
  impact on response to pressure, 111–12
  World Economic Forum index of gender equality, 111
Global Times:
  as propaganda source, 13–14, 88–89
  retractions, 151
Google 2010 dispute, 62, 78
Gorbachev, Mikhail, 9
Gu Yi, 151
Guangzhou discrimination, 82–83, 171
Guardian, The, 162

guiding public opinion, 68–69. *See also* Chinese Communist Party
Guo Jianmei, 109

Hafner-Burton, Emilie, 8*f*
Herald, The, 160
Hong Fincher, Leta, 102–3
Hong Kong:
    2014 protests, 65–67, 164–67
    2019 protests, 67, 166
    Causeway Bay Books, 71–72
    Chris Patten, 65, 116
    Hong Kong Human Rights and Democracy Act, 67, 191n.40
    identity in, 164, 165*f*, 166
    impact in China of pressure on, 66–67, 71–72, 91–92, 116
    impact in Hong Kong of pressure on, 164–67
    political polarization in, 164–67
    press freedom in, 165–66
    United Kingdom criticism of, 66–67, 71–72, 91–92, 116
hostile (foreign) forces, 46–47, 50–51, 63–64, 65–66, 97, 136, 151, 165
Hotan attacks, 142, 143*f*, 144
Hu Jia, 61
Hu Jintao, 53, 56, 58–59, 68, 90, 136, 137*f*
Huanqiu Shibao. *See* Global Times
human rights lawyers:
    Fengrui law firm, 64
    Pu Zhiqiang, 65
    Wang Yu, 64
Human Rights Watch, 30, 41, 54, 58, 92–93, 93*f*
hypocrisy, 52–53, 67, 127–28

India:
    domestic reactions to pressure, 155
    pressure on China in United Nations, 43
    protests on Tibet, 55, 58–59
informational argument for international pressure, 7–22, 35–36, 37
interest in foreign criticism, Chinese public, 88–90, 91–94
interfere in China's internal affairs, 51, 66–67, 85, 114, 129, 131
internet access growth, 36–37, 68, 69*f*, 158–59
Islamic countries. *See* Muslim countries
Israeli reactions to pressure, 153–54
ivory. *See* Chinese medicine

Japan:
    anti-Japan demonstrations, 45
    geopolitical incidents with China, 87
    rivalry with China, 27, 28
    whaling, 119–20
Jiang Junyan, 142
Jiang Zemin, 49–50, 51–52, 58, 86, 87–88
Jin Jing, 55, 57

Kang Youwei, 99, 100–1
Keck, Margaret, 100
Kelley, Judith, 111
Kerry, John, 104
Klaus, Vaclav, 55
Kuran, Timur, 7

Lam Wing-Kee, 150–51
Lee Bo, 71–72
Lee, Kim, 5–6, 102–3
LGBT rights, 109–10, 157–58
Li Changkui, 6
Li Peng, 58–59
Li Tingting, 97
Liang Qichao, 99, 100, 101
Lianghui, 84, 90
Liu Renwen, 6
Liu Xiaobo, 8–9, 14, 61–62, 76
Lu Jie, 138
Lü Pin, 102–3

Mao Zedong:
    Tibet crackdown, 42–43
    women's rights, 101
Martin Ennals prize, 8–9
melamine. *See* Sanlu scandal
Merkel, Angela, 3, 55, 66, 80–82
missionaries. *See also* Archibald Little, Mrs; Natural foot society
Moon, Ban Ki, 54–55, 103
Moravscik, Andrew, 11
Morocco, 22
most favored nation (MFN), 51
motivated reasoning, 17–19
Mugabe, Robert, 158–60, 161*f*
Museveni, Yoweri, 156–58, 158*f*
Muslim countries, 82

naming and shaming, 4, 11, 12, 29–30, 104–5, 109, 111, 170, 183n.5, 223n.16. *See also* pressure, response to
Nathan, Andrew, 5
National Endowment for Democracy (NED), 65–66
national identity:
    in China, 24–25, 100–1
    prime awareness of, 108, 111

See also nationalist/nationalism; national reform movement
national reform movement, 100–1
nationalist/nationalism:
   activists, 22, 45, 57–58, 63–64, 100–1, 119–20
   cyber- 22, 63–64, 67, 91
   disaster, 114
   education, 33
   events, 32, 87
   in *Global Times*, 14, 88
   measuring, 108, 111
   origins in Qing, 100–1
   protests, 3, 45, 57–58, 100, 113–14
   reaction to pressure, 3, 32, 57–58, 115, 119–20, 139–40, 140*t*, 143*f*, 152, 163–64
   See also national identity; national reform movement
NATO bombing of China Embassy in Yugoslavia. *See* Yugoslavia Embassy bombing
Natural Foot Society, 98–99
Neibu Tongxun, 49–50
New York Times, 36, 54, 68, 76, 84, 85, 93*f*, 168
NGOs, reported pressure in *People's Daily*, 80, 81*t*
Nie Shubin, 6
Nobel peace prize, 8–9, 14, 61–62
non-Western sources of pressure:
   censorship in China, 72, 82–83, 104–5, 107–8, 171
   impact on citizens in China, 107, 108–9, 108*f*, 122, 122*t*, 124–25, 128, 129–30
   probability reported in People's Daily, 77*t*
   theory of impact in China, 27

Obama, Barack
   criticism of human rights in China, 66, 78
   criticism of LGBT rights in Uganda, 157–58
   meetings with Dalai Lama, 60–61, 133, 134–36, 145
observable implications of theory, 35*t*
Occupy Central, 13–67, 164–67
Olympics. *See* Beijing 2008 Olympic Games
one-child policy, 30–31, 102, 121
organization of Islamic states, 82

Pakistan. *See* friendship deeper than the deepest sea, higher than the Himalayas, and sweeter than honey
partisanship:
   China, 24–25
   defensiveness, 20–21
   Hong Kong, 164–67

impact on response to pressure, 24, 155, 163–64, 165–67, 171–72
United Kingdom, 161–62, 163
United States, 20–21, 163–64
party's battle position. *See* People's Daily
'passing the buck'. *See* Pompeo, Mike
patriotic education campaign, 33, 49, 158–59
patriotic history. *See* patriotic education campaign
patriotism. *See* nationalism
Patten, Chris, 65, 116
Peking University's Research Center for Contemporary China, 27
Pelosi, Nancy, 80–82
People's Daily:
   delay in coverage of crises, 45, 46, 55–56, 65, 79, 89–90, 97
   number of articles about Human Rights Watch reports, 92–93, 93*f*
   number of articles about United States human rights reports, 86*f*
   number of instances of pressure reported, 74*f*
   probability different kinds of pressure reported in, 77*t*, 81*t*
   proportion of pressure reported, 69*f*
   reports of Dalai Lama meetings, 60*f*
   state control over messaging, 50
   as state mouthpiece, 13–14, 73–74
Philippine reactions to pressure, 152–53
Poland, 60–61, 80–82
polarization. *See* partisanship
policy implications:
   how pressure most effective, 171–72
   when pressure most effective, 169–71
political prisoners:
   Amnesty International, 44, 78, 168
   Congressional-Executive Committee on China, 68, 105, 168
   coverage of foreign pressure in state media, 61–65, 97, 104–5
   coverage of prisoners in state media, 62, 63, 64, 68, 69–70, 97, 105
   impact of foreign attention on release, 16, 103, 168
   See also dissidents; feminist five; human rights lawyers
pollution, air:
   interviewees' concerns about, 119, 120, 121
   interviewees' opinion of foreign pressure over, 122, 122*t*, 125–26, 128, 130, 131
   United States Embassy in Beijing readings, 131

Pompeo, Mike, 90–91
Power, Samantha, 97
praise, 19, 41, 89, 91–92, 142
press freedom:
    in China, 4, 7–8, 111
    criticism of, 7–8, 78, 93, 111
    in Hong Kong, 165–66
    in Uganda, 157
    in United Kingdom, 162
    in Zimbabwe, 158–59
pressure, definition of, 10–11
pressure, examples of:
    local calls for foreign, 16, 66, 166–67, 168
    nationalist backlash, 3, 119–20, 154–55, 157–58, 159–13, 214n.25
    successes, 4, 98–101, 103–5, 119, 168–69, 171, 183n.5
pressure, kinds of, 11
pressure, response to:
    activists, 23, 59, 66, 106, 168
    competing explanations – credibility, 36–38, 37t, 75–76
    competing explanations – informational, 7–22, 35–36, 37
    form: general, 29–30, 31, 35t, 51–52, 75, 76–78, 77t, 172
    form: policy, 30–31, 35t, 75, 76–78, 77t, 172
    form: specific, 29, 30–31, 35t, 51–52, 75, 76–78, 77t, 79, 109, 111, 172
    individual reaction: ideology, 31–32, 115, 141, 162–64, 165–67
    individual reaction: nationalism, 32, 35t, 115, 139–40, 140t, 143
    main predictions of theory, 37
    model of reactions, 24f
    private, 11, 31, 103, 186n.55
    relationship between source and target, 27–28, 35t, 83–87, 86f
    risks to regime from allowing, 22–23, 47, 49–50, 53, 59, 61, 64, 72
    source, 26–28, 35t, 80–83, 81t, 171
    target, 33–34, 35t, 171–72
    territorial issue, 28–29, 35t, 77t, 79, 171
    weaponization, 10, 25–26, 152–53, 167
prizes. See awards
Pu Zhiqiang, 65
public opinion:
    on air pollution, 119, 120, 121, 122, 122t, 125–26, 128, 130, 131
    on democracy, 138–39
    guiding and channeling, 68–69
    in Hong Kong, 164–60, 165f
    on human rights, 5, 126
    impact on activists, 6, 167–68
    impact on policy in China, 5–6, 109–10, 167–68
    on ivory and Chinese medicine, 119–20, 121, 122, 122t, 123, 125, 126–27, 128, 129–30, 131, 152
    nationalism in, 22, 45, 87, 91, 100, 113–14, 119–20
    opinion mining, 109–10
    and partisanship in China, 24–25
    on United States, 27
    on women's rights, 108–9, 108f, 111–13, 113f, 115–17, 118, 121, 122–25, 122t, 126, 127–28, 129–30
    See also activism; democracy; research methods; women's rights
Putin, Vladimir, 154–55

Qian Gang, 68–69
Qing empire:
    Cixi, Empress Dowager, 98–99
    and footbinding, 98–101
    lack of public support for, 100
    and reform, 100–1
quiet diplomacy, 130, 186n.55

rally 'round the flag theory, 19, 32, 115, 141
Ranger, Terence, 158–59
Renmin Ribao. See People's Daily
research methods:
    China as case study, 11–12
    ethics, 12–13, 116–17, 120
    interviews, 118–20, 131–11
    People's Daily databases, 73–75
    quasi-natural experiment, 133, 135–39
    survey experiment, 107–8, 109–11, 116–17
resonance of hostile narrative, 153–54, 156t
response latency, 219n.14
'revolutionary cascade'. See Kuran, Timur
Roberts, Margaret, 61–62
Ross, John, 66
Rudd, Kevin, 54–55
Russia, 154–55, 183n.3

sanctions, 46, 138–39, 154–55, 157–58, 159–60. See also boycotts
Sanlu, 89–90
Sarkozy, Nicolas, 3, 55, 57, 60–61, 80–82
Severe Acute Respiratory Syndrome (SARS), 89–90. See also censorship
Shambaugh, David, 73
Sharansky, Natan, 134
Shi Tianjian, 138

Shirk, Susan, 88–89
shortwave radio, 30–31, 47–48, 53, 55, 59, 172, 183n.3
Sikkink, Kathryn, 100
Simmons, Beth, 111
social identity theory, 18–19
social pressure, responding to surveys, 142. *See also* fear
Solzhenitsyn, Aleksandr, 3
South China Sea, 105, 110, 114, 120
Soviet Union, 4, 9, 26–27, 46
State department human rights report, 52–53, 86*f*
Stockmann, Daniela, 116

Tai, Benny, 66
Tajfel, Henri, 18
Tiananmen Square protests:
  anniversary and NATO bombing, 83–84, 85
  initial censorship, 46–47, 79
  open letter, 151
  reports of foreign pressure, 46–48, 79, 80
  shortwave radio, 30–31, 47–48, 183n.3
Tibet:
  1950s and 1960s crackdown, 42–43, 53
  1987 crackdown, 44–46, 47
  2008 crackdown, 3–30, 53, 54–58
  activists and protestors inside, 3, 23, 54, 55, 59–60
  experimental response to pressure on, 112
  forced relocation in, 41
  interviewees' response to pressure on, 123, 124, 145
  pro-Tibet demonstrations, 55, 57–59
  UN subcommission resolution on, 49, 50
  See also Dalai Lama
Tohti, Ilham, 8–9, 62–63
Trump, Donald, 67, 126, 163–64, 172
Turkey, 82
Tusk, Donald, 55

Uganda:
  response to pressure on anti-homosexuality bill, 157–58
  trust in president, 158*f*
Uighurs. *See* Xinjiang
Umbrella protests. *See* Occupy Central
United Kingdom:
  criticism of freedoms in Hong Kong, 66–67, 71–72, 91–92, 116
  cuisine, 19–20
  partisanship, 161–62, 163
  public reaction to pressure on COVID-19 162–63
  reaction to UN criticism of austerity, 161, 162
United Nations:
  Chinese citizens' attitudes towards, 128
  criticism of austerity in United Kingdom, 161, 162
  perceived hostility of pressure by Chinese citizens, 122, 122*t*, 125, 128, 129–30
  probability of pressure reported in People's Daily, 77*t*
  United Nations Commission/Council on Human Rights, 44, 48–49, 50–51, 80, 81*t*
  United Nations Convention against Torture, 44
  United Nations Environment Program (UNEP), 121–22, 125
  United Nations General Assembly draft resolution on Tibet, 43
  United Nations Sub-Commission on Prevention of Discrimination and Protection of United Nations Commission/Council on Human Rights, 48–49, 50–51, 80, 81*t*
  Minorities draft resolutions, 48, 49, 50
United Nations Environment Program (UNEP), 121–22, 125
United States:
  American friends, 85–86
  congress, 44–45, 51–52, 67, 85
  Congressional gold medal, 23, 59
  flags at Hong Kong protests, 67, 166
  geopolitical relationship with China, 27, 45, 52–53, 84–87, 86*f*, 107–8, 152–53
  hypocrisy, 52–53, 67, 127–28
  impact of foreign pressure in, 163–64
  NATO bombing of Chinese Embassy in Yugoslavia, 83–84, 85
  partisanship, 20–21, 163–64
  probability of pressure reported in People's Daily, 77*t*
  racial discrimination, 52, 82–83, 127, 171
  State department human rights report, 52–53, 86*f*
  US-China human rights dialogues, 86–87
  US-China meetings, 58–59, 84, 85–87, 86*f*, 88–89
  US-China tensions, 27, 52–53, 83–85
Ürümqi. *See* Xinjiang

visits abroad, Chinese officials, 58–59, 84, 85–87, 86*f*, 88–89
visits to China, foreign officials, 58–59, 84, 85–87, 86*f*, 88–89
  See also Beijing 2008 Olympic Games
Voice of America, 30–31, 47–48, 53, 55, 59, 172
VPNs (virtual private networks), 36, 68

Wang Yu, 64
Weibo posts:
  on air pollution, 131
  on COVID-19 90
  'gay themes' 109–10
  on Hong Kong, 65, 67, 115 n.88
  on human rights lawyers, 64
  impact on policy, 109–10, 167–68
  on political prisoners, 61, 62, 63
  public willingness to 'like' post in experiment on women's rights, 110, 110f, 111–12, 114
  racism and xenophobia in, 82
  on women's rights, 5–6, 106
  See also censorship
Wei Jingsheng, 61
weiquan. *See* human rights lawyers
Weiss, Jessica Chen, 57–58, 210n.70
Western forces. *See* hostile (foreign) forces
whaling, 119–20
Wildaid, 119, 121
women's rights:
  anniversary of the World Conference on Women in Beijing, New York 2015 105–6
  authorities' crackdown on, 97, 103–5, 109
  CCP role in promoting, 101–5
  Clinton, Hillary, 103, 104, 105–6, 109, 121, 127
  domestic violence, 5–6, 97, 102–5
  ethical implications of research on, 13
  experimental response to pressure on, 108–9, 108f, 111–13, 113f, 115–17
  impact of capitalism on, 102
  interviewees' knowledge of, 121
  interviewees' response to pressure on, 118, 122–25, 122t, 126, 127–28, 129–30
  laws on, 101, 102–3, 167–68
  Mao Zedong views on, 101
  modern activism on, 5–6, 97, 102–5, 106

and nationalist activists, 99, 100–1
one child policy, 30–31, 102, 121
Qing respect for, 98–99
World Conference on Women in Beijing, 1995 103, 105
See also domestic violence; feminist five; footbinding; one-child policy; Zhongze Center
Wong, Joshua, 66
World Health Organization (WHO), 89–90
World Values Survey, 8f, 18

Xi Jinping, 7–8, 12–13, 33, 52–53, 58–59, 71, 73, 87–88, 90, 106, 116
'Xi Jinping and his lovers' 71
Xiao Gang, 14. *See also* China Digital Times
Xinhua, 13–14, 73, 109, 150–51
Xinhua copy, use only, 55, 61–63, 73, 78. *See also* delay in news coverage of crises
Xinjiang:
  attacks in Hotan, 142, 143f, 144
  genocide, accusations of, 82
  Ilham Tohti, 8–9, 62–63
  international response to 2009 riots, 82
  Ursula Gauthier article, 93–94
Xu Zhiyong

Yang Dali, 142
Yugoslavia embassy bombing, 83–84, 85

ZANU-PF, 158–60, 161f
Zhang, Chenchen, 90
Zhao Suisheng, 100
Zhongze Center, 109, 110. *See also* women's rights
Zimbabwe:
  MDC response to sanctions, 159–60
  public trust in president, 161f
  ZANU-PF response to sanctions, 160

Printed in the USA/Agawam, MA
February 14, 2023

805803.021